Flower Drum Songs

Flower Drum Songs

The Story of Two Musicals

DAVID H. LEWIS

McFarland & Company, Inc., Publishers
Jefferson, North Carolina, and London

LIBRARY OF CONGRESS CATALOGUING-IN-PUBLICATION DATA

Lewis, David H.
    Flower drum songs : the story of two musicals / David H. Lewis.
      p.   cm.
    Includes bibliographical references and index.

    ISBN-13: 978-0-7864-2246-3
    softcover : 50# alkaline paper ∞

    1. Rodgers, Richard, 1902–   Flower drum song. I. Title.
ML410.R6315L48 2006
782.1'4 — dc22   2005032528

British Library cataloguing data are available

On the cover: *background* ©2006 PhotoSpin; *foreground* photograph
by Craig Schwartz/Mark Taper Forum

Manufactured in the United States of America

McFarland & Company, Inc., Publishers
  Box 611, Jefferson, North Carolina 28640
  www.mcfarlandpub.com

Remembering Mary and Miss Molly,
my friends across the street
when life was a flower drum song

Table of Contents

Preface

Some of my fondest memories of things past linger on in tiny little fragments. And one of the more remarkable fragments calls to mind the humble presence of two simple souls freshly arrived from China in an early scene from *Flower Drum Song* at the Curran theatre in San Francisco over forty years ago.

I see them up there on the stage singing about miracles happening every day — when Americans readily embraced such dreams. They are gracing themselves into the household of Master Wang Chi-Yang — and into an audience. I see them, in fact, more as real people than characters in a musical.

Surely I had gone expecting more boisterous things. To be amused by Juanita Hall belting out one of my favorite songs from the cast album, "Chop Suey." To hear the rousing "I Enjoy Being a Girl" or the dreamy "Sunday." And while in hazy recall I can visualize Hall and the chorus whooping it up about the great American melting pot, still, it is that softer scene in which Mei Li and her father, Dr. Li, first appear that flickers magically on like a musty silent film whenever I think back. Perhaps it epitomized how wonderfully different the show was from other musicals that had crossed the same stage.

Or ... was there not that much to remember? Had a Caucasian kid left the theatre entranced with the exotic circumstances, in effect humming the atmosphere on his way out?

Judging by what an emerging school of *Flower Drum Song* critics have had to say about the show, you might conclude that, indeed, that's all there was.

Enter this book, written to explore the musical's diminishing reputation over the years from a show that clearly charmed the masses (and most of the critics) when it first opened, to a show written off as a quaint, racially offensive relic. Therein lies a tale worth telling. There are, in fact, trails of misunderstanding, opportunism and deception to follow — clear back to the Chinatown of San Francisco in the 1950s, around which C.Y. Lee claimed to have fashioned a novel about the neighborhood; through the Rodgers and Hammerstein musical based upon that novel; through the movie version of the musical, which only added more controversy; and onto the political attack fields of Asian American scholars and students caught up in ethnic studies programs of the 1970s, citing alleged examples of stereotyping at the hands of two "white devils" of Broadway — Oscar Hammerstein and Joseph Fields — who co-scripted the musical.

Finally, the trail ends at the door of the Rodgers and Hammerstein Organization, whose granting one David Henry Hwang his wish to *totally* rewrite the show would set the stage for the most revolutionary chapter in Broadway revival history. Upon this heralded exercise, which audiences failed to support at the Virginia Theatre in 2002, an early curtain fell. And we are back, it seems, to square one, and to a number of questions not being asked very seriously within the musical theatre community. Among them, if *Drum* could not be revived in its original form — if, indeed, R & H are a hard sell on return trips to New York theatres — was that "golden age" not so golden after all?

While working on this book, I came upon an old diary of mine for the year 1960 and went searching through the pages, wondering what I might have written, if anything, about that long-ago day at the Curran. As it turned out, I had actually gone down to San Francisco on August 27 to see the Ringling Bros. Circus at the Cow Palace, and on my way I took in a matinee of the musical about Chinatown. A full-fledged critic in my own mind, I had things to write about both. John Ringling North's fourth all-indoor edition did not impress: "flat, dull, inactive, tired, and uninspired." Whew! Surely such thoughts were colored by the lingering anger of a young circus fan over Mr. North's having struck the big top for good only four seasons earlier.

Rodgers and Hammerstein fared better: "Saw first 'Flower Drum Song.' It was a light though great show. Loved the entertainment."

Light. I will not disagree. There is another word that describes what I feel whenever I strain to remember what I experienced that afternoon: enchantment.

That was, of course, long before this penultimate opus from two masters of musical theatre would take so many strange twists and turns over the intervening years, all of which I have tried to recount, as fully and accurately as possible.

This book would not be half the book it is without the generous sharing of those who have added so much to our knowledge and understanding. Among them, the very actor, Chao-Li Chi, who played the role of Dr. Li in that performance I saw in San Francisco forty-four years ago! Like those of many others who agreed to talk while a tape recorder rolled or to answer written questions, Chi's contributions would shape and inform this work in ways I could never have imagined. Indeed, never have I researched a project where I ended up knowing so much more than I did when I began.

So, a hundred million thanks to them all — to Chao-Li Chi and to my very first interview, Patrick Adiarte. To Sandra Allen, Ronald Banks, Eric Chan, Dean Crocker, Michael Feinstein, Arabella Hong, David Henry Hwang, Alvin Ing, Ole Kittleson, Thomas Kouo, Baayork Lee, Jared Lee, David Lober, Jodi Long, Wonci Lui, Tzi Ma, Blythe Matsui, Mary Rodgers, Harriet Schlader, Lea Salonga, Pat Suzuki, Ivy Tam, and Kim Varhola.

And to others who supplied information and responded to queries: Anne Marie Welsh, Don Shirley, Richard Chang; Robert C. Edgar; Jeannette Thomas, Scott Henderson, Bill Boles, Tim Dunn, John Hugh, Arthur Dong, Marion Suzuki, and Royce C. Young.

The San Francisco Performing Arts Library and Museum contains a wealth of material on the show's checkered appearances in that city, and those documents were generously made available for my use.

The wonderful photos that illuminate these pages are brought to you through the kind and swift courtesy of both Ron Mandelbaum at Photofest (great people to work with) and of the Mark Taper Forum's Craig Schwartz, whose extraordinary cooperation grants the latter-day *Flower Drum Song* its visual due.

I hope that what you are about to read amounts to a responsible beginning for a dialogue that deserves, I believe, to go on. Once lured by a friend into a Christian Scientist church service, I heard there something that I have never forgotten: "Truth can only destroy that which is untrue." What a truth.

Memory (I will speak for my own) can be a careless editor, and here you are about to travel a road now and then forged through the recollections, imperfect though some may be, of the theatre people who played a part in the creation of the two musicals. When accounts conflict, whom to believe? Against the best-assembled puzzle, even the most ill-fitting parts may bear degrees of truth. For example, consider the creation of the song "Don't Marry Me," detailed up ahead. There are in published accounts four different versions of how long it actually took Mr. Hammerstein to write the lyric and Mr. Rodgers to give it music. *Four.*

Maybe the truth of what was, like what may become, can sometimes be understood only at best in blurry outlines—like the distant planets, so real yet so mysterious. Like the human condition itself. I've tried my best — and what a fascinating journey it was—to cast the clearest lights upon it all.

— David Lewis

1

Seeking a Hit Back

Were Richard Rodgers and Oscar Hammerstein, the reigning giants of musical theatre, washed up? Suffering through the longest drought of their legendary career, the two men who had revolutionized stage musicals, landing nearly one huge hit after another on Broadway, had not had a single success in nearly eight years as they faced another opening night crowd. The world now seemed to be passing them by. Younger voices of rebellion within popular culture had been knocking on theatre doors of late: The year before, in 1957, a groundbreaking musical of brutal realism acclaimed by the critics—*West Side Story*—blasted a new path far removed from the relentlessly romantic one traveled by Rodgers and Hammerstein.

During eight luckless seasons, Dick and Oscar had no doubt observed the emergence of a new popular form of music rooted in blues, swing, and country. They might have watched and wondered in horror what it all meant when, one Sunday evening on the very same Ed Sullivan TV program that had routinely featured numbers from their own shows, a young troubadour from Memphis named Elvis Presley caused teenage girls to scream their heads off and a national TV audience to gawk over his raucous country songs and sexually suggestive hip swings. What, indeed, did it mean for stalwart traditionalists like Dick and Oscar? Considering how short-lived so many songwriting teams had been, insiders could well count them out.

"I'm tremendously worried right now about the next show," Rodgers told an interviewer. "It's very easy to fail and I've always known that. *Oklahoma!* didn't make me think for one second that we weren't vulnerable."[1]

They did not have to look or listen far to be reminded of how infallible they once were, for the musicals they had created during an incredibly prolific eight-year period still graced regional and community theatre stages from coast to coast. Their songs were still heard everywhere from small-town radio airwaves to big city cabarets, and recent movie versions of their shows were captivating millions of newfound fans and reaping more profits.

In 1943, Dick and Oscar had taken the stage with unexpected force, delivering what many considered to be the first truly integrated musical play. It was called *Oklahoma!* and it ran for an unprecedented 2,248 performances. Though each of its two creators had enjoyed prior success working with other partners—Rodgers with Lorenz Hart, Hammerstein with several noted composers, among them Jerome Kern on another ground-breaking work, *Show Boat*—in tandem they seemed to inspire each other to greater heights. Oscar's words were more finely honed; Dick's music, more seriously dramatic. Book, music and lyrics worked together in intricate ways to flesh out characters and locale and advance story lines.

Two years after the historic opening of *Oklahoma!* came what some would regard as an even finer achievement, *Carousel*. This was followed, in 1947, by the team's first failure, *Allegro*, and, then in succession, by two more monumental hits—*South Pacific* in 1949, which won the Pulitzer Prize for drama, and *The King and I* in 1951.

In every one of their stolidly upbeat offerings, the collaborators affirmed a sunny belief in the power of love to lift the human condition. Their songs soared romantically. Some probed controversial issues surrounding the characters. "The things that Rodgers and Hammerstein say live on beyond the close of the curtain," said Mary Martin at the close of a 1953 telecast honoring the music makers. "For they speak of love and faith and tolerance. That is the magic, the essence, the binding force that makes their work of a piece and alive. For it has the shine of forever."[2] So much magic, indeed, that the tribute was simultaneously broadcast from coast to coast on all *four* major television networks.

During their first eight years together, Dick and Oscar also turned out a fine movie musical for 20th Century–Fox, *State Fair*, based upon the 1933 Fox movie adapted from Phil Stong's novel of the same name. They infused it with a glib, high-flying score containing heart-stirring hits such as the ebullient "A Grand Night for Singing" and the wistfully lyrical "It Might as Well Be Spring." And during the same fertile period, the two giants found time to produce the work of others, their finest credit being a new musical by Irving Berlin, *Annie Get Your Gun*. They could do no wrong, it seemed.

Then came the 1950s, a decade as full of dissident voices below the surface as it was conformists on every street corner. After the *King and I*, R & H brought two subsequent shows to New York. Each contained

When everything was going their way: Richard Rodgers and Oscar Hammerstein in 1951 (Photofest).

winning elements in highly flawed books: *Me and Juliet*, in 1953, and *Pipe Dream*, in 1955. Why a couple of lackluster also-rans? Perhaps *Juliet* failed from the beginning, because the idea for a backstage musical was instigated by Mr. Rodgers himself, with which, it was said, Mr. Hammerstein reluctantly went along. It was an original, and they did not do well with originals. Few teams at the time were doing well with originals.

Then came their biggest flop, *Pipe Dream*, based on a work in progress by novelist John Steinbeck about a cathouse on Cannery Row in Monterey, California and the various and sundry fun-loving ne'er-do-wells in the vicinity, including a self-taught marine biologist, Doc. Oscar's tepid approach in addressing the central issue of prostitution rendered the libretto comically undramatic — the characters cheerfully vague. The critics shook their heads in dismay and disbelief. "Pretty much of a bust," summed up Louis Kronenberger in *Time*. "So warmhearted about a cold world, so high-minded about its lowlifes as to emerge more hootch-coated butterscotch.... What is meant to be low-down seems more like a hoedown."[3]

Helen Traubel and her girls sing "The Happiest House on the Block" outside a sexless brothel in the failed *Pipe Dream*. Based on a work by John Steinbeck, the musical marked Rodgers and Hammerstein's last serious foray into musical drama (Photofest).

Were the masters running low on inspiration? Nearing the inevitable end of a lush partnership — as all such associations must end? John Chapman saw just the wrong subject matter: "Perhaps Rodgers and Hammerstein are too gentlemanly to be dealing with Steinbeck's sleazy and raffish denizens."[4]

One of their most valuable fans, Ed Sullivan himself, on whose very first *Toast of the Town* television show back in 1948 and on many that followed, Dick and Oscar had appeared, would not allow his audience to even contemplate a flop from R & H. *Pipe Dream*, he would tell the world on his Sunday night telecast when Rodgers and Hammerstein dropped by to promote it, was a "smash hit," and, moreover, wasn't it "rather unusual," he asked the two, for them to have continued working on the show even after opening night?[5]

"No," answered Mr. Rodgers. "There's no reason in the world why the New York opening night performance should be the final version. Anytime we think of some way to improve the show, we like to do it."

Added Mr. Hammerstein, "Each audience is new. They're entitled to the best show we can possibly give them.... We've made vital improvements since the New York opening and no matter how much audiences may have enjoyed it at first, the audiences today are seeing a better show."

Some of *Pipe Dream's* intriguing songs and characters came alive on Sullivan's stage as members of the cast performed scenes from the show. Then, to conclude the pandering tribute, cameras panned to Dick and Oscar walking out onto the stage to take their bows, looking stone faced and reluctant — like a pair of humbled servants with little to show before a charitable king. The king's gratuitous endorsement could not turn a sluggish box office around. Whatever improvements R & H had made to their least successful musical did not rekindle the magic of their previous works.

In 1956 on the *Ed Sullivan Show*, less than three months after the failed *Pipe Dream* closed, Elvis Presley made his first earth-shattering appearance before a nationwide audience of 60,710,000 viewers— the highest rating in the program's history.

By that time, teenagers from coast to coast were rocking and rolling to a new beat, a much younger musical language in opposition to the sweetly shaped refrains of Jerome Kern and Richard Rodgers, of Cole Porter and Irving Berlin — tunesmiths who had helped write a Great American Songbook. Presley's assertive sexuality gave a populist voice to a counterculture already stirring underground in the larger cities of America, a movement that would change forever the social paradigm that Rodgers and Hammerstein had regularly lionized in song and dance. Indeed, Presley and his like, and their growing legion of teenage acolytes, rocked the tectonic plates of popular culture. Danny and the Juniors sang "At the Hop" while parents of restless teenagers who idolized such "noise" fretted the implications. And when a riot broke out at a rock 'n' roll show in Boston, Alan Freed, the promoter, was arrested for inciting it.[6]

In San Francisco's bohemian North Beach not far from Chinatown, a young novelist, Jack Kerouac, brought fame to the emerging beat generation *in On the Road* which became a best seller. In the movies, *Blackboard Jungle* portrayed teenage rebellion in big city school yards. Out of the film came the first bona fide rock and roll hit, "Rock Around the Clock." And just at the moment when the "space race" between the United States and the Soviet Union intensified as the Russians sent the first artificial satellite, Sputnik, into orbit, a best-selling novel about the end of the human race following a nuclear war reached eerie literary rapture when Australian Nevil Shute published his *On the Beach* in 1957.

In the theatre, two rather disparate worlds still coexisted. In the "straight play," voices of profound disillusionment echoed from Tennessee Williams to Arthur Miller. The average musical, however, continued to dispense charm, wit, splashy dance numbers and typical boy-wins-girl happiness by the final curtain. Meredith Willson's melodic valentine to Small Town USA, *The Music Man*, was launched in 1957. Already on the boards were long-running hits like *My Fair Lady* and *The Pajama Game*.

But ... nothing from Messrs. Rodgers and Hammerstein. To the public, however, their world was everywhere. Only four years earlier their names had flashed on four New York marquees when they had that many shows running *simultaneously*. They were the toast of TV specials, in which their shows were honored and their numerous songs sung over and over again by leading popular singers and Broadway stars of the day. Even their "flops" had supplied popular ditties to the airwaves: "No Other Love" from *Me and Juliet*, "The Next Time It Happens" and "All At Once You Love Her" from the raffishly incomplete *Pipe Dream*.

Three Rodgers and Hammerstein works—*Oklahoma!*, *Carousel*, and *The King and I*—had already made it to the screen. All were favorably reviewed and profitably attended. *South Pacific* would reach the Hollywood cameras in 1958.

By now, Dick and Oscar were closer in spirit to the warmer sentiments of TV sitcoms—to Beaver and Wally and David and Rick Nelson. And they refused to kowtow to the emerging cynicism of long-haired guitar-players and beat novelists. Doggedly, they continued affirming a devotion to canary yellow skies and to a lover's first kiss. To a scribe from *Cosmopolitan* magazine, who likened the Rodgers and Hammerstein office to "a large industrial organization," Mr. Hammerstein remarked, "I do all these foreign promotions, because Dick hates to travel—he hates flying; and besides, my wife loves England."[7]

The writer, Jon Whitcomb, noting that Hammerstein had once been called "the careful dreamer," raised the subject of a recent interview Hammerstein granted to TV newsman Mike Wallace, during which he was asked to comment on London drama critic Kenneth Tynan's ridiculing his work as "sacrificing wit and urbanity for sentimentality." In reply, Mr. Hammerstein argued that "not to be sentimental about babies and sunsets and falling in love is to be a poseur."

Of Mr. Rodgers, Whitcomb quoted Mrs. (Dorothy) Rodgers: "He has absolutely no temperament. He works in here at the Steinway with the door shut; in the country he can compose at the piano in a living room with no door. And you don't get killed if you walk in on him."

Mr. Hammerstein's wife, also named Dorothy, confided to the man from *Cosmopolitan* that her husband turned distant and remote while working on lyrics. "As for opening nights, Oscar has a tendency to go to pieces. We both get very nervous. We sit on the aisle, he'll sit there mouthing the dialogue and lyrics. Sometimes he makes hissing noises—very embarrassing."

Were these two poets of hope and good will on the verge of obsolescence? In a *Holiday* magazine piece, Cleveland Amory pushed them on the subject. And they replied undefensively, saying things that sounded almost scripted.

Answered, first, Richard Rodgers: "We don't say everybody has to love each other.... We just say that they might give a thought to trying to understand each other."[8]

"What's wrong with sweetness and light?" asked Mr. Rodgers' partner. "It's been around quite a while. Even a cliche, you know, has a right to be true.... The things we're sentimental about are the fundamental things of life, the birth of a child, the death of a child, or anybody falling in love."

So staunchly in unison were they on the subject, in fact, that when the two had turned to the work of adapting Ferenc Molnar's *Liliom* to *Carousel* in earlier years, they were unwilling to follow the author through to his pessimistic conclusion. "The way Molnar wrote it," explained Mr. Rodgers, "the man ends up hitting his daughter and then having to go back to purgatory, leaving his daughter helpless and hopeless. We couldn't accept that." So R & H figured out a way to end their *Carousel* on a more promising note by showing Julie Jordan learning how to express her feelings to others. "Molnar saw our final scene—which was the exact opposite of his," said Rodgers. "He told us it was the best scene in the play."

The "best" scene was penned by a man who admitted to having once "stolen" a radish from a blind man. The confession of Mr. Hammerstein to journalist Amory marked his most regretful departure from virtuous conduct, albeit with a redeeming caveat: While seated next to the sightless fellow at a dinner party—a fellow who could not have known there was a radish on his plate—Mr. Hammerstein shamelessly "grabbed the radish and ate it—and ever since has felt terrible about it."

The radish thief could also express profound unrest with a sometimes intolerant society in which he lived. During the Mike Wallace interview, Hammerstein was asked what he thought of African American singer Paul Robeson, who had appeared in his and Jerome Kern's *Show Boat*. He replied, "I knew Paul very well and I used to admire him. It troubles me to sit as a judge upon Paul, because I think of myself and wonder how I would feel if I were the son of a minister—if I had been a Phi Beta Kappa man at Rutgers, an all–American tackle, a tall handsome man, a singer and actor and athlete, and could not live in the same hotel with the other members of my theatrical troupe. I would be good and sore and I don't know what I might do."

To which, Oscar's wife, Dorothy, added, "I watched the broadcast from the house, and I just forgot I was married to him. I felt like getting up and applauding."

Hope. Faith. Dreams. Love. Courage. Tolerances. Sharing. Sunsets to sing about. Young lovers to sing about. Bigotry to address. Old forgotten river hands toiling all day long and making but a few pennies, and getting up and doing it again — more fodder for thoughtful lyrics. Rodgers and Hammerstein, in the public's mind, stood for the best American ideals. *Newsweek*, in identifying "the new empire of the American musical," proclaimed them its international ambassadors, and the State Department used their shows as a "high visibility component of its racial and cultural diplomacy in Europe and Asia."[9]

Behind their noble facades built on indisputably high artistic achievements— behind the carefully controlled image of two upstanding songwriters skillfully in tune with Judeo-Christian values, perfectly suited to each other's talents and at ease with each other in their respective homes— each man quite alone suffered his own demons and doubts. So ill-inclined or unable, in fact, were the two to communicate on a personal level that each, privately, at different times in their partnership wondered just what the other was thinking, and how long it would be before the other might go his separate way. They were, after all, laboring in one of the most wickedly competitive fields of show business. While they had long maintained an arm's-length relationship almost out of an unspoken understanding that such collaborations were fraught with peril, they had scarce reason by the late 1950s to see themselves going much farther as a team.

Hammerstein could relive the nightmare of a long, eight-flop drought he had endured through the 1930s before teaming up with Rodgers, when Larry Hart, nearing his end, had grown erratic and unproductive, lost in personal loneliness and drowning in alcohol. No matter what Hammerstein said to the press, he had plenty of time to ponder the tart criticisms of Kenneth Tynan and other theatre commentators who questioned his Pollyanna brand of theatre, when all around him society was growing much more hip and rebellious. If Oscar Hammerstein could not bring himself to face the real music of prostitution in *Pipe Dream*, how would he ever be able to adapt to the changing mores? Or had Oscar and Dick only been bowing all along to mainstream culture in order to sustain their ivory reputations and stay out of the reach of Joseph McCarthy's witch hunt?

The insecurities of Richard Rodgers were of a different sort — a vast cornucopia of phobias. Afraid of travel, afraid of heights, afraid of riding in subways, surely he feared above all the possibility of writing another flop. Even more than his more philosophically grounded partner, he lived for musical theatre. And all of these fears drove Mr. Rodgers deeper into association with another partner — the bottle.

Another of his ongoing dreads was the attention he resented having to pay to his wife and two daughters, Mary and Linda. Although he seems to have deeply loved his wife Dorothy in the beginning, as the years and the shows took their toll, Rodgers grew to resent her presence whenever he was at work composing the next song — and then to resent everything about being at home when he was not at work on a show. Worse yet, Mr. Rodgers was observed by both his daughters to be distinctly uncomfortable with their presence. While not working on the next show, he spent a lot of time in bed — with the next woozy sip nearby.[10]

Indeed, the lives of Oscar and especially Dick hardly resembled the rosy picture put out about them by an ever-respectful media. Wrote Cleveland Armory in Holiday, "Neither Rodgers nor Hammerstein smokes, drinks more than occasionally, or favors night life, nightclubs, all-night parties or even, strangely enough, theatre first nights."

The public knew virtually nothing about the souls behind those faces — certainly not about their stilted relationship as collaborators.

To his credit, during work on *Pipe Dream* through the summer of 1955, Rodgers had survived a humiliating cancer operation to remove his left jaw. That and the abysmal critical and box office reception to *Pipe Dream* left him engulfed in a lingering depression, which television helped alleviate for a spell. From the dominant new force in popular culture came an invitation to the creators of hit musicals to produce one for CBS: a musical version of "Cinderella." Even then, Mr. Rodgers was beset by such depression that for a troubling spell he was unable to compose a single note. To his partner in November 1956, he wrote, "Apparently, I picked up a bug or got some bad food and in some mysterious manner my central nervous system was affected. I couldn't retain my balance. I walked unsteadily and kept bumping into things. I couldn't even sign my name properly. Milton [Rosenbluth, his doctor] wanted to send me to a neurologist, but I was so fed up with going through my history with doctors that I begged him to wait a few days and see if I didn't improve spontaneously. That was exactly what I did."[11]

The composer's unsettling moods did not prevent him from fashioning a wonderful set of brand new melodies for *Cinderella*, itself an unprecedented success. A production starring Julie Andrews was presented on

March 31, 1957, before 107,000,000 television viewers—nearly twice the number who had watched Elvis Presley's first appearance on Ed Sullivan. No original musical ever attempted before or since on television would come close in quality.

There to behold at every moment was the indelible R & H magic. Rodgers delivered two of his most thrilling waltzes ever. Hammerstein penned a parade of ear-catching lyrics, from dreamy to worldly to the unexpectedly thoughtful ballad, "Do I Love You Because You're Beautiful?"

Now Dick and Oscar faced a new panel of judges: Television critics. They did well enough overall, though some of the scribes noted pallid stretches, others a nagging schism in style and tone: "Hammerstein's script kept shifting uneasily between the sentimental and the sophisticated," regretted *Time* magazine's Lester Bernstein, "and made each seem less than the other."[12]

The script dabbled in touches of worldly relief. A video of a full dress rehearsal of the show before rolling cameras—requested by Dick and Oscar for editing and polishing purposes—reveals a modern sensibility during "Waltz for a Ball," when the two male cooks, overcome with the music, lock arms in jaunty affection and add their agreement to the swirling ensemble. Out it went. Out, also, inexplicably, went a more masculine and assertive performance turned in by neophyte actor Jon Cypher playing the prince.

In the *Daily News*, Ben Gross did not say the sort of things that the chronically insecure Richard Rodgers liked hearing: "Rodgers' music, gay and tuneful as it was, in its innocent simplicity, lacked the surges of inspiration found in *Oklahoma!, Carousel*, and *South Pacific*." There, again, were those earlier mega-hits, still haunting Rodgers. But why not *The King and I?* This could be read as another omission easily turned into an insult by the paranoid composer, who on occasion would peevishly refer to the "mixed" notices he remembered (somewhat incorrectly) for *The King and I*, holding them aloft like a pouting child scorning any gift under the Christmas tree that had not come off the most expensive shelf at Macy's.

Left still wondering when and if he and Oscar would ever turn out another big one, back into acute depression sank the troubled tunesmith. About this, he wrote: "One thing that might have triggered the situation was my returning to work so soon after the cancer operation…. Whatever, it is the only reason I can come up with for an extremely baffling and frightening period in my life."[13]

Post-*Cinderella*, Dick and Oscar were still without the right book or novel to adapt. Years earlier, they had spent fruitless sessions together trying to figure out a way to set George Bernard Shaw's *Pygmalion* to lyrics and music. When they gave up, they opened the doors for Alan Jay Lerner and Frederick Loewe, who came in and turned the play into one of Broadway's greatest milestones, *My Fair Lady*.

A stage version of *Cinderella*? A major rewrite of their favorite flop, *Allegro*? Nobody knows how many books and plays they rifled through in their search for the right property, nor how many ideas had been urged upon them by friends and colleagues, or by Broadway stars wishing to be cast in a musical by the giants. By working agreement, if either did not like an idea, not a word more was said.

Meanwhile, Mr. Rodgers' lingering depression became so unbearable that in 1957, as recalled by Mary Rodgers, "He was barely able to function. They had put him on tranquilizers, which was normal in those days. They didn't recognize that its effects on the brain are similar to those of alcohol and the synergistic effects could be lethal. He had ground to an absolute halt. Essentially he was not there anymore."[14]

On July 4, largely at the suggestion of others, Richard Rodgers voluntarily committed himself to the Payne Whitney Clinic, a high-priced sanatorium complete with in-house psychiatric counseling for the troubled with money. Placed by apprehensive doctors on the suicide floor and treated there for chronic depression, the theatre's most famous composer agreed to slow down, study some real sunsets, possibly hum a few of his favorite tunes to himself, and relax. And relax. And relax some more. And he did, for twelve rejuvenating weeks. And when he got out of the place, at last, nearly at hand was his next show to write.

Came a call from script writer Joseph Fields, whose father, Lew, had been a close friend of Rodgers' family and who had given Rodgers and Hart their start in the theatre. Joseph had just read a new best-selling novel, *The Flower Drum Song*, by a young Chinese-American writer, C. Y. Lee, about the generational conflict in San Francisco's Chinatown between a rich refugee widower and his two sons over dating patterns and marriage. Seizing upon the book's dramatic potential, Fields approached Mr. Lee for the stage rights, offering him a modest $3,000. About the same time, a movie producer, who desired to retain all rights, offered the novelist $50,000.

The stagestruck Lee had a heck of a time deciding between a huge amount of money in Tinseltown and a likely entree to the New York theatre. He retreated to the Filipino nightclub downstairs from where he was living in San Francisco and lost himself in a drinking spree. The next morning, the telephone rang. It was his agent. "Congratulations," she said. "You made the right choice!"[15]

Lee could not remember calling anyone to accept any offer, although somebody called Joe Fields to accept his.

From there, Fields shopped the novel to R & H, believing they could create a quite lively and lovely little musical comedy, both contemporary and exotic.

Dick and Oscar immediately saw the potential and agreed to sign on. They had excelled with oriental themes and characters, both in *South Pacific* and *The King and I.* Broadway was still a place where a young man meeting a young woman and falling in love (with complications) was the thing people paid good money to see. Creative juices began to flow. The trio of collaborators— Fields would co-script the libretto with Hammerstein — were soon combing the pages of Mr. Lee's poignant prose for characters and story lines to focus on. Since Mr. Fields had specialized in comedy and since Mr. Rodgers and Mr. Hammerstein were evidently in no mood to embark on another risky project like *Pipe Dream*, musical comedy it would be.

The creators of *Oklahoma!,* the two men who had done more than anyone else to define and advance musical theatre as a valid dramatic form, were about to embark on a project of unseen consequences that would stretch far beyond their time on this earth.

Foremost among the immediate problems was the unprecedented casting of the show itself: all Asian, and contemporary. This would be the first musical of its kind. So what? Dick and Oscar had spent their lives innovating from one idea to the next. In the beginning, there was sufficient novelty to stimulate them and, once word got out about what they were up to, the public as well.

In the fall of 1957, a few weeks after the trail-blazing *West Side Story* opened at the Winter Garden Theatre, on a day when newspapers headlined Nikita Khrushchev's offering America "Moon, Missiles for Pact on Arms," Fields and Hammerstein were out by San Francisco's Golden Gate, dining at Lamps of China on Grant Avenue, chatting with C.Y. Lee about his novel, and taking questions from a local reporter.

"We are getting ready for the fall of 1958," said Mr. Hammerstein. "We are delighted with the book from beginning to end."[16]

A possible tryout in the city that gave birth to the novel?

"Not very likely," replied Fields.

Mr. Lee beamed with pride, telling the reporter how he had hoped to become a playwright, but, failing that, resolved instead to try writing a novel that could be turned into a play. His meeting that day with Hammerstein and Fields was "the culmination of a ten-year plan to sneak into the theatre via the back door."

The men posed for pictures. Since a real flower drum was nowhere to be found, the photographer returned with a bogus drum "decorated with a fresco of flowers."

Protested the novelist, "That's not a flower drum."

Asked just the same, to pose with it, Mr. Lee graciously complied, and while flashbulbs popped, he wanted to make it clear: "I have to tell you that this is not authentic."

That night, Mr. Fields' new comedy, *Tunnel of Love*, which he had adapted from the novel by Peter DeVries, opened at the city's Alcazar Theatre to critical nods.

Earlier in the day, Lee, Hammerstein and Fields had walked the streets of Chinatown, stopping at another local restaurant for lunch, where the two theatre men were shown how to use chopsticks by Mr. Lee and Mrs. Johnny Kan, wife of the eatery's owner. They took in the sights and scents of America's largest Chinese neighborhood, cable cars clanging up and down California Street crossing Grant, sharp fish and other strange aromas seasoning the cool sea air. Oscar, his eyes scanning the scene for research, tried to picture a musical comedy drenched in the rare atmosphere — beyond that, people standing in ticket lines around the block, thousands of miles away, after a victorious opening.

Back in New York City, Mr. Rodgers, whose assorted fears had ruled out his making the trip west, was once again looking forward to working on a new show, struggling to stay semi-sober and semi-happy, to believe in himself and to be well and ready for the next new typed lyric sheet to arrive from Oscar. In his hands, it would likely bring him the solace and a calming sense of purpose that only the theatre could give him. He would feel a life-affirming desire to set Oscar's words to music. He would find a way.

He would be Richard Rodgers once more.

2

Above Grant Avenue

From his office window looking down upon America's most famous Chinese thoroughfare, a struggling young Chinese American immigrant writer, C. Y. Lee, banged away at a typewriter, translating English news stories from San Francisco papers into Cantonese for *Chinese World*. Barking out orders nearby was the boss, who ran not just the newsroom upstairs but a teahouse down below. Cable cars clanged up and down the steeply rising hills, their shrill music piercing fog and sun.

The young journalist pored over pages from the local dailies, ever on the lookout for juicy reports of robberies and rapes, murders and escapes with which to enthrall local Chinese residents who were all eyes for tabloid tales. Especially did the locals delight in misfortune within their own neighborhood, rarely reported in the English dailies. "Ugly family scandals should never be exposed to foreigners," went an old Chinese saying. Mr. Lee, off hours an aspiring novelist, lent a writerly bent to his translations, adding "more spice to make it more tasty. It was very good practice for a fiction writer."[1]

Chinese World catered mainly to an elderly Cantonese readership of aging bachelors— the predominant population of Chinatown. It was a "big letter" broadsheet, peddling local stories that San Franciscans by and large did not get to read. From the family associations, Mr. Lee received for publication elaborate write-ups on weddings and funerals; the Chinese held a longstanding fascination with death. The larger the family roster the more impressive the report, for family size counted for prestige, and the nuptials and obits were a free form of advertising. Their solemn announcements comprised the bulk of the so-called "ad revenue," of which there was little.

From his desk window, Lee could gaze down upon the tourist-busy street laden with curiosity seekers from far and wide. Shoppers mulled over paper parasols, lion mugs and ornate Chinaware, pennants and little silver and gold tea cups, stately black teapots and paper dolls. He could smell incense and sea fish, turtle and snail and all the assorted foods which fairly shocked the Western eye. Up and down the street, he could view the gay parade of pagoda arches bathed in red and gold, calling to mind a distant world on the other side of the ocean.

"To the refugees from mainland, Grant Avenue is Canton. Although there are no pedicabs, no wooden slippers clip-clapping on the sidewalks, yet the strip of land is to the refugee the closest thing to a home town. The Chinese theaters, the porridge restaurants, the tea houses, the newspapers, the food, the herbs ... all provide an atmosphere that makes the refugee wonder whether he is really in a foreign land."[2]

When Mr. Lee walked the streets below, he could imagine himself thousands of miles elsewhere as he glanced upon familiar objects in store windows: "the bamboo baskets, the miniature trees, the lacquer, the silk, the tiny porcelain, the jade, the silk brocade of gold and lavender."[3] He might look upward at a panorama of tiled and stately rooftops leaning in quiet splendor against the cool blue sky....

He knew many things not known to the casual tourists— things that lurked behind the well-orchestrated store fronts bursting with discount souvenirs. Indeed, back of Grant Avenue's crowded bustle, discounted by one scholar as "looking like a China that did not exist ... the way Americans thought it should look,"[4] there lay a far more real view of this imported China, where old mainland customs doggedly persisted. Local scandals went unreported to the larger world. The Chinese family associations, oblivious to the surrounding culture, continued to uphold and enforce ancient familial control as best they could. Young men and young women were still treated as unequals.

Remembered a one-time second-generation resident, Esther Wong, "My brother has a great deal of spending money and a bank account of his own and can do just about as he likes. We girls are expected to do everything and to pay for our room and board."[5]

The younger generations still had to endure the pressures of parents trying to marry them off, a practice which, only a few decades earlier, was virtual law. In 1920, Ms. Wong was driven nearly insane by her mother and father not being able to agree on the right man for her to marry. The mother favored a distant cousin whom the daughter hardly knew and whose interest she had never suspected. The father, very much against the cousin, wanted Ms. Wong to wed a thirty-seven-year-old divorced man, hated by the mother. "Divorce nearly always means something queer in

China. I was seventeen-years old. I finally said, I would pack my suitcase and go, if they did not stop this torture. Then my sister, who was only fifteen, had a suitor, too, and she used to tell him to his face, 'I don't like you! I won't have you!'"

Many young women reluctantly accepted a man's hand in marriage for sheer survival, and many lived to regret their acquiescence: "You either get a divorce or stay with your husband and fulfill your duties. Fulfilling your duties is the only way to save your marriage. It is disgusting work but you must think that you get paid for it and are assured a comfortable old age."[6]

A gaping disparity then existed in the number of men to women in San Francisco's Chinatown — seven to one, a ratio that exacerbated the loneliness of aging bachelors, most of whom had given up on ever finding a mate. They were content to stay put. They settled for prostitutes, who comprised one-half of the female population. They drank and gambled, sat on benches, talked to each other and dreamed of the land they had left behind to seek their American fortunes.

C. Y. Lee could identify with them. He, too, would have to compete with his fellow expatriates for the affections of a woman, statistically in demand. Unlike his cohorts, though, Mr. Lee was well educated with a dignified job, however little it paid. His downtrodden peers bore the lingering scars of age-old prejudice and persecution at the hands of their ambivalent foreign hosts.

In previous generations, their forebears had come by the thousands across the sea, many from depressed southern China, first drawn by tales of gold at Sutter's Mill. Others later emigrated to join the ranks of railroad builders brought over by California industrialists to blast their way, inch by inch, explosion by explosion, through the punishing rock mountains of the 7,000-foot Sierra Nevadas, to burrow out tunnels and lay tracks through the dark passages and around treacherous mountainsides for the Central Pacific Railroad. Their American employer was engaged in a furious competition with the Union Pacific — itself laying down tracks from the East — to join rails somewhere in between and link the coasts with silver ribbons of transportation.

The men with whom Mr. Lee rubbed elbows were the sons of the Chinese pioneers whose indomitable work ethic had built the railroad. These humble immigrants from China were the men who accepted low wages, who endured snowbound winters under freezing tents, who hammered and chipped away and blasted forward and helped shape a new American empire, their collective achievement considered "probably the greatest engineering feat" of that era.[7] Yet these same men, once their jobs were done, had to face not just ingratitude but hostility when they went to other places in search of new employment. These same men came back to San Francisco to accept domestic work in the homes of the rich; they bussed dishes in restaurants or turned out hundreds of shirts a day in local laundries.

Chinatown then housed thousands of ex-rail workers in tiny, windowless rooms crammed together in back street tenement dwellings. They suffered the same bigotry as African Americans and Indians. In San Francisco, posters on street corners read, "The Chinese must go!" The vocally intolerant protested, "The Invasion of Asiatic Barbarians!" Chinese laundries— a source of employment for one-third of Chinese males and a constant threat to white laundry owners— were torched.

In 1879, the United States Congress passed the Chinese Exclusion Law, effectively denying Chinese laborers the right to apply for citizenship or to call for their wives from the mainland. Ironically, one of the law's supporters was California senator Leland Stanford, president of the Central Pacific Railroad, whose tracks were almost entirely laid by Chinese hands. "The word liberty," wrote Saum Song Bo in 1885, "makes me think of the fact that this country is the land of liberty for men of all nations except for Chinese."[8]

Laying low to avoid further persecution and risk being deported, the men shunned western society, including its medicine. As a result, they suffered not just abject loneliness but malnutrition, tuberculosis and alcoholism. They coughed and drank and gambled away their time, sought fleeting pleasure in rooms of ill repute with what little money they had, and slept in seedy barrack dorms in the crowded and disease-ridden back streets of the other Chinatown.

"You know, when I first came over here as a teenager to work on the levees," recounted Lew Wah Get, "we were stoned when we got off the ship. We weren't allowed to leave Angel Island because they said our faces had worms in them. They fed us like pigs because they thought we were filthy. Finally, a group of old men came and led us into Chinatown. But on the way, people shouted 'Chink! Chink!' and threw stones at us again."[9]

Thousands of girls were auctioned off to pimps who set them up in back-alley brothels amidst aging apartment buildings where families lived sometimes five or six to a room, the rooms as confining as five feet by ten feet. Dim, musty halls led to community kitchens and common bathrooms, to which long lines formed all day. Family meals were cooked in well-ordered shifts. Back of colorful Grant Avenue, Chinatown was an unhealthy ghetto of fifteen thousand souls contained within the space of five by four blocks.

C.Y. Lee was lucky to have his own little one-room apartment. By the early 1950s, when he arrived to work for *Chinese World*, he was taking up residence in the largest Chinese American community in the United States—and one of the world's most congested slums. It had the highest tuberculosis rate in the U.S., among other unflattering public health statistics.

Concentrated up and down its back alley sweatshops were thousands of subservient seamstresses who hunched over sewing machines from morning till night, toiling in depressing anonymity behind morosely drawn curtains in the dark-stained windows of capitalism's netherworld. Did Mr. Lee ever look into the pitiful wages doled out? Did he ever poke about the tenements teeming with families or through the forbidding old rooms up and down rickety staircases where, not so long ago, the Tongs had fought their bloody turf wars over gambling and prostitution?

The ghosts of the gold rush and its lure ... of coolies pouring into California to join the Central Pacific gangs ... of murdered mine workers and submissive cooks and manservants ... of laundry slaves and bus boys ... they all hung about the place like old air trapped in a boarded-up museum.

By now, the aging "bachelors," many of whom actually had wives back home, had gained nominal respect in the new world. The 1906 earthquake had delivered the perfect excuse to claim natural citizenship. Since virtually all documentation had gone up in flames, the typical Chinese resident need only tell the authorities, "I was born in America." End of dispute. He was free to stay.

In 1941 came additional political reasons to tolerate — and use — these industrious, loyal immigrants from China: the war effort needed the men to join the armed forces, the women to work the Kaiser Shipyard across the bay in Richmond. The women were so exemplary in their work habits that they were honored with special citations.

Chinese Americans took double pride in helping to defend both their homeland and their adopted country against a common enemy: Japan. President Roosevelt took note of their devoted citizenship and publicly declared the "exclusion law" to have been wrongheaded, to have been a "historic mistake." With that, it was repealed. Then came subsequent acts of Congress favoring genuine Chinese political and social integration: the War Brides Act of 1945, the Displaced Persons Act of 1948, and, finally, the Refugee Act of 1955.

So the Chinatown into which C.Y. Lee entered as a young journalist reflected both a hideously unfair past and a promising American future. He could tread the crossroads of oppression and opportunity beneath his feet. He could view the invasion of Yankee night life, which already flourished in North Beach only a few blocks to the north from his neighborhood. There, on the Pacific avenue that was once called Barbary Coast, men flocked to dance bars and strip joints. And similar amusements were now noisily in operation along Grant Avenue. The Chinese Sky Room — a nightclub designed to capture the American dollar — had opened in 1937.

A couple of years later, just outside Chinatown on Sutter Street, Charlie Low opened his Forbidden City. It offered an all–Asian revue of dancers, singers and comedians performing American fare, as did five or six other clubs in Chinatown that would spring up in those years, between which a coterie of Asian entertainers moved back and forth. Low's shows were particularly aimed at a white clientele of tourists and locals.

At first, Mr. Low had shunned what North Beach sold the eager male. And besides, local Chinese girls would not dare bear in public generous portions of their anatomy for fear of societal and parental rejection. The female dancers who answered the Low call came from cities in the Midwest where they had been raised among Caucasians. Most of them were Japanese and Filipino. A few, Chinese. Not until somebody suggested adding a stripper to the bill did Charlie Low realize the meaning of profit. Low hired Noel Toy — soon dubbed the "Chinese Sally Rand"— to do a bubble dance and bare all. He cleverly billed her act, "Is It True What They Say About Chinese Women?"[10] Overnight, throngs of servicemen formed around the block, eager to watch the bubble dancer. Eager to see if it *were* true. The bar became submerged, night after night, four-deep in sailors. A dollar fifty got you dinner and the show, and you could dance till last call.

> Come along with me, please …
> I'll show you how to have fun in Chinese!

Forbidden City pulled in over two thousand customers a night. Handsome crooner Larry Ching, his velvet pipes as smooth as the smoothest, sang audience favorites like "How High the Moon." Dorothy Toy and Paul Wing danced up an articulate storm, every bit as spectacular in footwork, dash and crisp unity as Astaire and Rogers. All around the room went Mr. Charlie, the affable owner, patting backs and sprinkling delicate Chinese cheer.

Local residents frowned on the degrading "amoral girlie revues," of which there were at one time quite a few throughout the neighborhood, continuing to favor local Cantonese opera companies. In fact, by the time that Mr. Lee arrived to begin his stint with *Chinese World*, the opera theaters were still actively in operation, while, ironically, Forbidden City, a place Lee could ill afford to patronize and probably never did, was on the wane.[11] All of the sailors and soldiers whom the war years had delivered to its doors were now raising families out in the suburbs. And they had another reason to stay home at night: television.

Chinatown's culture was undergoing inevitable changes as its second-generation members were less ready to take marital marching orders from their parents. More and more they began to embrace western ways. More and more they ventured out of the land of Forbidden City into mainland San Francisco. More and more, the women refused to subjugate themselves to boyfriends or husbands; instead, they reached out to take advantage of the educational opportunities all around them. Many of them assumed greater power in the average Chinese American family. The male holdouts, increasingly ignored, stayed behind to nurse their wounds, to have their tea with each other, to relive the gold old days and to sit on Portsmouth Square benches, recite Confucius to themselves and rue their declining authority.

At his brother's insistence, in 1943, the 25-year-old Mr. Lee had come to the United States, selling everything he owned on the black market to raise steerage. He would never see his parents again. He arrived in New York with a bachelor of arts degree from the National Southwest Associated University in Yunnan, a wartime refuge college in China. First admitted to Columbia University, he later transferred to Yale, where he received, in 1947, a master of fine arts degree in drama. He hoped to become a playwright, but his efforts in that direction went nowhere fast — like a new show stranded out of town in New Haven.

He moved to Los Angeles near Union Station, ready to return home without prospects for employment. "Let them deport you," friends urged him. "You don't have to buy a steamship ticket."[12]

Down to his last fortune cookie, Mr. Lee walked over to Chinatown and spent twenty-five cents for a bowl of noodles, free tea and a copy of a San Francisco–based newspaper, *Chinese World*. In it, he read of a job opening for a column in English. He shot off three sample articles and was hired to write five a week under the banner *So I Say*. Each byline drew him five dollars. At twenty-five bucks a week, he could afford "a lot of noodles."[13]

Lee's daily prose became so popular that the publisher offered him full-time employment over a typewriter up in San Francisco. He accepted, and there the column was retitled *Grant Avenue*. And there, the writer was soon made city editor. Bilingually adept, Lee worked on both English and Chinese editions.

While in violation of the law — technically a student, Lee had taken a job — he was sending off short stories to publishing houses, having been encouraged during his Yale days by a New York agent to switch from playwriting ("no market") to fiction. He won first prize in a short story contest from *Writers Digest*. An additional $1,500 came from *Ellery Queen* magazine for reprint rights. He took the money and the certificate down to the immigration office which granted him a five-year extension. He could now apply for citizenship.

Wanting more time to concentrate on his novel, Lee changed employers, taking up with the more established *Young World*. Work there began at noon, allowing him late nights for his own writing. "It was a very good job for free lance writers," he noted, "because they supply three meals, they supply room upstairs, and they said, 'If you want to keep your job we can supply a coffin.' So that gave me a lot of security. That's how I forced myself to get into Communism ... I mean, journalism."[14]

Lee declined the dormitory room upstairs on Sacramento street, opting instead for his own private apartment over a very public and noisy Filipino nightclub on Kearney. For a time, he also contributed feature copy for *Radio Free Asia*. He became intimately familiar with the neighborhood, finding intrigue and amusement in the ongoing conflicts between the older generations and their westernized children.

Now he began in earnest on a novel about life in Chinatown. He envisioned the story through the eyes of an atypically well-to-do family, caught up in sometimes comical, other times tense and pathetic generational conflicts.

"In Chinatown, I knew everything that was going on," he said years later, looking back. "Out of that I created characters, using everybody including my own family and my friends, plus a lot of invention from the air."[15]

The central figure is Wang Chi-yang, a very old-acting, 63-year-old well-heeled refugee from the Hunan Province in central China. He has fled to America to escape the Communist devils, and he wishes only to preserve his pampered life in the two-story house he owns three blocks from Grant Avenue. Wang Chi-yang speaks only in the Hunan dialect; in English, he has mastered two words—"Yes" and "No." In his home are the cook and the two servants he brought from China. Next to his bed stands a lovely little garden, and around it, a mosquito net. Under his rug, he hides all his money. He spends a lot of time reading Confucius, writing famous poetry on rice paper, and practicing his calligraphy. All "foreigners" to him look alike. His chronic cough is actually a source of satisfaction: "He didn't want to have it cured completely. Coughing, in his opinion, was sometimes a pleasure and it seemed to increase a person's authority in his household."[16]

Wang Chi-yang's late wife's sister, Madame Tang, who comes regularly to hound him with advice, is a more progressive spirit. She has been attending American citizenship classes at an adult school in the Marina, patiently matriculating despite not knowing when the Immigration Service might allow her to attend a preliminary hearing. "Her teacher, Miss Shaw, had commented in her class that Madam Tang was the only student who hadn't missed a single class during the past two years and could recite everything she had learned."[17]

While not being badgered by his sister-in-law to get a real bank account or to purchase something modern to wear ("In this country you truly look like a stage actor in that satin gown"),[18] Wang Chi-yang is constantly at odds with his two sons, whom he considers the only "impure" elements in the house. Wang San, the youngest, is infatuated with baseball, junk food, and rock and roll. "What a barbarous way of eating," his father says. "Use your chopsticks."

Answers Wang San, "You are not supposed to eat a sandwich with chopsticks, father. This is American food."[19]

The eldest son, Wang Ta, has just graduated from the University of California in Berkeley. Unable to find suitable employment, yet feeling "ashamed to receive money from his father," in desperation he takes a job washing dishes at Fisherman's Wharf. The proud father is so embarrassed, he orders Wang Ta to quit at once. As a face-saving device to postpone the painful ordeal facing a well-educated young Chinese American man in a biased job market, Wang Ta returns to college to study medicine. Three more years in limbo.

Wang Ta's fate is shared by a good friend of his, Chang, who has a Ph.D. in economics and is working as a grocery clerk.

The story turns to comedy when Wang Chi-Yang tries arranging a bride for his son, announcing to Madame Tang, "I have negotiated a wife for him through a go-between in Hong Kong at the recommendation of a herb doctor. Day before yesterday I received a girl's picture. She is not bad looking, and was born in the year of the rabbit."[20]

In fact, Wang Ta is not having much luck on his own. He has dated numerous American women but finds them devoid of "serious intentions." And he has perused many Chinese girls, some from the mainland and many of them "stiff and polite" or too full of themselves owing to the extreme advantage they enjoy outnumbered by eligible males.

Wang Ta wanders aimlessly through a trio of romantic interludes. First to snare his interest is Linda Tung, a divorced war bride from Shanghai, where she danced in nightclubs and slithered her way through a string of brief marriages, the most recent supplying a boat ride to

America. Here in the wide-open states, Tung has become a practiced gold digger who strings men along like so many cheap pearls—to each representing that any other man who happens to drop in and out of her life is her "brother." Miss Tung has a lot of brothers, and they each give her a lot of money and things. She most definitely enjoys being a woman living a fast life.

Once Wang Ta gets wind of Linda Tung's one-person Chinatown dating service, he drops her. On the rebound he is seduced by the pathetically conniving Helen Chao, a lonely pockmarked seamstress with whom Ta has been having a mentally stimulating platonic friendship that he never intended would go beyond coffee and conversation. He quite appreciates their intellectual companionship. Chao has all along wanted more. At her apartment one night, after serving Ta another elaborate meal, Chao softens up her friend's defenses on alcohol, begs him to sleep it off on her bed, and then goes to work. Waking up out of love the next morning, the mortified Wang Ta, a gentleman at heart, succumbs to the offer of an affair, spending regular nights with Miss Chao, though he quickly ends up feeling terribly guilty, unable to be seen any longer with her in public, and breaks it off.

Finally, Wang Ta finds real love in a demure, submissive little country lass from the mainland, Mei Li. She and her father, Dr. Li, have entered the county illegally and are now walking the streets of Chinatown, singing little flower drum songs to raise money for a restaurant they hope to open, unaware that the man whom they are banking on to fund their project has passed away. By accident one evening, outside the front door of the Wang Chi-yang residence, they are greeted by Wang Ta, who is so taken with the charming young Mei Li that he invites her and her kindly father into the household, where the two succeed in winning over the father and finding a place to stay in return for modest domestic chores. Sings Mei Li:

> Sad is my fate
> I married a man with a flow'r drum
> Stupid is he,
> Oh, how stupid and dumb
> All day long he beats his singsong drum ...

Sings the old man Li ...

> Sad is my fate, oh how sad!
> To spend my life with such an ugly mate
> Of all the women you ever did meet,
> My wife has the largest pair of feet.
> Largest pair of feet.[21]

By the end of Mr. Lee's narrative, the father's control is slipping hopelessly away. Wang Ta vows to wed Mei Li after she, falsely accused by a

pair of jealous house servants of stealing a clock, has run off in humilia-
tion. Wang Ta also agrees to become partners with his friend Chang in the
grocery business.

How to find a publisher for his newly finished work, which he called
Grant Avenue? Mr. Lee remembered the agent in New York who had encouraged him during his Yale years. To her he sent a copy, and she agreed to
shop it around. After a year of being bounced from one house to the next —
too "quaint and episodic" — the manuscript fell into the hands of a very old
reader at Farrar, Straus and Giroux. Confined to a sickbed and without the
energy to complete a full report, the reader was sufficiently excited by Lee's
prose to write on the manuscript, "Read this." And then he died.[22]

And it was read — by an editor who saw a best seller in the making
and who urged that it be retitled *The Flower Drum Song*. Released in the
spring of 1957, it was greeted with generally warm acceptance. "A first
novel that is always fascinating, and by turns amusing and pathetic," wrote
the *Chicago Sunday Tribune*. "A novel written with grace and decorum in
the even, unimpassioned narrative style that is characteristic of classic Chinese literature."[23]

Lewis Gannet, reviewing for the *New York Herald Tribune*, remarked,
"It is called a novel though some day it will undoubtedly make a play.
It presents, with lingering charm and affection, a preposterous cast of
characters ... and after dawdling for two hundred gently witty pages,
it suddenly piles enough action into the last chapter to make another
book."

The *San Francisco Chronicle* found it a "pleasant, sentimental novel
on the life of a young immigrant in search of love and its happy ending."

For the *Times of London*, charm and levity overcame structural flaws:
"simple, even clumsy, but it is worth reading not only as a fascinating picture of Chinatown, but for its tranquil humor, of which the author seems
almost unaware."

While Mr. Lee may well have captured a realistic panorama of colorful Chinese customs, rarely did his rich narrative venture too far or long
beyond the duplicitous facades of the Grant Avenue it so commercially
evoked.

Noted the *New York Times* reader, "Mr. Lee writes with no omission
of slang and sex and every regard for popular tastes ... absent are the deeper
notes and the finished hand of the craftsman."

Notwithstanding a reviewer's inability to spot the darker moments,
one thing was certain: Mr. Lee's portrayal of life inside the Chinatown he
chose to see was replete with abundant plot twists, with engagingly drawn

characters, with ample amusement and poignant drama. And when Oscar Hammerstein and Joseph Fields got down to the business of adapting it into a working libretto, they had more than enough material from which to choose: familial strife and misunderstandings, callous dames on the make, youthful rebellion, striptease and forced marriages and chop suey jokes, wife beating and suicide. And a discriminatory job market not open to the young Chinese male.

C. Y. Lee was observed to have stood amiably by, never once daring to question any of the decisions being made about how his book should be turned into a stage musical. At the age of thirty-nine, he was nearly a celebrity himself. He had written a best-selling fiction of Asian themes that was about to take him up a strange Confucian path to a place where in his youth he had longed to begin: the theatre.

3

Hold the Snails, Please

Within the darker pages of *The Flower Drum Song*— like the cruel and twisted back alleys of Chinatown itself — there lurk a collection of disturbing tales that were bound to have stirred the serious dramatist in Oscar Hammerstein.

At the center of Mr. Lee's portrait looms the old master of the house, Wang Chi-yang, a walking compendium of ancient superstitions and rituals bordering on the bizarre. Stubbornly resistant to change in his well-insulated word where a simple kiss between a man and a woman is tantamount to falling in love, Master Wang attends Cantonese opera theaters, and, among many rituals he honors in order to preserve the life he left in China, he acquires two gigantic cockroaches to make the house resemble his old home on the mainland.

Whenever Wang's youngest son, Wang San, displeases him, the boy risks a mild whipping and a route to the corner to study Confucius and recite it back. Wang San complains to his older brother, "I don't understand a word of that junk."[1]

In the absence of Master Wang's long-deceased "cheap wife," he tolerates her sister, Madam Tang, who nags him to break free of himself and embrace change. But he sees only a crass and disrespectful culture unworthy of his standards. During an uncustomary walk through the international settlement outside his neighborhood, Wang Chi-yang ventures by accident into a sordid North Beach nightclub and, just to save face, becomes a reluctant patron "to contribute something to the friendship between Chinatown and North Beach." Mistaken for a fellow in search of a good time, he is nearly assaulted by a dedicated stripper. In horrified retreat, he upsets the small table at which he is seated and scampers disdainfully out the door, his cough reaching Stravinskyan dissidence. "It was bad luck to have a woman jerk the lower part of her body above his head like that. He must hurry home and bathe himself and fumigate his head with incense."[2]

Along the street, Wang Chi-yang spots his eldest son, Wang Ta, in the window of a small café sitting across the table from a woman — Helen Chao — whose pock-marked face resembles, to him, that of a Taoist priest. Just another pitiful example in the father's eyes of his son's vulgar choices in women.

Determined to select a mate for his son, Wang Chi-yang confronts Wang Ta with news of the bride whom he has arranged for him to marry. The two argue furiously. Wang Ta, refusing to buckle under, walks out in disgust.

Linda Tung and Helen Chao both experience acute adversity in the novel. The cavalier Tung, divorced from her G.I. husband and out to get even with all men, dates too many too dangerously. During a Chinese celebration, she becomes the center of a jealous exchange of gunfire between two rival boyfriends after dancing with one of them — whom she calls her "brother" — at a businessmen's club on Sacramento Street and then being discovered by another "brother." She ends up, soon after, freelancing down in Los Angeles, essentially expelled from Chinatown.

"Another case of destruction," explains Wang Ta's friend, Chang. "That's what you get by mixing up with a girl like Linda Tung. It could have been you, you know…. Brutality distorts the picture of Chinatown. I think this shooting is again a result of this peculiar situation — not enough women to go around. In Shanghai, girls like Linda Tung are a dime a dozen. Nobody would lift a finger for her, let alone shoot!"[3]

Far worse is the tragic fate suffered by the lonely Helen Chao, ironically unable to land a man in a place teeming with too many men for too few women. Pathetically determined to win over Wang Ta, she subjects her face to a punishing sandpaper treatment that leaves it temporarily full of swollen red spots, and before it can heal she throws herself at Wang Ta, pleading with him to marry her. "I'll do anything for you!" She promises him, on the word of her doctor, that her skin will soon be perfectly clear. "I have his written guarantee. I can show it to you if you want to…."

Wang Ta refuses her pathetic offer. "Just come once a week," she begs him, willing to continue the affair on any terms.[4]

While Wang Ta tries to extricate himself from a hopeless situation — from Helen Chao's "birthday party" to which he was the only person invited — she crushes a wine glass in her hands by nervous accident, and her fingers bleed profusely. After Wang Ta has left, in utter devastation Miss Chao drives herself out to Ocean Beach, gets out of her car for the last time, and walks into the ocean and never looks back.

Two other unhappy characters in C. Y. Lee's wide-ranging panorama are a pair of servants in Wang Chi-yang's household: the deaf and dumb Liu Lung and his berating wife, Liu Ma. Fearing that Mei Li and her father, who have ingratiated themselves into the graces of Wang Chi-yang with their flower drum songs, may replace them, the conniving Liu Ma plants a valuable clock treasured by the master inside a suitcase of Mei Li's. Liu Ma figures its discovery will paint Mei Li as a thief and result in eviction for her and her father. This hoary incident brings the novel to a harrowing climax, fraught with quite enough bitter cross-accusations, vindictive violence and family meltdown to fill an entire second act of a musical drama.

Wang Chi-yang lashes out at Wang Ta for having invited the two now-suspected thieves into his home in the first place.

"We are busy locating your mother's clock," he bellows, "which is more precious than your worthless life!"[5]

The frame-up is exposed — ironically by the deaf and dumb Liu Lung, whose desire to right the evil committed by Liu Ma inspires him to utter the revealing words. Wang Ta, sensing Liu Lung's anger with his wife, hands him a bamboo stick, and Liu Lung proceeds to whip his wife "so violently that she finally retreated toward the door, shrieking and swearing. Liu Lung chased her to the backyard and presently a sound beating was heard."[6]

Wang Ta decides to follow after the falsely incriminated Mei Li, with whom he has fallen in love, and her proud father. To his own father, Wang Ta declares, "I am going to tell them that we are the real thieves. We have stolen their happiness. I am going to beg for their forgiveness and ask Mei Li if she still cares to marry me…. Frankly, I am disgusted with this house and everybody in it."[7]

On the verge of losing his oldest son, Wang Chi-yang struggles to understand the damage he has caused everyone inside his shattered home.

"Suddenly, an unbearable loneliness closed in on him. He felt as though he were sitting alone in a small boat on a vast ocean, without a speck of land in sight, with dark clouds looming in the distance."[8]

Wang Chi-yang leaves the home and heads up to Grant Avenue. Passing by the herbalist store run by a friend, he decides not to stop in — not to prolong any longer his fixation on all the customs that have set him at odds with his son.

"Perhaps in fifteen years most of the familiar sights and smells of Chinatown would be gone. Perhaps there will be no more clatter of Mah-Jongg behind closed doors. No more operatic music of drums and gongs…."[9]

Instead, Master Wang finally acts upon his son's advice to see about his chronic cough when he notices ahead the Tung Wah Hospital. He admires the characters on the hospital sign: "Well written, although lacking in strength in some strokes, but on the whole they were the product of years of patient practice in the Sung School."[11] Swallowing his Confucian pride, Wang Chi-yang moves up the marble steps and through the doors of the building.

Any of these elements could have supplied the premise for a taut dramatic work — could have. Mr. Hammerstein and his colleagues were evidently in no mood to write a musical drama or even to invest their comedic approach with dramatic counterpoint of the sort that Jud Fry had given *Oklahoma!* Helen Chao's pitiful descent into suicide could have been that departure — but it was not to be.

In any event, a daunting task faced Rodgers, Hammerstein and Fields: Focus. Focus. Focus. Hammerstein had been around long enough to respect this cardinal rule of musical theatre. Indeed, without the discipline to adhere to one major premise, he and Fields would be risking dramaturgical disaster. A musical simply cannot survive the narrative scope and spread of a novel.

What is somewhat puzzling, however, was Hammerstein's apparent ignorance of the probing realism in Mr. Lee's work, revealed in remarks he made to *Newsweek* magazine just week's before the show's New York premiere. "There isn't much plot to the novel," he said, "but it's strong on character and background, like a Chinese 'Life with Father'; I just fell in love with it."[11]

What he fell in love with — or went along with — was the image of a sunnier *Flower Drum Song.* It may have been a matter of his deferring to the comedically savvy Mr. Fields, who, after all, had acquired the rights to the book and had offered it to R & H as a three-man collaboration. Fields' formidable Broadway track record in comedy plays (*My Sister Eileen, Junior Miss, The Tunnel of Love*, to name but a few) was heavily weighted against his agreeing to take a chance on a dramatic musical. In fact, his one attempt at serious playwriting (*The French Touch*) had met with short-lived failure. He had contributed the books to three musicals— a pair of laugh hits in *Wonderful Town* and *Gentlemen Prefer Blondes*; a dud in *The Girl in Pink Tights.*

Rodgers, Hammerstein and Fields took the safest commercial route by following the eldest son's search for love — the most popular theme at the time with Broadway audiences. All three of Mr. Lee's principal female heroines— Linda Tung (whom they renamed Linda Low); Helen Chao and Mei Li — were incorporated into their libretto. At this troublesome juncture, R & H, needed a surefire hit. Romance and comedy promised the greatest chance, and judging by the work that ensued in fits and starts in between respective trips by all three men to hospitals and sickbeds, they were fairly adept at finding the right formula and in capturing C.Y. Lee's characters without following any of them to their unhappy ends. Excluded from their treatment were the two bickering servants; nor did Wang Ta's supportive friend, Chang, make it to the stage. Chi-Yang's sister-in-law was renamed Madam Liang.

By playing up the romance between Wang Ta and Mei Li, they in effect aimed the follow spots onto the two least dramatic characters. Both Mei Li and Wang Ta are essentially very good, very sensitive souls — and also rather passive. They are people to whom things happen. Neither is all that ambitious, and certainly not neurotic or conniving.

Two other characters, both worldly and conniving, would drive the Hammerstein and Fields adaptation, and one of them wasn't even in the book. His name is Sammy Fong, invented to serve the role of a wisecrack-ing nightclub owner of the Celestial Bar (the name possible inspired by the real-life Chinese Sky Room in the real-life Chinatown). Some, includ-ing film maker Arthur Dong, would see Sammy Fong as a reflection of For-bidden City's affable, fun-loving owner, Charlie Low, and Forbidden City itself as the model for an all–Asian nightclub scene written into the script which was nowhere to be found in C.Y. Lee's novel.[12]

Sammy Fong becomes the resentful recipient of a mail order bride ordered from China by his mother, herself anxious to see her playboy drifter of a son married off and domesticated away from frivolous nightlife trysts. The bride's name is Mei Li. None too smitten with this soft-spo-ken country lass, Fong sees her as a natural for love-starved Wang Ta, who himself is currently infatuated with Fong's on-again off-again girlfriend, Linda Low, not realizing she is a stripper. And so Fong offers Mei Li first to Ta's father for his inspection.

Sammy wants to keep the bed sheets reserved for Low, who works in his nightclub. So it is these two characters who form and propel the conflict, with Mei Li and Wang Ta meeting and falling timidly in love and muddling their way through a thicket of standard plot complications, the most vexing of which is Mei Li's discovery — in Helen Chao's apartment — of evidence that her new American boyfriend has been sleeping around.

Events come to this point — and to a dramatic head — in a second act ballet which depicts Wang Ta's confused romantic longings through the three women, culminating in his waking up in Helen Chao's bed. In the scene that follows, Mei Li, having dropped by to pick up some repaired clothes for the Wang Chi-yang household, gets wind of Wang Ta's involve-ment with Chao. There, too, after Wang Ta leaves, Chao discovers that the

Cheered by the critics for her work in *The King and I* and as a soloist with the Martha Graham troupe, dancer Yuriko assumed the role of Mel Li in the dream ballet (Photofest).

calling card she has just handed him has been left indifferently on her bed. In this one poignant intersection, all three lovesick principals experience various degrees of pain. Here, the musical realizes its deepest chords.

As a result of the prominence assigned to Wang Ta and the three women, the father's story was minimized. While many of his amusing eccentricities remained, the internal drama that makes him so compelling in the novel was fairly lost in the adaptation. The tension between father and son over the latter's willfully independent dating habits comes to a climax at the Celestial Bar when Wang Chi-yang, his sons, and Madam Liang pay a visit. Leading up to this moment, Sammy Fong, having spotted the perfect opportunity to sabotage Wang Ta's relationship with Linda Low, persuades Low to perform her strip number before Wang Ta's father. (The comical outcome calls to mind the International Settlement episode in the novel wherein Wang Chi-yang ends up in a strip joint and exits in coughing disdain.) Fong is now closer to reclaiming Low for himself. Meanwhile, can Mei Li and Wang Ta get back together? That's the question for intermission talk.

In their second act, Fields and Hammerstein continue the father-son conflict in a humorous vein with a song, "The Other Generation." This number allows Wang Chi-yang and Madam Liang to vent their exasperation in trying to understand and guide the two boys.

Meanwhile Helen Chao, like the brooding outsider Jud Fry of *Oklahoma!*, is there. Unlike Jud Fry, she is not given much to do. Certainly, not as much trouble to cause. Even so, she pushes the play into its darkest corners, few though they are. In effect, she serves potentially the same purpose as Jud, whom Hammerstein once called "the bass fiddle that gave body to the orchestration of the story."[13]

It is tempting to contemplate how differently the script might have turned out had they followed Chao's sad suicidal tale all the way out to the beach and into a consuming sea — had they allowed audiences to witness her desperate last journey. Richard Rodgers and Oscar Hammerstein, if not Joseph Fields, had plenty of the experience required to integrate such a tragic turn into the second act. In their interview with the man from *Newsweek*, they proudly reminisced over some of the daring and acclaimed departures they had made in prior work.

"You wonder about what's acceptable and what isn't," began Oscar. "Dick and I once made up a list of things people told us we couldn't get away with in a certain show — things like not having a chorus come on until the show was 40 minutes old, and like having a killing five minutes before the final curtain. *Oklahoma!* did all that, though. I had a murder in *Rose Marie* in 1924, miscegenation in *Show Boat*, and a suicide in *Carousel*."

Onto the subject, then, of the new musical on which he and his partner were at work up in Boston. It didn't "break any new dramaturgical ground," stated Hammerstein. "We wanted to put together an entertaining show."[14]

At the same time, it is also useful to note the numerous pitfalls that have doomed musicals that try to do too much, especially those which consciously set out to be musical comedies. Musicals that lack a strong central focus, that stumble gracelessly from comedy to pathos, can stumble just as gracelessly at the box office. Also worth noting is that Joe Fields, a far less seasoned librettist, came to the project with a track record in comedy.

Dick and Oscar, eager to forge a workable book and recapture a place on a Broadway marquee, deferred to what Fields had been demonstrably good at. Forget about advancing art. So clear-headed were they about this, they even refashioned from morose to cheerful the pervasively downbeat flower drum songs contained in Mr. Lee's prose. In the novel, Mei Li sings about stupid husbands and ugly mates, about poor men's sons being sold out of town; in the play, Oscar rhymes, instead, of children learning to walk, of the ever-changing spectacle of stars and rain, and of a hundred other miraculous happenings along the yellow river of Tibet. Nary a line about any of the attendant misfortunes and heartaches that befall the same souls in the same region of the world.

In one of his early drafts of the song, Hammerstein alludes quite profoundly to the uncertainty of knowledge; a lyric referred to the act of viewing a swan in flight and seeing black or seeing white depending upon one's personal perspective. Alas, this lyric — by far the most brilliant verse crafted for the new musical — did not make it into the working script.

Hammerstein chose not to wander too far off the Grant Avenue traveled by entranced tourists.

4

Slanting All Eyebrows

Finding the right approach to adapting C.Y. Lee's novel might have been a cakewalk for Dick, Oscar and Joseph. Finding the right actors to fill the parts, however, was anything but. Instead of the usual "cattle call" of dancers and singers by the hundreds showing up to audition, when it came time to cast the show, so few sufficiently talented Asians turned out that the producers were forced to reach well beyond Broadway. With arms outstretched, they turned themselves into beggars struggling to talk others (which sometimes meant the *parents* of others) into giving them a chance.

By luck and serendipity, they gradually assembled a company of some forty souls. Many of the new recruits came from the amateur class. Some of them might have joined out of a sense of ethnic duty, willing to postpone medical school or other ambitions.

The challenge of casting *Flower Drum Song* was rooted in two historic problems. Problem number one: A dearth of Asian roles in stage and film had done little to inspire Chinese youngsters to pursue careers in entertainment. While all across the United States, into hundreds of tap-dance schools in towns large and small went little white tots (mostly girls), their Chinese counterparts were far better off leaning to sing in Cantonese for Chinese opera. Hollywood had not helped any by routinely casting Caucasian stars in Asian roles. (Nor had American audiences, who regularly accepted the resulting oddball makeup jobs without protest.) Los Angeles–born screen vixen Anna May Wong was one of precious few exceptions to this casting practice. Wong was the real thing — a bona fide Chinese actress of beguiling beauty who enjoyed a fairly illustrious career in the movies. And to succeed, Wong had to die a thousand deaths rather than offend white audiences by ending up in the arms of the numerous white actors against whom she played.

Reason number two: As a rule, Chinese parents viewed the acting profession with acute disdain, horrified over the thought of their sons or daughters donning scanty attire and making clowns and sex objects of themselves performing to vulgar western music. "The motives which impel some mothers to drag small children down the byways of Broadway, and teach them spelling by neon sign, move the Chinese not at all," wrote Joanne Stang.[1] Certainly true in predominantly Chinese neighborhoods.

Andy Wong, who ran San Francisco's Chinese Sky Room, recalled how difficult it was when he opened the club in 1937 (the first of its kind in Chinatown) to assemble a local chorus line. To his doors, and to the doors of like-minded clubs that followed, came Asians of mostly Japanese and Filipino ancestry from small midwestern towns. They came with less guilt, having grown up immersed in Caucasian culture. Better still, they could be far enough away from their parents to avoid being berated for undignified behavior. A boy or girl raised in or around a Chinatown was not likely to work for an Andy Wong.

Along this barren, Asian-resistant landscape there were some wonderful exceptions—the kids who grew up in homes where one or both parents performed professionally, or at least encouraged their children to develop theatrical gifts. Young Patrick Adiarte, a Filipino whose mother earned a living as a ballet dancer, started dancing himself at practically the same time he learned to walk. He was cast in Rodgers and Hammerstein's *The King and I* at the age of six or seven. Sometime later, his mother joined him in the company.

Adiarte proved naturally adept at moving to music. Agreeably, he moved the way he was told to move, like a kid taking directions on how to deliver the afternoon paper route. He so impressed *The King and I's* reigning star, Yul Brynner, that he was promoted, while doing the road tour, from chorus boy to the crown prince, a part he would also play in the movie. Adiarte believed it was Brynner who made it happen. "I looked like I could be from Siam."

For his *Flower Drum Song* audition, the young teenager sang a chorus of "Kansas City" from *Oklahoma,* the legendary first Rodgers and Hammerstein show. A little later — in show biz years—"when I got older, I started reading that Rodgers hated anybody to sing his songs, cause he goes crazy. But I guess a little kid singing was okay."

For Gene Kelly, engaged to direct the new musical, Pat tried a few dance steps, and Kelly, viewing the boy's ability from different angles, would say, "Try this way. Well, try it that way...."

By now, Adiarte had adopted a rather blasé attitude to his increasingly sophisticated stage assignments. Says he, with a retrospective yawn, "I wasn't interested in theatre like everybody else was."

Seems it was his mother.

By that time, Pat was taking tap lessons with Paul Draper, the black-listed hoofer who liked to click his heels to Bach and Beethoven. And Pat had landed a scholarship to ballet theatre just before he struck R & H as being ideal for the role of Wang San, the youngest son of Wang Chi-yang, who loves baseball, burgers, and rock and roll, and hates Confucius.

Japanese-born Miyoshi Umeki, the last of nine children to a father who operated an iron factory in the hilly bayside town of Otaru on the northern Japanese island of Hokkaido, grew up in semi-favored circumstances. Also under the same immense roof were a couple of servants and seven extra boys who apprenticed at the father's firm. Miyoshi took a liking to the local Kabuki Theatre. Her brother enrolled her in tap and harmonica classes. From there, she tried her hand at mandolin, which she did not like, and then piano, which she did. "I just loved any sound that you could do it with instrument."[2]

At home, she sang, sang, sang. The tunes were mainly from America. Her mother and father mainly did not like them. So the 13-year-old sang at night under the blankets; during the day, with a water bucket over her head. She was also developing a wry sense of humor.

After V.J. Day, U.S. ships docked in Otaru Bay. So did Miyoshi's first audience of fans. She was awed by the tall G.I.s, three of whom were invited into her home by Miyoshi's English-speaking brother. One of the towering visitors, Ed Giannini, played the clarinet in the 417th Army Service Forces Band. Many nights through the early winter of 1945, Miyoshi, now 16, sang not a word but enjoyed watching the servicemen carry on. One evening — about the time that *Carousel* was opening across the sea — they teased Miyoshi into singing a song. Now she had a real audience, not cringing in cultural shock like her mother and father. She sang and received instant adoration. Giannini told her, "Don't feel ashamed of your voice. Song is not only voice; is heart, mind."

When the war ended and the three visiting G.I.s left, Miyoshi was haunted by memories of music and acceptance. She sought out opportunities to sing with G.I. bands at various service clubs in Otaru, and she made a little money doing it. She spent her free nights listening to the army radio station. She heard Peggy Lee and Doris Day. She landed air time on Japanese radio and TV, singing. Listeners approved.

Three years later, inspired to make the big break and try her luck in the States, Miyoshi started singing in small U.S. nightclubs. In one, she was noticed by agents. Gigs in tiny towns from coast to coast ensued. From there she swiftly ascended — onto guest spots with Tennessee Ernie Ford's television show and with Arthur Godfrey's morning program. She was spotted by a Warner Bros. casting director who routed her into an audition with Josh Logan, then preparing to direct his next film, *Sayonara*. Miyoshi was offered the part of Katsumi. It won her an Academy Award.

It also won her the attention of Rodgers and Hammerstein. Miyoshi looked and sounded perfect for the part of the demure country lass, Mei Li. Moreover, she came with marquee value. With the added personal endorsement of Logan, who had directed both the stage and film versions of *South Pacific*, the Umeki casting seems to have been wrapped up in quick order. After *Sayonara*, Miyoshi had been getting $2,500 per week for singing engagements, and Jerry Lewis had offered her a neat fifty thousand dollars to appear with him in his next movie, *Geisha Boy* (she did not). For Dick and Oscar, Miyoshi agreed to work for $1,500 a week. Nightclubs paid more in money; Broadway, in fame.

Another major casting find was American-born Pat Suzuki, signed to play the brassier Linda Low. Given the name Chiyoko at birth, she was nicknamed "Chibby" (little squirt) by her dad, and later "Pat" by a local grocer who had a hard time with "Chiyoko." Pat grew up on a small California farm in Cressy, population 400. She learned her ABCs in a no-frills two-room schoolhouse. She swam and rode horses bareback. She spoke Spanish to migrant farm workers.

"I could hardly wait to grow up. I didn't like being a kid, because I always had certain feelings I couldn't explain. The only things I could dream about in those days were the trucks going by on the highway all night long. I used to dream of all the places they had been that I would like to go someday."

With no place yet to go and little to do in Cressy, Pat sang songs to pass the time. She sang songs at church, her first solo at the prima age of three and a half years. During an Easter service she blared out "White Lilies" with such hallelujah verve that all of the other children hushed to let her go it alone.

Everybody waited to hear more Pat-power whenever she dived into her next vocal rendition. During a few county shindigs, she brought the show to a standing ovation when she tore into "I Am an American!"

Not quite. She was treated decidedly more Japanese, as were other families of like heritage at the outbreak of World War II. In Pat speak, " … Wham! Pearl Harbor."

The Suzuki family members were interred at the Amache Relocation Camp in Lamar, Colorado. Pat was said not to have sung much during those bleak years of national isolation. Her memories of the time consist of thunderstorms and of watching Nisei boy scouts every dawn battling proudly against windy sand to raise high the American flag.

Following the war, the Suzukis returned to Cressy. Pat was ready for bigger and better things in bigger and better cities. She had been listening to a radio program from the Edgewater Hotel in Chicago which gave her glamorous visions of city life near a lake and beach. Her father endorsed her dreams: "As you get older, you get afraid to take chances. When you're young, you have the drive. You should use your youth."

The advice taken, Pat Suzuki, the same year Rodgers and Hammerstein were writing *South Pacific*, left Cressy for Oakland up north, attracted to Mills College. She worked for a spell as a receptionist in a Chinese restaurant, and in short order switched down to Modesto Junior College, nearer to her home. Still restless, she tried some classes up in San Francisco at City College, then settled down for two years at San Jose State, where she took courses in philosophy, biology, art, art history, woodworking — and voice. On the weekends, she sang in local clubs.

Europe was her next intended destination. The year was 1954. Pat got as far as New York. Running out of money, she ran into a stroke of good fortune. In the Big Apple, Suzuki snared a minor role in the road company of *Teahouse of the August Moon*. When the company got to Seattle, the girl from Cressy mustered the nerve, after finding herself inside the Colony, a bohemian supper club, to needle its owner, Norm Bobrow, for a fling with the band. Her impromptu vocalizing rocked the room, and a star was sort of born that night. Three sizzling Seattle years later, Suzuki was a regular at the Colony.

"How long will she stay?" one of her fans asked the owner.

Answered Bobrow, "Until Rodgers and Hammerstein write a musical for her."

Who knows? The prophetic remark, as later reported in *Time* magazine, may have actually been made.

During Pat Suzuki's Colony days, Bing Crosby saw her perform, and he returned three more times, bowled over by the young Japanese-American dynamo. He told many of his friends, "She's a great bet for the big time!" The jacket notes for Pat's first album were penned by Crosby.

Along the way, she had impressed critics and tickled crowds in Kansas City when she played Dorothy in a Starlight Theatre production of *The Wizard of Oz*. Pat could be Merman. Pat could be Garland. Better than that, Pat brought her own brazen oomph to the stage — the essence of a true star. Pat could be Pat.

By the time that Dick and Oscar got around to appraising Suzuki, she was a newly established New York fixture, having lit up the television night appearing on a number of shows from Ed Sullivan to a Frank Sinatra special before ascending to the top of the heap as a guest on Jack Paar's nationally riveting *The Tonight Show*. Richard Rodgers, Suzuki is not the first to suggest, likely discovered her when she sang for Paar's audience. Perhaps Rodgers saw her the night when she was asked by another guest, "Tell me, do Japanese dogs talk differently than dogs in America?" To which Suzuki replied: "Yes, of course. In America, the dogs go bow! wow! wow! And in Japan, they go wan! wan! wan!"[3]

Suzuki believes that if one could survive the trauma of appearing for the neurotically unpredictable Jack Paar, whose reputation for off-the-cuff candor kept many performers in a state of panic, one was ready for the comparatively genteel world of Rodgers and Hammerstein. And they were ready for Suzuki — she in whom they could see their Linda Low. For the Japanese singer's one audition, when it came time to read, the only script they could find was a copy of *Lady in the Dark*. Suzuki remembers not doing justice to Moss Hart.

A few other actors nearly cast themselves into the show on the basis of career portfolios. Keye Luke, famous as Charlie Chan's number one son in the film series, was signed to bring Master Wang Chi-yang to the stage. He would also be bringing strong name recognition to the playbill, which just might attract some of the Asian Americans who usually shunned such entertainments.

Whom to cast as the brooding, desperately seductive Helen Chao? Classically trained Arabella Hong, full of steamy gravity (though perhaps a little too beautiful for the role), had been giving concerts for many years. She was out of the country during the initial audition hubbub. Upon her return to New York, she read about *Flower Drum Song* in the papers, and, without representation, immediately called the office for an appointment to try out. Backstage during auditions, she was approached by agent Ray Coleman, who offered to take her on as a client.

"I believe in fate," says Arabella, who sang "Steal Me, Sweet Thief" from *The Old Maid and The Thief* by Gian Carlo Menotti. By coincidence, the song had the same feel as a new ballad which Dick and Oscar would eventually write for the Helen Chao character.

Came two callbacks for Hong, these before Richard Rodgers. She sang "My Man's Gone Now" at each. "I didn't know what they were looking for," she remembers.

Evidently, they were looking for her.

Another new working professional who answered the call was film actor and dancer Chao-Li Chi. He had appeared, with Arthur Kennedy and

Dick Kiley, as "a Korean soldier torturing American prisoners" in his first play, the 1956 stage production of *Time Limit!*

Chi held a masters from New York University in physical education with a major in ethnic dances. He had performed with New York dance troupes. Although he auditioned as a dancer for Gene Kelly, whom he regarded as "a gentleman in every sense of the word," the director saw Chi as right for the part of Mei Li's father. So Chi was about to go into rehearsal playing a major role in a new musical, and that should be worth a giant feather in his cap. To the chosen few — among the few — went many golden opportunities.

From the alumni of *The King and I*, they drew two or three kids. One was Baayork Lee, of Chinese and Indian descent, who started dancing at the age of three and, as a child, played the parts of an Eskimo in Irving Berlin's *Mr. President*; a girl in *Harlem*; and a shoeshine boy in *Golden Boy*. Like Adiarte, Lee can only mistily recall how it all happened, or even whether she had to try out. Agentless like Hong, Lee showed up on her own. "Rodgers and Hammerstein remembered me, so when it was time to audition the show, they put me in."

At the moment, the new R & H musical was but one of four other shows with all or partly Asian casts gearing up for their first nights on Broadway. For Wonci Lui, another young *King and I* veteran, it gave her heady visions of a promising new era: "All of a sudden — Hey! Asian casting! Get with it!"

Indeed, for a time it looked like the Great White Way was about to become a pan–Asian corridor, what with *The World of Suzie Wong* getting ready to face the critics, and with three other new plays headed for Times Square — *Kataki*, *Rashomon*, and *A Majority of One*.

Lui was offered parts in both *Suzie* and *Drum*. At auditions for the latter, choreographer Carol Haney sent strong we-want-you signals.

"She was marvelous," says Wonci. "'Can you do that?' she would ask. 'Dance with me.'"

Lui was assured by the stage manager, "No matter what, I want you in the show."

For a time, she had the rare luxury of having to decide between two shows. Her friends asked her, "Are you going to be in *Suzie Wong*?" "Are you going to be in *Flower Drum Song*?"

"A strange time for Asian acting," she remembers. "I had to choose. I'm a dancer. I'd rather go with a possible hit."

While they did well casting most of the principals, the chorus was still full of empty slots. The auditions were running up against a counter-productive feature of Asian culture, as articulated by casting director Eddie

Blum: "The biggest headache *Flower Drum Song* presented was finding actors. The problem is that Asians are generally very poor actors because they are too shy…. I remember when Miyoshi Umeki came to us. She was very shy but fortunately, she had a wonderful sense of humor."[4]

So, out to the major cities went Gene Kelly and Carol Haney, to Boston and Philly, to Los Angeles and San Francisco in search of the elusive "Chinese" chorus line. Taking advantage of all the publicity generated about their ultra-conscientious coast-to-coast search for the missing talent, they cast a wide net, extending as far west as Hawaii, where nightclub singer and dancer Ed Kenney was seen and signed to play the eldest son, Wang Ta.

It is puzzling that they did not find more bodies at San Francisco 's still-vibrant "Chinese" nightclub, Forbidden City — or, for that matter, at any of the other night spots in the pagoda district. Although it had seen its better days, Charlie Low's club still put crack entertainers before a discriminating public. They spoke and sang English. They crooned and amused. They dazzled with pizzazz and snappy footwork. Toy and Wing were an absolutely first-rate pair of hoofers. Might they have stolen the club scenes in *Flower Drum Song*? Might they have settled for a couple of cameos?

Perhaps the sensitive Gene Kelly was disinclined to raid Low's ensemble. And perhaps Toy and Wing would have taken too much focus off the principals.

Ivy Tam, Low's wife and the club's costume maker (and, within a year, a dancer herself), does not recall any formal *Drum* auditions anywhere in Chinatown, Forbidden City included. Neither does anybody else. Tam saw Gene Kelly and other Hollywood stars coming and going at the time, sitting down to enjoy the floor shows. They had ample opportunity to watch and appraise. During social chats with Gene over drinks, Charlie and Ivy exchanged the usual pleasantries.

Tam did not believe that

Hawaiian nightclub singer and dancer Ed Kenney played the eldest son, Wang Ta, whose search for love formed the main plot (Photofest).

Kelly or his colleagues were going out of their way to discover hidden talent on the premises. She thought they were there to drum up free publicity and have a good time. From all of Chinatown, only one person was picked up: Jack Suzuki, who changed his last name to Soo. A regular at Forbidden City, under contract to Low, Soo worked as a comedian and emcee stand-in for Low. Kelly is said to have spotted him.

Charlie Low was proud and supportive, remembers Ivy Tam, and let Soo go with his blessing, believing the Broadway break was to important to turn down.[5]

Soo landed the minor role of Celestial Bar comedian Frankie Wing — a role he may have inspired, it seems so tailor-made to his work at Forbidden City and there is nothing like it in the novel. Why they did not see Soo as perfect for the larger part of nightclub owner Sammy Fong would become one of many casting-related mysteries. Soo's deadpan expressions were alone worth a dozen well-reviewed laughs.

With rehearsals approaching, and still without a full cast, they began resorting to some unusual measures. After placing ads in New York Chinatown newspapers soliciting audition candidates and receiving replies from a grand total of *one*, they put on their walking shoes and hit the pavement. With a grinding determination reminiscent of the days when a young Richard Rodgers and Larry Hart trudged fruitlessly from one publishing house to the next, they trudged from church to church and from tap school to tap school seeking promising young talents to sing and dance in a new musical.

"A number of doors politely but effectively slammed in their faces."[6]

Rodgers spent some afternoon hours writing letters to a number of school principals, striving to gain their allied cooperation to allow 17-year-old Mable Wong to appear in the show's understaffed chorus. His letter-writing paid off.

They stalked the streets at large, gazing hither and yon for anyone who kind of looked Chinese and might be amenable to a quick theatrical makeover. A Revlon sales clerk, Marie Huie, was nearly scared out of her wits, feeling she was about to be held up or worse, when suddenly stared at on Sixth Avenue by a strange man from out of nowhere.

"How would you like to be in a Broadway show?" he asked.[7]

Miraculously, she joined the growing ranks of a cobbled-together cast, reluctant or otherwise. The amusing tale, codified in the pages of *Time* magazine, seems more a testament to effective press agentry than to a genuine talent-finding coup. Not only were R & H making hay with their colorful tryout techniques, they were also insulating themselves against possible bad reviews pointing to personnel shortcomings.

And all along, too, they were admitting into their quasi–Chinese company some veteran actors who did not arrive with slanted eyebrows or far east accents. Bring on the oriental makeup specialists. One dancer who would need a lot of it was David Lober, a Russian who had performed in a number of shows from *Bloomer Girl* to, most recently, *John Murray Anderson's Almanac*. A pro he was, with a veteran's knowledge of musical theatre and his own discriminating views on the endlessly debated subject. Lober was about to observe a number of things that he would privately question.

In particular, says he, "They made some extraordinary strange choices in casting."

Lober could never understand why the role of Sammy Fong, the irascible nightclub owner in love with the equally raffish Linda Low, went to a *Caucasian* comedian, Larry Storch. Two years before, Storch — who hailed from Texas — had earned his principal Broadway credit, along with other newcomers Joel Gray and Tammy Grimes, in a 32-performance blowout, *The Littlest Revue*.

"It really didn't make much sense," says Lober

To casting director Eddie Blum, it made sense, for in Blum's curious opinion, "there are no oriental comedians."[8]

Shawnee Smith, not quite off the reservation, was half Hopi and Indian and half English. Of Italian descent came Victor Duntiere, another veteran. The names Ahumanda and Lorca, Young and Ribuca, and Jim and Ellis Griffith showed up in the program credits, as did one Vicki Racimo. "The scouts ... settled for any vaguely oriental features," wrote *Time*.[9]

They settled, too, for even less than vague. Juanita Hall, featured in a 1955 flop, *House of Flowers*, and before that, beloved for her performance as Bloody Mary in *South Pacific*, was chosen to play Wang Chi-yang's late wife's sister, Madam Liang. Hall, the only seasoned stage vet among the principals, was a light-skinned African American. (Some would try to pass her off as a Polynesian.) To her credit, with makeup and a wig, and with her natural otherworldly air, Hall cleverly managed to look kind of Asian. "Kind of" was fast becoming a standard.

There might have been a second African American in the original cast had an idea of Mr. Rodgers, possibly inspired by the impressive example of Ms. Hall, panned out, orientally speaking. The composer, who was rumored to have fancied ladies in his employ, approached a young Diahann Carroll, whom he may have fancied. Another former resident of the folded *House of Flowers*, Carroll was asked about possible work in Dick's new "Chinese" musical. Might she consent to an extensive touch-up job

African American Juanita Hall, left, with Miyoshi Umeki and Keye Luke, was one of many non–Asians cast in the original Broadway production (Springer/Photofest).

by makeup artist Eddie Senz, to see if she could be made to blend in with other quasi-orientals? She quite nicely consented.

It didn't work, recounted Carroll. "By the time Eddie Senz was through, the powder and paint was so thick that I could barely open my mouth. Rodgers dropped the idea but promised there would be another show some other time."[10]

(That "some other time" came four years hence when Carroll was cast to play the lead role, a real African American woman, in Rodgers' *No Strings*.)

By the time they were on the road, going through shakedowns before out-of-town audiences, R & H were turning their colorful casting travails into the stuff of legend — talking them up to reporters as if they still needed more free press to stimulate an already booming advance ticket sales campaign. A color photo of twelve members of the cast that reached the cover of *Newsweek* revealed nine reasonably Asian-looking women and three generally whatever-looking men, none of whose altered eyebrows could quite disguise who he really was. The overall impression, nonetheless, was exotically if vaguely appealing, thanks possibly to one Eddie Senz.

Gene Kelly was high on the young, eager recruits, most of whom were about to appear in their first Broadway show. And maybe, with a little help from Mr. Senz, their first hit. Fresh innocents, indeed, any one of whom might turn out to be *Flower Drum Song's* surprise star....

"What most of them lack in show business experience, they more than make up for in willingness, charm, and inherent talent," beamed Kelly to *Dance* magazine. "I mean to say, I'm crazy about them."[11]

5

Starring the Director

Gene Kelly. Two magical words. Two words synonymous with movie musicals. The star of *Singin' in the Rain*, Kelly danced and sang through the most revered sequence in any musical ever made when, alone one dreamy night on a small rain-splattered city street and having just fallen in love, he ambled up and down with an umbrella in hand, sloshing his blissful way through puddles and grinning at raindrops, his face wondrously aglow.

"He was a sweetie," marvels Pat Suzuki. "Just like the movie. He had that incredible smile and he was graceful in person."

In the twenty-seven film musicals in which he appeared, Kelly, who had started out in Pittsburgh running his own dance school, leapt across rooftops, skated through city parks, sauntered up hillsides of heather with the girl by his side. He jumped like a sailor on leave, pranced in clown face, fought off pirates. He danced around Paris fountains, and did it all with the casual grace of an average sort of guy—the guy you might see next door mowing the lawn or building a barbecue out back.

Unlike his one filmland equal—suave top-hatted hoofer Fred Astaire—Kelly took the earthy route, delivering songs in an oddly faint voice, cracking jokes like a garage mechanic on a break. Making it all look natural. His genius for portraying an American everyman informed and lifted the 102 glorious minutes of *Singin' in the Rain* into cinematic rapture.

Richard Rodgers, then working with Larry Hart, had given Kelly his first important break on Broadway back in 1940, casting him, ironically, to play a lowlife gigolo in their ground-breaking musical of unsparing realism, *Pal Joey*. From there, the dashing new dance guy who looked like no other dancer on the lot was stolen away by Hollywood. Among a slate of cinematic treats to which he lent his understated charm, there was *On*

Pat Suzuki, left, and Miyoshi Umeki take direction from Gene Kelly for publicity photographs (Springer/Photofest).

the Town (with Frank Sinatra), *The Pirate, Invitation to the Dance, For Me and My Gal, Brigadoon,* and the award-winning *An American in Paris.*

By the time Kelly finally returned to the stage, thanks to Richard Rodgers and colleagues offering him a second big break — the chance to direct his first Broadway musical — his name, as measured in type size contractually granted for billing purposes as well as marquee value, would loom high above all others save for Richard Rodgers and Oscar Hammerstein. Even Joseph Fields settled for a smaller-sized credit.

Kelly had also co-directed and co-choreographed *Singin' in the Rain,* as he did a number of his other films, for which he received high honors, once earning an honorary award by the Academy for "brilliant achievement in choreography."[1] Striking out on his own, he had shown directing savvy in Hollywood the year before when he took the big chair on the set of the Joe Fields comedy *The Tunnel of Love*. And in later years, he would direct five more films, a rather inconsistent batch including *Hello, Dolly!* and *The Cheyenne Social Club*.

Biographer Alvin Yudkoff believes that a big reason for Kelly's being offered the *Drum* assignment was his easygoing way, a quality that could help soften the potential trauma for a cast of neophyte Asians working on a new show headed for the big time. "It was a task that required far more than theatrical know-how and had much to do with why, surprisingly, Gene had been chosen over many directors with many more credits listed in Broadway playbills." Gene's natural friendliness among people of different races was a factor evidently valued by Rodgers and Hammerstein. "He was one of the very few who could direct a story about a clash of a gentle Asian culture against the bristling modern American world without being patronizing or insulting."[2]

Kelly, in fact, tolerated a lot of different people in a country still riven with bigotry. When blacklisted Hollywood film director Jules Dassin, who had fled Los Angeles during the House Un-American Activities Committee hearings after being named by another director, received a best director award in 1955 at the Cannes Film Festival for his *Rififi*, he was ignored by former colleagues wherever he went; they would either gaze down at their feet or "hide their faces" behind raised glasses. Only one American celebrity had the courage to speak with Dassin at Cannes. Gene Kelly.[3]

Actually, he was also something of a chameleon, for there was another, much more artistically ruthless Kelly that his *Flower Drum Song* charges would not see. Well known, at least to those with whom he had labored in Hollywood, for a demanding perfectionism with dancers, Kelly had an ego and would stop "short of nothing to get what he wanted."[4] Evidently, with sweet-tempered Carol Haney officially handling the choreography, there was little risk of this tougher, more driven Gene Kelly surfacing.

Was he really their first choice to direct the show? Not according to two authors, each of whom cites exclusive accounts, none substantiated, in other relevant books covering the personalities in question. Meryle Secrest, one of numerous Richard Rodgers biographers, noted that they had first gone to Yul Brynner. Brynner had to decline because he was tied up with a film, *The Sound and the Fury*, for 20th Century–Fox.[5] In another tome, *The Wordsmiths*, it is written that Jerome Robbins was the first choice to direct. He, too, was previously engaged, then working on *Gypsy*, although it would not open for another six months.[6] All other sources cite Kelly as the number one candidate.

Kelly received a cable from Oscar Hammerstein, who was in London on business, inviting him to meet at the Claridges Hotel, where he was staying. There, while Oscar sat on the edge of his bed, he told Gene of a new show he and Dick were writing, and asked him if he would be interested in directing it.

A few months later at Hammerstein's Pennsylvania farm, Gene and Oscar, together again, discussed the still incomplete script and worked out a number of details. When Gene said "Yes," he likely envisioned a stable project of the sort Dick and Oscar were known to run, sans temperaments flying and script doctors coming and going. Hardly could Kelly have imagined all of the daunting obstacles which lay ahead to test his good nature.

The first of a series of dispiriting setbacks to the director-designate was the fragile physical condition of both Oscar and Richard. The show was originally slated to begin rehearsals on the stage of the Plymouth Theatre on September 1, 1958, but the date had to be moved back by a fortnight to give Hammerstein more time to recuperate from a recent double operation in the hospital. Both his gall bladder and prostate were removed. The gentle giant was in considerable pain in the late days of the trying summer of '58, behind in his lyric-writing by at least three songs when the first cast readings finally got underway. One of the unfinished songs was to be a ballad for Arabella Hong.

During the delay, Pat Suzuki and a few others in the ensemble were sent off for tap dance lessons. Pat was also turned into a publicity machine for the show when she and her father started getting sent out by R & H to do radio and television interviews. "He was good company, and good to be interviewed," says Suzuki, who adored her dad. From out of nowhere appeared a public relations firm approaching Mr. Suzuki about representing him and his up-and-coming daughter. Said the man from Cressy in reply, "Well, I'm a farmer, and I don't know anything about this business, but I'll tell you: When I have a good crop, I put on fertilizer. You guys are hired."

Kelly had no idea how really ill Hammerstein was, for he had never heard him complain. Once he got wind of the situation, he felt sure they would postpone things until Oscar was well enough to proceed. Rodgers and Fields, taking charge, proceeded anyway. "They already got an opening date set for the St. James Theatre and Oscar, apparently was insisting that there should be no postponements. Both Dick and Oscar, I discovered, were extremely strong-willed men.... They were fighters, both of them, and I admired this quality tremendously."[7]

So Rodgers, minus Hammerstein during most of the early rehearsals, kept an active eye on the developing situation, along with Joe Fields, who himself was not shy about asserting his authority and whose fragile heart was a ticking time bomb ready to send yet another of the creative triumvirate to a hospital emergency room. (Such were the perils of the profession. In 1960, as Alan Jay Lerner, on the road with the Broadway-bound *Camelot*, emerged from a hospital having survived a heart attack, he noticed the show's director Moss Hart being wheeled past him on an incoming gurney. Hart had just suffered the same setback.)

Kelly's next obstacle: the unfinished script and score. They began rehearsing the young cast while Oscar labored over fresh verse in the making, sometimes at home in bed too weak to get up, other times down at the theatre, leaning over a piece of paper on the stage apron with a pen in hand. Nonetheless, the unflappably upbeat director, Mr. Singing in the Rain himself, cast a wide nurturing smile across the entire company from wherever he stood or sat in the empty theatre.

While Miyoshi Umeki was learning one of her big numbers, "A Hundred Million Miracles," Kelly moved his head back and forth to the tune, shaping the words with his mouth without singing them, just to demonstrate for the sweetly complaint lass from Otaru, Japan.[8]

Dancer Wonci Lui was disarmed by the director's embracing manner, as was, indeed, most everyone in the company. "He would say, 'Okay, just sing with me! Let's see what range you are.' ... He would start us off. We would start singing, then he would fade off and let us continue."

"Gene!" shouted Dick Rodgers. "I'd like to borrow Pat Suzuki, take her downstairs and run over that thing we started this morning."

Composer and first-time star retired to a basement lounge for song practice. Exhorted the tunesmith to the singer from Cressy, California, "Forgive me, darling, but that beat comes a little sooner than you think it does."

Suzuki gave the song another try.

"Exactly! Don't ever do it better!"[9]

The brash, fun-loving singer, who joined the company with scarce apprehension (well, she had endured those nerve-rattling nights on the unscripted Jack Paar program), bore a rather blasé attitude, figuring that if things didn't work out, she could always rejoin her "buddies in Seattle" at the Colony nightclub. And in her nervousness, she turned to teasing Mr. Rodgers "mercilessly."

When first introduced by Rodgers to one of her solos, "I Enjoy Being a Girl," Suzuki was disappointed, comparing the number in her mind to the jazzier stuff she had been belting out in cabaret. Nor was the number easy to learn, with Rodgers insisting on a certain delivery. "He always had a very definite idea about the timing because it was important that the words were emphasized in a specific way."

Struggling to comply, Pat brashly blurted out, "It's hard to sing because it's really square!"

Undaunted, Rodgers kept her at it until she understood exactly what he was after.

Despite her reservations, Suzuki mastered the number in a way that would make audiences take note and give the show a compelling pulse. "It showed off your voice a lot."

Back to the song about miracles happening every day: Mr. Kelly, who by some accounts dreamed of making this a dance show — perhaps the most danced of all the Rodgers and Hammerstein vehicles, and why not? — was coming up against another big setback in the form of Miyoshi Umeki. She and Chao-Li Chi, paired up to play Mei Li and her father, Dr. Li, were being instructed on how to dance while singing their flower drum songs.

Recalls Chi, "Gene Kelly had the idea that I would be a good Dr. Li. Unfortunately, they got Miyoshi Umeki fresh from triumph with Academy Award playing cute cute cute."

Through no fault of her own, the actress could not dance. Neither could she move around very much while singing.

Kelly strove to give her a few simple steps to complement the number.

"First of all, Miyoshi could not move two arms at once," continues Chi. "And she has two left feet. She was tripping over herself. Gene Kelly tore his hair out."

He kept at it. Nothing registered.

"Miyoshi," said the director, "if you don't know how to move, then don't move. Just stand there and sing."

Miyoshi felt awkward not knowing what to do with her hands. She had strapped the drum around her waist, but it would turn over on her. She tried the steps once more.

Suggested Kelly, "Miyoshi, if it's difficult for you to walk, then two steps forward, one step back, three steps to the left, three steps to the right."

She had trouble with that too.

"If that's too much, then don't move. And hold the drum so you can't move two arms at once. So, never mind the strap. Hold the drum so it doesn't turn over on you, with one arm, and hit only with one hand. Never mind the stick."

Vivid are Chi's memories of Umeki "hugging the drum desperately under one arm and slapping it with her one hand."

Kelly was fast realizing that many of his ideas would never make it into this show.

Chi's primary skill as a dancer may have sealed his early demise in the role of Mei Li's father. Kelly was also bothered by how ill-matched the pair looked in their disparate facial structures. So Chi was tactfully removed from the part of Dr. Li, and, in compensation, offered the smaller role of Dr. Lu Fong and a double understudy position for both Wang Chi-yang and Dr. Li.

If Kelly had not sensed lightweight scripting during the preliminary talks with Hammerstein, he soon grew concerned over a certain lack of depth to the property as he worked with the actors blocking out scenes. Gradually, he came to feel that his first musical could not be another *South Pacific* or *Carousel*, so he decided to compensate with as much comedy shtick as he could get into the show and onto the actor's faces— with gags and with cakewalks, all the usual stuff that can keep a borderline musical at least theatrically appealing.

At the same time, the director apparently tried to inject as much dramatic tension as was practically possible. In the scene between Helen Chao and Wang Ta, shortly after Ta wakes up to find himself by mistake in Chao's bed and just before he exits indifferently, Kelly instructed Hong to throw herself at Wang Ta in a desperately pleading fashion, in essence recreating a scene from the novel.[10]

However Kelly viewed the libretto, a lifelong hoofer of his passions might have wondered what he was doing directing book scenes and not the big dance numbers. His more-than-capable colleague, choreographer Carol Haney, had her dancers in promising motion and under control. Something of a celebrity herself, Haney had recently taken the stage to sizzling acclaim when she introduced "Hernando's Hideaway" in *Pajama Game*, dancing to the footwork of choreographer Bob Fosse, who himself favored hot visceral jazz.

Haney had started dancing at the age of five. Ten years later, she opened her own dance studio for youngsters in her hometown of Bedford, Massachusetts. Within three years she was on her way to Tinseltown, where she did the drugstore waitress thing by day. Up in San Francisco, she landed sporadic club work. Back in L.A., she broke into pictures— and promptly injured her knee. Once recovered, Haney became Jack Cole's partner in the clubs. She was hired to assist Gene Kelly, guiding many of the partners with whom he danced in film musicals. Leslie Caron was taught the American way by Haney. While at work with Gene on *Brigadoon*, Haney auditioned for George Abbott, who had co-authored and was about to co-direct, with Jerome Robbins, a new show, *Pajama Game*. Haney landed a role which would win her a Tony for best supporting actress.

Loved by all, choreographer Carol Haney, center, with Richard Rodgers, left, and Joseph Fields, appears to be welcoming a new recruit to the chorus (Springer/Photofest).

Now she was teaching again, this time endeavoring to turn a chorus of fresh-faced young Asians into stageworthy pros. One of the kids was Baayork Lee, who adored Haney and her Jack Cole–inspired style of dance.

"Fantastic. I admired her so much. I wanted to dance like her."

Did Haney strive for some sort of an Asian motif?

"No," answers Lee. "It had the Jack Cole kind of smooth aggressiveness. There were these furies that came out, and they did slides going from one side of the stage to the other on their knees."

David Lober adds, "Filtered through Carol, what came out was strong and fluid. Cole's moves tended to end in sharp holds of position. Carol's tended to flow through. There was a different kind of continuity."

Haney liked the way Lee moved, so she put her in some of the adult dance numbers, too, including, to Lee's delight, the dream ballet. "We had these little tinkle things that we carried, and she allowed me to be in that."

Wonci Lui remembers the endless tinkering with "Chop Suey." Haney could not make up her mind. "We felt as if it was offensive.... 'Put your fingers up!'"

So they raised their fingers up one way. Then another way. And still another....

"We'd sit around and watch and say, 'Okay, here we go again!'"

Patrick Adiarte's flashy, energetic dancing made him a favorite with the company.

"Pat was loved by Gene Kelly because he tapped," said Lee.

Adiarte, in turn, found Kelly much more relaxed than Jerome Robbins. More prone to "let you go. Hollywood people tend to be like that."

The dance numbers involving Adiarte were put together without his initial participation, after which he was brought in, taught his steps and integrated. He doesn't recall Haney ever correcting him.

"She was marvelous," states David Lober, "perhaps too overly sweet a woman. She was a superb dancer. She got her work done. She was extraordinarily easy to get along with."

Lober feels that Haney's contributions ranged from exceptional — he lauds her "beautifully done ballet" — to "just schlock."

"She had a magnificent sense of rhythm," he says. "The choreography was somewhat inconsistent from my point of view but filled with fine rhythm and movement inventions in certain areas. She seemed given to neologisms such as calling one section of the ballet danced by three girls in tight oriental skirts 'the Onions.' ... She evoked fondness in the people she worked with."

By all reports, Haney enjoyed definite autonomy, although Lober recalls that the "very smooth, very pleasant" Kelly choreographed the soft-shoe routine for "Sunday" — "probably the best thing he did." Kelly also apparently had a hand in setting a few other minor dance sequences. He and Haney got along well, conferring a lot in private over the unfolding saga, the drama both on stage and off — not all of it flattering to Kelly. Only a few days into rehearsals, Oscar's son, James, was not liking what he saw. He shared his doubts with his dad, who was still recuperating at home. Oscar was warned of a show already "in trouble," the blame being placed at the feet of Kelly, who "seemed confused and unconfident."[11]

Any musical going up for the first time falls under the constant scrutiny of almost everyone connected to it, from star to prop hand. "Hit or miss?" they ask themselves every day — everyone a professional critic in his own mind. They sit out in the seats or stand in the wings when they have the time; they watch bits and pieces being slogged together and pulled apart and reslogged or discarded. They fail to imagine how the whole thing might look and sound opening night. All they see are the things *they* would never let happen were *they* directing the mess.

Victor Duntiere, left, and Susan Lynn Kikuchi (Yuriko's daughter), right, in "Sunday"—the one number staged by Gene Kelly, with costumes by Irene Sharaff stressing degrees of assimilation (Photofest).

James Hammerstein's alarm bell to his ailing father was not an act of pure selfless feedback—not considering his own obvious ambitions to stage direct himself. And added to the son's mounting worries were the natural insecurities of the largely virgin cast. By and large, actors do not like tentative or fumbling stage masters, no matter how good their work turns out to be after anxiety-raising experimentation on the road. Most actors prefer to be told exactly what to do. For all their railing against the abusive words and demands of a tyrannical taskmaster like Jerome

Robbins, still, when all is said and done, a Jerome Robbins is the director they will respect and praise, regardless of whether he deserves it.

While Kelly may have only been trying this and trying that in order to shake out unworkable ideas and build upon unforeseen good ones, the cast quickly sensed an unsure hand. Stage veteran David Lober, who had worked with some of the best, regards Kelly's direction as "mediocre." Arabella Hong was not impressed, remembering that R & H did not find Kelly "up to the task."

Chao-Li Chi saw a man losing faith in the materials at hand. "He was giving up because there was no integration like *South Pacific*, all those things that are woven together, belong to the story. But what happened, because the pilots were gone, the people just followed and followed along as much as they can and ... the whole thing was put together piecemeal."

Richard Rodgers was there every day, fussing over details, making curt corrections when quarter notes were issued as half notes, sharing caustic doubts in letters to his wife, Dorothy, who was traveling abroad: "Oscar has slowed down again. Joe is doing nothing. Gene is paying too much attention to details in directing, and I'm the only one who's fault-less. Aren't you proud?"[12]

Faultless maybe — when not dozing off in an orchestra seat. Under the effects of fatigue or alcohol, he did not always stay awake. When they lost him out there, quickly the house lights were struck to keep the sleeping composer out of the gaze of an apprehensive cast.[13] This also put novelist C.Y. Lee, another lone figure in the empty seats, in the dark. Never asking impolite questions, never daring to suggest a different approach to anything, Mr. Lee was noticeably thrilled with all the attention being lavished upon his book. "He was so delighted that his play was being done," recounts Chi, "that he just sat there with a silly grin. He never spoke a word.... He never made a suggestion."

James Hammerstein asserted more authority, edging his way up onto the stage to assist Joe Fields in blocking some of the scenes. Just how he and Fields got into the act would never be officially explained. Likely, though, their presence was the source of the friction that led to a "fracas" between Kelly and Fields some three weeks into rehearsals. As good natured as Kelly was, he also was known for guarding his authority and not liking to share it with others. Upset, he asked to see Rodgers and Hammerstein between rehearsals that night. About the meeting, Rodgers wrote smugly to his wife: "Gene had nothing new to say and could have said it today. Neurotic?"[14]

In the murky world of *Flower Drum Song*'s erratic creation those first confusing weeks, Kelly's power was on the wane. He was far from a fired

employee, though. Arabella Hong observed Kelly — "one of the most beautiful persons you could ever meet" — losing control and fading off into the
background, where he spent more time helping Haney on the dances. Chi
remembers Joe Fields directing book scenes, and Wonci Lui recalls that
Jimmy Hammerstein "seemed to be involved a lot in the directorial....
They kind of reached for him and thought that maybe he was closer to the
original idea." The direction, in Pat Suzuki's words, was "pretty collective."

As they continued reaching, probably the most formidable challenge
to Kelly's withering authority were the producers themselves, who happened to also be the writers. Any gripes Kelly had with his co-creators
would have to be taken up with his co-creators. And together, the three
of them were damn near a foundation. Between them, Dick and Oscar had
amassed 92 musicals. Fields had worked on three shows. In the theatre, a
track record often trumps a job title, especially when the backstage buzz
does not favor the director of record. Actors exchange their own notes.
Stage managers see themselves rescuing a property in trouble. Lyricists
suddenly burst onto the stage, ready to take over for the latest director
felled by the latest heart attack. (Read Alan Jay Lerner.)

A searchlight of seasoned eyes studied every move made by Mr. Kelly.
If, indeed, he had been demoted, he carried on as if he were still singing
in the rain — still spreading loads of good will, getting along with a song
in his heart for everyone out there in the whole human race. Those running about in the rain of a confusing rehearsal period without their
umbrellas could at least count on Mr. Kelly to keep them from crashing
into one another.

Patrick Adiarte was oblivious to any power struggles. "I was so young,
scared and in awe of everyone at the time that I didn't really know any of
the rumors and gossip.... I was just trying to hit my marks and say my
lines."

The looming figure of Oscar Hammerstein, when he did come around,
did not settle the young actor's nerves. "I was scared of him. He had a
pockmarked face. I didn't understand him. He seemed quiet all the time....
Rodgers was a little more friendly, and had a kinder face to me at the time."

Another fear that kept young Patrick on edge: "You're always afraid
you're going to get fired. At least I was."

What bothered Arabella Hong more than the lack of a strong director was the lack of her solo number, yet to be written. By now, she had
naturally assumed she would be learning it. Three weeks into the
rehearsals, she wasn't. The song, whatever it might be, remained uncom-
posed. Hong decided to approach the master from whom the notes would
flow.

"Everybody had gotten their song. I hadn't gotten mine. One day after rehearsal, I was standing up on the apron of the stage and Dick was out in the auditorium, and the only one there. And I said, 'You know, Dick, everybody got their song. When do I get mine?'"

Rodgers paused.

"Don't worry. I'll give it to you before opening."

Hong had heard through her agent that a new lyric of Oscar's, "My Arms Are Not Being Used," was not getting used by the composer. "Dick couldn't hear any music to that."

Her agent told her that they wanted to write something for her like "You'll Never Walk Alone."

The prolific songwriters went away for the weekend. On the following Monday afternoon during rehearsal, they returned with sheet music for a new ballad, which they placed in Hong's hands, asking her to give it a try. While the rehearsal pianist played the music, Arabella Hong sang "Love Look Away."

"So really," she says, "I felt like it was written for me."

Then she was subjected to a cycle of notes from its creators as she endeavored to master the number.

"Too operatic," she heard them carping over and over.

Hong also had to learn a very long verse that introduced the number, "a whole piece" in itself. When she first sang it in the Linda Low dressing room scene, audiences were ill-prepared for such a soliloquy from a character, as Hong recalls, not very well developed up to that point. So they decided to strike the long-verse version and substitute a brief blare of trumpets.

The mood of the company became more serious and tense as the time neared to board the trains for Boston. R & H were privately sharing grave second thoughts about Larry Storch. Was this Caucasian really right for the part of a Chinatown nightclub owner in love with a Chinese stripper? Gene Kelly tried working with Storch.[15]

The director kept his spirits high. One night after a long, grueling day of run-throughs, Kelly showered the cast with another pep talk.

"Think of the fun we're having," he started, flopping down into a chair. "Look, kids, I know some of you are not used to these notes and changes, but you must get used to them because this process goes on." He noted the confusion that abounded — a cast replacement, a new number, a pause to work out orchestrations. He assured them they were all doing fine — "But now we've got to go over these readings again and again until we get them, and then I want them to stay that way."

He shone a weary smile over the exhausted crew.

"You're all tired. Go home and get some rest."[16]

And the next day it all resumed.

Freelance writer Joanne Stang, granted rare access to cover the show in preparation up close and down deep (sometimes from the orchestra pit), listened to Richard and Oscar confess "feelings of bewilderment, frustration and terror" during the rehearsals on all their shows. Nonetheless, reported Stang, they "smiled when they said this, and looked placid."[17]

Indeed, placid they stayed. En route by rail up to try the show out in Massachusetts, Hammerstein, moving through the cars, was stopped by one of the girls engaged in a crossword puzzle with David Lober. Could he give them a better word for "mountain"? The towering lyricist thought for a moment and supplied a synonym — *Tor*.

On October 23, 1958, at the Shubert Theatre in Boston, *Flower Drum Song* went through its paces for the first time on a stage full of sets and props. The workouts began at eight that evening. Actors could hear directions being shouted at them from semi-obscure figures somewhere out there in the seats.

"Don't stand in front of the street light! It looks like it's growing out of your head!"[18]

Platforms rolled across the stage like railroad cars off the tracks. Upon them stood actors clinging to each other for dear life. While rehearsing one of her numbers, Miyoshi Umeki almost walked into the wrong set. Later during tech shakedown, the lights went out — not by cue — and stayed out for an eerie long while.

Yelled Joseph Fields from the darkened house, "It's a good spot for a number!"

Yelled Richard Rodgers, "A number? An opera!"

Once illumination returned, Gene Kelly was raising his strained voice to the girls, wherever they were, who'd just been given a new entrance: "Girls! Please enter!"

The company took a brief break at one in the morning. Between taking catnaps, Rodgers voiced his correcting orders to off-key musicians and confused singers.

A Chinese lantern fell to the stage. Luckily, those standing beneath it were not touched.

At three A.M., they called it a night. To the Ritz Hotel went Rodgers, Hammerstein, Fields, Kelly and Haney. They would review the day's catastrophes and plot tomorrow's solutions.

They had four nights to right their wrongs. Four nights to smooth out the technical problems, perfect the dances, pace the entrances and exits.

Four nights to make it all work.

Four nights to the Boston opening.

Four nights until the first critics with sharpened pencils— Elliot Norton of the *Boston Herald*, Peggy Doyle of the *Globe*, and the man from *Variety* — would take their seats and judge a brand new musical by Rodgers and Hammerstein and render their verdicts to a waiting world.

Gene Kelly would be there, too, backstage and out front, through the lobby and behind the flats, smiling and tossing notes, grinning and kidding and goading and flattering. Wonci Lui remembers his upbeat presence. "Whenever he came in, we felt that he was contributing to whatever."

If he, in fact, had been ignored or actually superseded, who outside the company would ever know? To the writer from *Newsweek*, in town to report on the return of Rodgers and Hammerstein to Broadway, Kelly chirped, "These guys are a joy to work with. There are no heavy hands, no temperament. They make no major decisions without me. I could louse up the directing but that's my problem. As far as I can see, I'm in the catbird seat."[19]

In a higher sense, while the others were scrambling around in circles like so many self-appointed captains on a small, slightly rocking boat nearing an iceberg, Kelly had ascended to the highest mast above them all. He was calming nerves, waving the troupe onward, shouting down, "All clear ahead!" like a cheering father figure. By default, Mr. Singing in the Rain had become the show's true producer.

6

Clocking the Laughs

"FLOWER DRUM SONG IS ANOTHER R & H SMASH," rang a *Boston Globe* headline. "ELLIOT NORTON WRITES: FLOWER DRUM SONG CAN'T MISS BEING HIT," proclaimed the *Boston Herald*.

Variety concurred: "The much-heralded Richard Rodgers and Oscar Hammerstein (with Joseph Fields) show, an offbeat oriental musical, opened in Boston to a wham reception. It delivers a one-two click punch with petite, winsome Miyoshi Umeki winning all the way and Pat Suzuki belting out songs."[1]

That "wham reception" so elated the hit-starved Mr. Rodgers that several times during the opening night performance he jumped for joy out of his seat, paced up the aisle to the rear of the theatre in search of anyone to hug. Now, he could imagine being back on Broadway with another smash — at last — after nearly eight long years of depressing disappointments following an equal number of seasons turning out almost one hit after another with Oscar. The two partners might once again bask in the glory that had been theirs. Let *Flower Drum Song* resume where *The King and I* had left off.

The first critics to examine their new opus declared that a probable new gem from the masters of musical theatre was on its way to New York. What powered the Boston endorsements was Umeki and Suzuki and, additionally, the winning razzle-dazzle of young hoofer Patrick Adiarte; comedian deluxe Larry Storch; the overall exotic glow of the production itself; and the relatively contemporary score from R & H, whose snazziest songs tended to jump, swing, belt, cha-cha and even *rock*.

Reported the *Boston Herald's* esteemed drama critic Elliot Norton, "When they trim it down a little and tighten it up a lot, and get it to move with even speed from first curtain to final gaiety, *Flower Drum Song* will surely rank with the major works of Richard Rodgers and Oscar Hammer-stein."[2]

Norton described the show as "warmly humorous, tenderly roman-tic, rich in melody, gay in the best of its dancing, and strikingly beautiful in the lovely sets of Oliver Smith and the costumes of Irene Sharaff." He termed the work of both Suzuki and Umeki "extraordinary," declaring Suzuki "a singer of astonishing power and variety, an absolute star in her own right who lights up the stage and brings down the house." Several of the Carol Haney dances, Norton noted, were "spectacularly lovely." And of the new Hammerstein lyrics he had "nothing but praise," writing, "Nowhere has he written with more felicity the following words to suit the spirit of the songs."

To Norton's slightly skeptical ears, the new tunes themselves were almost as good: "Although the music has a faint hint, at times, of some-thing familiar, it is all extraordinary and it includes at least four songs that no one but Richard Rodgers could have written." In part, Norton cited "A Hundred Million Miracles" ("almost a miracle of delicate lyrical beauty"), "She is Beautiful" ("magnificent"), "I Am Going to Like It Here" ("ten-derly humorous"), and "Sunday" and "I Enjoy Being a Girl" ("uproarious numbers").

In the *Globe*, Peggy Doyle expressed keen pleasure with the two female leads, and she also liked Ed Kenney, "a leading man who has looks, a fine baritone and too many girls in love with him." The sets, she noted, "trans-port us to that colorful sector like nowhere else in the world." She also praised Storch, calling him "a robustious character as full of flavor as he is of expediency." In total, predicted Doyle, "It would look like still another hit for the greatest theatrical team of our time."[3]

Variety's man saw much the same promise, registering only a few quibbles. He, too, thought that Storch was just ducky, "neatly cast as the unwilling suitor, a nitery operator, and makes the most of his comedy opportunity." For that matter, he tossed kudos to nearly everyone, pro-nouncing Ed Kenney, in particular, as being destined for "stardom." In summation, reported he, "It's a fundamentally basic show built around family pride, love and the right man for the right girl. Should please the family trade, and despite a few side meanderings looks like a sure winner for a long run."

About those "side meanderings," Norton and Doyle, less charitable with their reservations, saw a show in the rough, in need of polishing. Doyle pounded on the "last quarter," opining that it needed "jacking up and one character could be eliminated to the show's advantage." Inexplic-ably, she did not specify whom, although her complaint about too many women for Wang Ta might imply that the peripherally placed Helen Chao was that character.

Norton noted pacing problems and some extraneous plot developments that veered too far off the central premise. "When it gets away from that, it sometimes seems a little strained, or even wooden." Of the male leads, only Patrick Adiarte earned a nod from Mr. Norton — "dances with dazzling grace." Two others earned no-confidence votes: Ed Kenney, he complained, didn't "look Chinese, and while his manner is pleasant and his voice remarkably beautiful, he is not a good actor." And of Larry Storch, about whom Dick and Oscar had been nursing their own misgivings in private, Norton issued a terse two-word dismissal: "Too brash." Coming from a critic to whom R & H had turned for valuable out-of-town feedback in previous years, probably this crystallized their decision to take action. They would wait, however, for a week or so.

The critical qualms with pacing and focus were nothing unusual or ominous. By tradition, most musicals open on the road way too long and way too slow. Such deficiencies are normally remedied as the show is judiciously pruned, as cast members settle into their roles and master their blockings, and as things start to flow. This company had good reason to feel part of a winner in the works, but also to expect frenzied revisions around the Boston clock.

By the next morning, the euphoria had vanished like last night's confetti. Time to cut and shift and hone. Time to build on what works the best. Carol Haney was loudly counting "two-three-four-five" to the dancers. Gene Kelly was going over scenes with the actors. Dick and Oscar were off stage somewhere, huddled in seclusion, furiously trimming words and lines and beefing up the finish stretch. Joe Fields, talking about it all to a reporter at the back of an empty house, was sharing a veteran's wisdom: "We can't depend on the audiences any more to tell us how we're doing. The notices were good and they'll come and enjoy themselves and laugh at everything. That's wonderful, of course. But it's the amount of work done on the road that determines whether you have just a good show or a smash hit when you get to New York. We all intend to work very hard."[4]

And then Mr. Fields proceeded to suffer a heart attack, rendering him fairly useless. Once out of the hospital, he was taken back to New York for rest and recuperation. Less input from Fields had to mean more input from the healthy Mr. Kelly, still upbeat and still dispensing savvy advice with smiling good-guy encouragement.

Now, the creative staff turned away from their own opinions about how things should be altered as they listened with intense scrutiny to the audiences. Nobody was more shrewd in reading the clues of a crowd than Oscar Hammerstein, who had practically made an art of it since long ago learning that, above all else, audiences follow the story. He could tell by the sounds—too much coughing in unison, too many noisy seats—how things were proceeding up on the stage. C. Y. Lee, who remained on the sidelines in quiet fascination, remembered Oscar's modus operandi, eyes closed, ears to the chairs: "because chairs would squeak if the people watching were restless. And he told his secretary, 'Mark that.'"[5]

Rodgers was more the stage watcher, a hawk-like monitor impatiently waiting for the next flaw to appear in the fabric, for the next sloppy entrance or the next dropped beat. He knew, like Fields, how crucial were the days spent on the road. So crucial, that Mr. Rodgers quipped to a reporter, "I wouldn't open anything, not even a can of sardines, in New York. You gotta have that out-of-town shakedown."[6]

And so, shake they did. Rodgers stood his ubiquitous vigil night after night, barking out reprimands like a village taskmaster: "Terrible! It's slow, slow, slow! Where are all those long pauses coming from? They're not in the script! Let's have a sharper second act, and for God's sake, let's have a better show tonight!"[7]

For God's—*and* for Richard Rodgers'—sake. Although the company was not thrown into a Bob Fosse–induced panic, the relentless changes made during the final out-of-town days drove more than a few of them a little "wacko," in the word of Wonci Lui, recalling a kind of confusion that would leave her with a lingering lifelong memory of something that never quite came together into an impressive whole. "There was a lot of fumbling a couple of nights when we didn't know what was exactly happening. A lot of changes."

In their listening to what the Boston patrons were most being entertained by, Dick and Oscar and Gene came to a pragmatic conclusion that they had on their hands a women's musical.[8] All three female leads earned consistent valentines from critics and crowds. Alvin Ing, who had tried out but was not cast, recalls that "the show did not come to life until Pat Suzuki stepped on the stage and sang 'I Enjoy Being a Girl.' She lit up the stage. She had a wonderful belting voice and a wonderful personality that just exploded across the spotlights."

Given the crowd-pleasing impact of Suzuki and Umeki against the mixed reception accorded Ed Kenney ("not that good and not that masculine," according to James Hammerstein),[9] R & H decided, it would later be recorded, to transform the script from a story "about a sensitive, transplanted Chinese man to a routine musical comedy-fare about two couples."[10] As recounted by Hugh Fordin, script rewrites enlarged the parts played by Suzuki and Umeki, while diminishing "those of the weaker characters."

At this tricky stage, audience reactions held much more weight than a roundtable discussion about thematic or dramaturgical integrity. They were capitalizing on what worked. Their growing confidence in the two leading ladies drove them to downplay the role of Helen Chao, played by Arabella Hong — whose good looks, oddly enough, were proving a certain liability.

During one telling Boston intermission while Dick and Oscar were hanging out in the lobby, straining to hear every little comment made by the chattering masses, they heard a lady wondering aloud why Wang Ta did not just go for Helen Chao. "She's better looking than the other two."[11]

That did it. Not good. Not good at all. They could not risk having Hong upstage Suzuki or Umeki.

"They already had two leading ladies," recalls Arabella. "So what they did, they completely changed the scene [between Want Ta and Chao after the seduction]. They took the depth away."

Kelly rescinded the way he had originally directed Hong to fall to her knees, pleading with Wang Ta to marry her. Moreover, Hong's physical appearance was altered to make her look "frumpy," she says. The skirt she had been wearing was replaced by a longer, drearier dress. From high heels to flat shoes, she was refitted. From long hair in a bun to short bobbed locks she converted. Everything to downplay the scene and make her look "as matronly as possible."

The drastic changes so infuriated Hong that she called up a close friend and told her she was going to quit the show.

"Oh," responded her friend, "you don't quit Rodgers and Hammerstein!"

On her own, Hong

Ed Kenney as Wang Ta and Miyoshi Umeki as Mei Li (Springer/Photofest).

decided to redirect the scene herself. "To me, they took the guts out of it, so I had to put it back. I took the scene and dramatized it."

This she achieved by reblocking it herself. She figured out the most poignant way to discover her calling card which she handed Wang Ta on his way out, left behind as a painful symbol of his utter indifference. How to run with it to the door, but then how to stop short just before reaching after Wang Ta one more time. How to accept the inevitable by resuming the ballad ... love look away!

Recounts Arabella, "I directed it myself. Excuse the expression, I milked the scene."

Another act of self-direction by default was Pat Suzuki's ad-lib strip number, still without official dance steps from Carol Haney. Clomping around the stage, Suzuki felt like "a gal who never showed up for rehearsal and then suddenly is in front of the club audience, and there you are just trying to fake it." During the first run-through, Rodgers, Hammerstein and Fields were so amused that they hesitated to let Carol Haney do anything with it. Explains Suzuki, "They saw that I was always kind of jerking around to see were the hell we were, because I was not a very good dancer, and they thought it was the funniest thing on wheels."

Unbeknownst to Pat, they told Carol Haney to leave it alone. On opening night in Boston, Suzuki panicked big time, realizing that her parents were in the audience and were about to watch their little girl reveal a whole lot of woman. "I was mortified. I was worried about my folks out there with me stomping and making a damn fool of myself."

After the first act curtain, she ran across the stage back to her dressing room, bursting in tears. Soon after came Richard Rodgers, knocking on the door.

"Hey, hey!" sang he. "I think it's going well! Don't you?"

"My folks are out there! I'm so embarrassed!"

"You'll get over it."

Suzuki continued pressing Haney for a real choreographed routine to perform, each time being put off.

"Oh, God, Pat! We have the ballet, and we're really really in deep deep trouble. Can we do it Monday without fail?"

Monday never came around.

Six months into the run, Haney leveled with Suzuki.

Another thing soon made clear by the sound of the seats: They had a show that sang exceptionally well. The cast of some forty-six, of whom twelve were actually Chinese, delivered an atypically jazzy R & H score, termed by *Variety* "exuberant ... a dozen rollicking songs." Less serious, more glib, its appeal was immediate and breezy, and easy to take. And if it failed to reach the depths of a *Carousel* or *The King and I,* still it did not lack the inventive detours that only Dick and Oscar could have given it. In "I Am Going to Like It Here," a remarkably slow-moving number full of contemplated atmosphere, Oscar's lyric followed an ancient Malaysian form, the "phantom," in which the second and fourth lines of each four-line stanza become the first and third lines of the succeeding one. The quiet enchantment of the song perfectly suited Miyoshi Umeki's delicate character.

For the greater part of the evening, Dick's compositions bristled with populist pizzazz. Significantly absent was a waltz — not a single waltz from a composer famed for rousing three-quarter beats. In fact, this would be the first R & H musical not to offer one. "I Enjoy Being a Girl" pulsed with fresh excitement. "Like a God" blew across the stage with exhilarating force — again, freshly formed. "Grant Avenue" had a funky, get-down swing to it. Cheesy, maybe, and impossible to resist. A quasi cha-cha beat underpinned the raucous, roof-raising "Chop Suey," driven by Hammerstein's clever if corny rhymes satirizing diverse icons of the American landscape from hula hoops to Maidenform bras, Dr. Salk to filter tips to Gabor, Capote and Como to nuclear war. They even stepped head first into the fifties youth culture with a modestly revolutionary theatre number, "You Be the Rock, I'll Be the Roll." Backwards, too, they glanced, sending the dreamy "Sunday" into soft-shoe heaven.

The outstanding ballad "Love Look Away" is arguably the most tautly crafted blues song Dick and Oscar would ever create. A spare economy of both words and notes combine to evoke the stark loneliness of unrequited love in a great big beautiful city overlooking a bay. Arabella Hong continued struggling to make her rendition sound more musical theatre. "Too operatic" she kept hearing. Notes and more notes.

Oscar Hammerstein told her with a twinkle, "You know, Arabella, you have a Cadillac motor in a Ford chassis."

And the struggle went on. In exasperation, she mustered the nerve to approach the composer — once more. "You know, Dick, all my training is in opera. If you could tell me, tell me note for note how to sing 'Love Look Away,' I would be only too grateful."

"Okay," said Mr. Rodgers in his terse fashion.

Two days passed without a word from anybody.

On the third day came Colin Romoff, up from New York, who helped Hong to de–Wagnerize the number.

She stopped getting notes.

Soon after, Oscar came backstage to her dressing room. "That was wonderful!" he said. "Do you know what you're doing?"

At another performance, on her own Arabella tried bluesing up the number. Later on she asked Dick, "How did you like it?"

He hesitated. "You weren't even in the show."

One problem song that proved unsolvable was the lyrically inconclusive "My Best Love," delivered by Keye Luke. It had not been going over well, taking audiences on a lovely if yawning ride to nowhere: Why does one's "best love," according to Mr. Hammerstein, necessarily come after all the others? The verse failed to strike a persuasive closing chord. Nor did the scene between the father and son in which it was set have much traction.

"Then we gave it to Juanita Hall," remembered Rodgers. "And that didn't work either. Then Oscar and I decided to scrap the number completely and write something new for another character in the same scene."[12]

This they accomplished after deciding that Larry Storch had to go and replacing him with another Caucasian, Larry Blyden.

The exit, on the surface polite and brief, was not without internal controversy, nor would it ever be forgotten by Storch, left embittered by a lost Broadway opportunity. The man who took Storch's place did not seem better suited to the role, especially to insiders noting his relationship to the choreographer as her ex-husband. R & H had waited for about a week of Boston previews before informing Storch of their decision. He was said to have taken the news in stride. The views of cast members, queried on the matter, are as varied as were Storch's reviews.

"He was there one day, then the next day he wasn't there anymore. We never understood that," says Baayork Lee.

"He should never have been fired," states David Lober, who considered it a likely act of raw nepotism. "He did a good job. It was a very strange show, and for me it was my first experience being a minority."

In Lober's skeptical view, Blyden "couldn't have been more wrong for the part.... Larry Storch had a lot more edge, and a lot more that was like the ultimate performance that Jack Soo eventually did." (Soo took over the role midway through the run)

However, Pat Adiarte remembers Storch being "not Asian enough ... too American." And Arabella Hong recalls Storch's inappropriate projections. "He kept playing to the audience, rather than doing regular proscenium playing. So he kept entertaining instead of acting."

As detailed in the *Newsweek* story, the Bronx-born Storch "played the comedy lead more like a dead-end kid than the good-time Charlie he was supposed to be."[13]

Once the switch was made, out went the meandering "My Best Love" as fast as a comedy number for Blyden and Umeki could be written to

Strange casting: Larry Blyden as Sammy Fong (second from right), with Pat Suzuki, replaced another Caucasian, Larry Storch, during Boston previews. Also seen here are Eileen Nakamura, left, and Chao-Li Chi, right (Springer/ Photofest).

replace it. Keye Luke, possibly feeling a bit abandoned, was left without a song of his own. He would have to settle for his share of the comedy lines in "The Other Generation."

The lyricist retired to his suite at the Ritz-Carlton Hotel one afternoon, where he began work on the new number, "Don't!" He returned sometime later—anywhere from that same day a couple of hours later to four days hence, depending on four different accounts. Author Ethan Mordden wrote that R & H together completed the number in two hours flat.[14] Gene Kelly recalled a five-hour period. Either of these accounts, if true, transformed the ordinarily time-consuming poet into a wordsmith of hurricane penmanship.

"So you see," recalled Kelly, "slow as Oscar was reported to be, he was the complete pro. Dick was always fast, but so was Oscar that day. And Dick took me out to the ladies' room and said, 'Listen to this,' and I said,

'It's fine, I'll stage it, I'll have it in the show tomorrow.'" "I'm glad you like it," he said, "because we think it's terrific."[15]

According to Kelly's account, it took Rodgers the same amount of time to set the music as it took Hammerstein to write the words. After retiring with Oscar's new lyric to the women's lounge, he plunked himself down at a grand piano and labored for five hours to come up with a tune. The ailing, alcohol-dependent Rodgers may have spent a part of his creative hiatus dozing off or indulging. This was the same man who had composed "Bali Ha'i" on a table napkin in five minutes.

Another Haney-related appointment brought in her current boyfriend, Hugh Lambert, to serve as her assistant and to understudy for Ed Kenney in the ballet. "Totally inappropriate," says David Lober, describing the simplicity of Kenney's ballet steps (a few moves and one lift) as "essentially an acting role" and noting how Lambert himself "could not have looked more Anglo-Saxon."

Out front, they kept their ears to the seats and listened for coughing sounds. Shamelessly, they were "clocking the show for laughs," in the wry recollection of Chao-Li Chi, who rued the demise of "My Best Love," believing all along that the number, "more Chinese kind of sentimental," deserved serious respect. "They took out Master Wang's song. It didn't get any laughs or anything."

Chi watched with mounting dismay as "the committee" (including Kelly, Hammerstein, and Haney) geared audience reactions to their comedy "with a stop watch."

"They sat in the audience and clocked the laughter. If a line got a laugh, it was kept and doubled, and if it didn't get a laugh, out it went.... Gene Kelly was going to make this a dance show, but instead, they turned it into a burlesque ... one joke on top of another, which would be booed off the stage if they weren't done by Asian faces."

Kelly was doing everything he could to compensate for a script which he felt lacked the substance of a *South Pacific*. "But it had a warmth and a sweet sentimentality about it," he said, looking back. "I knew that as long as I crammed the production brimful of every joke and gimmick in the book I could make it work, but this was always an audience show rather than anything for the critics."[16]

Arabella Hong shared Chi's despondency. She saw Kelly as a weak director who went along with the commercial compromises made by the others. He did not push for the depth that another director (like Moss Hart) might have been able to draw forth. "There wasn't a director," Hong insists, "so they took over, and they went for the laughs all the time, whatever went over with the audience, like 'All white men look alike.'"

Pat Adiarte did not realize the historical significance of a little throw-away dance number he introduced — virtually the first self-consciously rock and roll ditty ever sung in a Broadway tuner. Adiarte saw it as just another audience-pandering gag. "It was corny stuff … put in there to get a laugh."

Yet the song, "You Be the Rock, I'll Be the Roll," typified the show's modern slant, a quality of spirit much admired by the first critics to lay eyes on *Flower Drum Song*.

"The production is an achievement of pure delight," wrote *Variety*, "coming up with absorbing, exciting musical of conflict between the old and the new in San Francisco's Chinatown."

"A great musical show in the making," predicted Elliot Norton. "In four Boston weeks, it should come to full fruition."

And while it matured theatrically, Chi and Keye Luke would go out for chop suey and bemoan the missed opportunities — the bittersweet experience of watching two "top notch creators" turning a touching little novel into a lightweight song and dance diversion. "We had high hopes," said Chi, "but the high hopes dissipated once we started rehearsals, because both Hammerstein and Rodgers were in the hospital. So it was done with Gene Kelly and Mr. Fields, and of course Carol Haney." When they started out, explains Chi, there was a basic story, "but we really didn't know what to do with it, and the script was not quite finished." With a huge advance ticket sale trumping artistic considerations, they rushed ahead, ill-prepared, as Chi sees it. "We had hoped that it would have been a Chinese show, and we know that we trust Oscar Hammerstein's intelligence and experience, [that he] would have made it a real drama, kind of comic, but dramatic also."

"It wasn't the show it could have been," concedes Arabella Hong. "I think it has some of the most beautiful music that Dick and Oscar have ever written. The show, if directed properly, could have been a great show. As it is, it was a good show."

Whom to believe? Cast members are rarely in a position to offer objectivity, not as long as they are up on the boards and in the show. They can also be unduly influenced by personnel conflicts, by personal grudges and preferences behind the scenes. Nonetheless, this company had clearly hoped for something more dramatically noteworthy from the masters, even if they had been told flat out that they had been cast in a musical *comedy*. Not a musical drama. Not a musical play.

The "committee" kept clocking the laughs. And the new song they had inserted about the pitfalls of ending up married to the wrong mate, the retitled "Don't Marry Me," was drawing plenty. The cakewalk done by

Umeki and Blyden to end the number, as Chi recalled, noting the novelty of an Asian doing it, "brought down the house." The seats were sounding wonderfully squeak-free. And Gene Kelly continued adding more fail-safe gimmicks, gags and jokes to the enterprise.

Adding up in his mind all of the changes they had made in Boston, Oscar Hammerstein treated them as minor modifications to a fundamentally viable work. To a reporter he remarked, "This is the first show I've been connected with that's needed very little cutting for length or pace. Oh, we've made changes of course, plenty of 'em, but not the kind you make when a show's in trouble and you need a whole new second act. I've been convinced that we had a hit in 'Flower Drum' ever since opening night."[17]

By December the New York advance had soared to over one million dollars (ten million in today's dollars). A huge number of performances were already sold out. Boston word-of-mouth spelled long lines at the box office. Theatregoers hungered for another bona fide hit from the masters.

Cast and crew boarded the trains back to New York. The new Oliver Smith flats and drops swung into position on the stage of the St. James. Dancers stretched out over the boards. Kelly and Haney put the cast through its paces. More notes were given. Tech people fussed over last-minute glitches. Dick and Oscar were ready. Gotham's critics — the world's toughest, and let nobody tell any of *them* what to think — were ready. The night of ultimate judgment was at hand.

7

Opening Night Blossoms

Boston was but a promising prelude. Could the "wham reception" it gave that new musical about Chinatown be duplicated down in Gotham? Shows that wowed 'em out of town did not always leave 'em raving at the St. James or the Majestic or the Winter Garden. *Flower Drum Song's* innocent young cast was about to face seven of the toughest theatre critics in the world.

Brooks Atkinson, of *The New York Times*, had started out as an English teacher at Dartmouth College, then turned to police reporting in 1917 for the *Springfield* (Mass.) *Daily News* and later for the *Boston Evening Transcript*, where he was made assistant drama critic in 1919. He joined the *Times* in 1922 as book review editor and was offered a drama desk in 1925. He also served as a war correspondent while on leave, winning a Pulitzer Prize for his reports filed from Russia. Noted more for his trenchant analysis of new plays than of musicals, Atkinson was the most respected and feared of the bunch. He had found *The King and I* "no match for *Carousel*,"[1] and of *Me and Juliet*," he grumbled that it "has just about everything except an intelligible story."[2]

Another formidable force was the *Herald Tribune's* brilliant theatre essayist Walter Kerr. A man of the theatre himself, Kerr had co-authored, during his teaching days at Catholic University in D.C., the scripts for three tuners, two of which he also directed. Against normal odds, all three advanced from school stages to Big Apple boards. Kerr's latest effort away from reviewing was another new musical that he had directed and helped write, *Goldilocks*, in its second fragile month at the Lunt-Fontanne. Like his colleagues, Kerr had long run out of patience with R & H, calling *Me and Juliet* "a show without a show,"[3] *Pipe Dream* a tame party missing "that gallon jug of good, red wine."[4]

With the *Daily News* since 1920, John Chapman had stared out in 1917 reporting in his hometown for the *Denver Times*. A few years later at the *Daily News*, Chapman moved among many desks, first turning in police reports, then serving as a Paris-based photographer, as drama editor in 1929, and as a Los Angeles columnist in 1940 before settling down as a drama critic in 1943. Chapman demonstrated a canny knack for appraising new scores.

Ostentatious southern-born gentleman Robert Coleman, who sported side whiskers, had toiled for the *Daily Mirror* since 1924. At the age of ten he began in show biz passing out flyers for a touring minstrel show, in whose box office he later worked during his teen years. Coleman argued that *Me and Juliet*, too much in need of "revamping," should never have come to New York in the first place.[5]

John McClain, at the *Journal American* since 1951, joined the *New York Sun* in 1929. By the early forties, he was out in Hollywood writing screenplays for MGM (*Lady Be Good*). During World War II, McClain won a Bronze Star at Iwo Jima serving as a navy commander. Back to the *Sun* he returned to write a column, in 1951 switching to the theatre. He had found Rodgers and Hammerstein's *Pipe Dream* "a far cry from the exalted talents that produced *South Pacific*.... They must be human, after all."[6]

One-time editor-in-chief of the U.S. Office of War Information in Chungking, China, Richard Watts, Jr., working for the *New York Post*, had been dishing — and dissing — out film and stage notices for over thirty years, going back to *Desert Song's* New York premiere in 1926. Watts' notices were considered reliable and savvy. *Pipe Dream*, he had judged, was "oddly lacking in the sense of excitement that had been hoped for."[7]

And, finally, neophyte Frank Aston, of the *World Telegram*, was still in his first year covering opening nights.

These New York scribes had seen little to cheer about in the last two offerings from R & H. The theatre world was changing, although during the previous season, the critics had enthusiastically embraced both the past and the future in two disparate new works: Meredith Willson's expertly wrought small-town charmer, *The Music Man*, and the bristling and brittle inner city masterpiece from Leonard Bernstein, Arthur Laurents and Stephen Sondheim about racial tension between knife-wielding teenage gangs, *West Side Story*.

Through the 1958 season, already the reviewers had sat through the first-night humdrum of too many new shows ranging, in their varied opinions, from mediocre to abysmal: *Oh, Captain!*, which picked up fair reviews; a roundly panned three-performance loser, *Portfino*; the so-so *Say, Darling*, which drew more mixed notices; and an opera by Gian Carlo

Menotti, *Maria Golovin*, touted by its producer David Merrick as a "new musical drama," which folded after a split critical tally and five performances. The critics also had to review one of their own with the opening of Walter Kerr's *Goldilocks*, written with his wife Jean to the music of pop king Leroy Anderson. The lumbering hackwork, which drew a politely tepid response, lasted for a paltry 161 shows. Only one musical to open so far in 1958, the imported *La Plume de Ma Tante*, earned a socko reception — great reviews and a great run.

One month later, now it was Dick and Oscar's turn to face the big pens. To be toasted or questioned, cheered or jeered. The house lights dimmed at the St. James Theatre on December first. Conductor Salvatore Dell' Isola raised his baton. A staccato roll of drums beat out the first notes of "A Hundred Million Miracles." Would there be any tonight?

The curtain rose on the plush Victorian Chinese living room of Master Wang Chi-yang — an artful blending of San Francisco and Hong Kong featuring straight-backed chairs, lamps, a miniature garden on a low table, and the god of longevity on a wall looming over the room. A large window and a door opened onto a street.

While Wang San (Patrick Adiarte) was seated in a chair munching on an apple, Madam Liang (Juanita Hall) stood next to a telephone, talking into it as the house servant Liu Ma stood by with a list in her hand.

"Hello ... Is this the Ping Wah Super Market? This is Madam Liang. I would like to place my order. How is your octopus today? Oh ... No, never mind. Then send me two pounds of sea horse, one pound of dried snake meat and a box of longevity noodles."[8]

As the story began to unfold, the seven fourth-estate judges surveyed the passing sets, gauged the lines and jokes, studied the characters and the unfolding conflicts, listened intently to new songs and tried to decide — Great? Good? Not so good? And against all of their individual passions and preferences, the elements together began to make an impression, either positive or negative or somewhere naggingly in between. And when the final curtain fell, there were heard the usual opening night cheers from an audience dominated by well-wishers, friends and relatives and curiosity seekers and hard-core R & H buffs.

Then everybody went their separate ways to wait out the reviews. The critics who would write them hurried back to city desks around Times Square, or to nearby pay phones, there to call in their formalized evaluations to be transcribed and rushed into hot lead type for the rolling presses and hustled out through the night to newsstands and front porches for tomorrow morning's readers. Atkinson and his colleagues were terrifically fast on their feet, summing up in mere minutes what would resonate down through the ages whenever the new musical being first seen and appraised that fateful New York night would be talked about, written up: What were the *reviews*? Always, the tale would begin with the opening night reception from the New York seven.

The cast and crew, in keeping with nail-biting tradition, adjourned with fake gaiety to Mama Leone's, there to act wonderfully hopeful and happy. Chocolate cake for Arabella Hong, among others. They had gotten through opening. Wasn't that a wonderful reception! What applause! All the while, they silently fretted about the ultimate feedback from the feared seven. What would *they* say?

Novelist C.Y. Lee, left, and Arabella Hong, who played Helen Chao, at the Mama Leone's opening night cast party in 1958 (Courtesy Royce O. Young).

The answers came in one notice after another through a long anxious night. Dick and Oscar might have been the most nervous of all — they had so much riding on this show. In came the words of Atkinson and Chapman, of Coleman and Watts, Jr., under headlines mostly bearing nuggets of welcome sunshine: FLOWER DRUM SONG A BIG HIT ... SUMPTUOUS FLOWER DRUM SONG CREATES A DANCE FAN'S DREAM ... MUSICAL BY R & H GARNERS A POSY ... FLOWER DRUM SONG FILLED WITH TUNES, COLOR AND SWEET ROMANCE.[9]

They grabbed the newspapers and tore through pages to find the reviews, their hungry eyes glued to every word. "Rodgers has composed one of his most persuasive scores," wrote Coleman. "And Hammerstein has written lyrics that are moody and amusing. The new arrival comes with precision and inevitability of a perfectly adjusted clock. It has bounce and color and humor."

Reported Frank Aston, "It was as if some genius of an engineer had arranged a tried and true assembly line and was showing right before our eyes, exactly how a perfect show is put together."

John Chapman wrote, "It is unlike anything they have attempted before. In its exotic setting and with its cast of Racial types, it is somewhat like *The King and I*. In another sense, it is like the first Rodgers and Hammerstein musical, *Oklahoma!*"

Robert Coleman lauded Larry Blyden's Sammy Fong, finding his presence "fuel for a jet-propelled performance. He's cunning and brash — a likable heel." Coleman called Miyoshi Umeki "captivating," Pat Suzuki "quite wonderful as a rock and roll stripper, pretending to be a lady." He dubbed the entire enterprise "a hit of gargantuan proportions."

Like a few of his colleagues savvy to something delightfully different in the air at the St. James, Coleman defined his enthusiasm: "But *Flower Drum Song* is a show worth the digging and the waiting for. We found it a delight, as did the initial ticket holders.... Everything about it is just right. From authors to principals to chorus, it clicks on all cylinders."

For Aston, the show was "a dance fan's dream." He echoed Coleman's high regard for the exceptional stagecraft on display throughout the evening. The show had "true heart," he wrote, praising the comedic flair of Mr. Blyden, the understated whimsy of Miss Umeki. "She owns the St. James and everyone in it.... She is a rare gift from Broadway to the ticket buying public." Pat Suzuki also made Aston's A-list, as did Carol Haney's "spectacular" choreography and Gene Kelly's overall direction.

Aston stopped tellingly short of an unqualified rave. "There is a formulaic air about *Flower Drum Song*, but there can be no doubt about it — here is a walloping hit."

The resident expert on first-night score appraisal, John Chapman, heard songs that were sufficiently satisfying. He, in fact, liked everything about the new show to a measured degree: "Lavishly colorful, delightfully tuneful and thoroughly sentimental ... a lovely show — an outstanding one in theme and treatment. But I shouldn't go to it expecting to be bowled over by sensation; it is a sweet gentle story, sweetly and gently treated."

Just as they had done up in Boston, Umeki and Suzuki carried the notices. "Enchanting," "ineffably lovely," and "tenderly endearing" were the adjectives awarded the demure one, while the brassier dame from Cressy, California, who played the brassier Linda Low, got nearly equal mention for gusto and personality. Surprisingly, Ed Kenney fared better in New York with the critics, Frank Aston noting that the young Hawaiian "probably will soon be the talk of the town with his voice, dancing, and looks."

As Oscar and Dick, Gene and Joseph and Carol dug deeper into the write-ups, they discovered in a few of them nuances of equivocation and doubt. The show's subtler mannerisms and older-fashioned virtues did not win everyone over. Indeed, those very same qualities that supplied theatrical unity also constrained the work's reach.

New York opening night curtain call, left to right: Gene Kelly, Pat Suzuki and Richard Rodgers (Photofest).

About *Flower Drum Song* there was, to be sure, a certain rarefied air caught and affirmed by a majority of the seven. To listen to the song "I Am Going to Like It Here" is to feel the calming mystery of a number — and a show — that dares now and then to take its own reflective time, as does the character, Mei Li, who sings it. New to the Wang Chi-yang household, she is entranced with the romantic opportunities that lie ahead. The little song, so tenderly different, is, to use Chapman's phrase, "unlike anything" that the boy wonders of musical theatre had attempted before.

Sympathetically inclined Walter Kerr fell mildly in love with a musical whose "precise character ... ambles." Kerr offered the comedy song that had been written up in Boston as a prime example of the show's unique spirit: "As the fetching rhythm of 'Don't Marry Me' begins to make itself felt, she is willing to follow her renegade suitor into a lazy investigation of light and easygoing American footwork.... She takes Mr. Blyden's hat into her upraised hand and waves it loyally as she joins him in a delectable double trick ... a joyful experiment in innocence flirting with sophistication."

Most of the show, reported Mr. Kerr, "is as easy as that: placid, unruffled, cheerfully confident." Not a collaboration that would "mark the more daring and buoyant of the Rodgers and Hammerstein masterworks," said he. No, a work of "quieter pursuits" which would stand as a "modest and engaging leaf from a very full album ... the atmosphere is attractive, the score is ingratiating, and the company good."

Knowing exactly what it was up to was good enough for John McClain, who issued a modified rave. So what if, in his tempered opinion, nothing about the new R & H trick was "sensational." In matters of taste, humor, book, music and lyrics, the show, he predicted, was destined to "grow in stature as it is recorded and re-recorded.... *Flower Drum Song* is a big fat Rodgers and Hammerstein hit, and nothing written here will have the slightest effect on the proceeds.... There will be 'national' companies and road companies. The dramatic society of Tiffany High may attempt it in a couple of years, and it will be translated and played in Swedish, German, French and Chinese."

As the night wore on and morning began to break through, a couple of other notices cast ominously dissenting verdicts. Neither Brooks Atkinson nor Richard Watts, Jr., found much magic or invention at the St. James. Atkinson's tepid endorsement read more like a veiled autopsy; straining for words to convey minimal recognition for a crowd pleaser, he resorted on three instances to the smugly diffident adjective "pleasant." Wrote Mr. A, it was a "pleasant musical play." It contained a "pleasant score." And in redundant conclusion, it offered a "pleasant interlude among some most agreeable people."

Far less pleasantly tolerant was the rather exasperated Mr. Watts, who got to the point of adversary fast: "It is astonishingly lacking in distinction." A "touchingly romantic tale" it might have been, he conceded. "But the spirit of the strip-tease girl and the finagling nightclub man appears to have descended on the authors, and an air of Broadway brashness dominates the delicacy of the romance, giving *Flower Drum Song* the quality of a good, routine musical comedy of the conventional school, instead of the imaginative freshness we have come to expect of the authors of *South Pacific* and *Carousel*." To Watts' eyes and ears, the atmosphere was "pseudo Chinese," the overall effect, "minor Rodgers and Hammerstein."

There were sufficient raves to splash in huge boldface type across full page ads in *Variety* and Sunday newspaper theatre sections. As well, there were enough carping non-believers for the unenchanted to ask, had Dick and Oscar lost their magic touch? Beyond the first night notices, which by sacred tradition stood for final judgment from on high, other reviews followed in the days and weeks ahead from other papers and periodicals. Standing snidely apart from even the equivocally downbeat Richard Watts, Jr., was English wonder boy Kenneth Tynan, who reviewed for the upscale Manhattan-centric *New Yorker*, and whose brief love affair with Rodgers and Hammerstein (he had "wept" over South Pacific)[10] had long since tanked.

Tynan's acerbic diatribe against *Drum* struck like a poisonous snake, lancing all the sunny endorsements, popping every party balloon in its path and setting into wicked motion a counter-movement against the R & H school of sentiment. Tynan was about to make musical theatre history when he, to encapsulate his revulsion, coined the wickedly memorable zinger, "The world of woozy song."[11]

Another dart thrower was Marya Mannes, dissing away in *The Reporter*, "The Chinese in San Francisco cannot be quite as quaint as Rodgers and Hammerstein make them. It is pretty to look at and pleasant to listen to, and it is very reminiscent, in a faded way, of Rodgers and Hammerstein. The critical sprite lay quiet all through, lulled into apathy."[12]

Chao-Li Chi remembers one critic cracking that, apparently, in the world of R & H any non-wasp can pass for a Chinese.

Came, too, yet more ringing endorsements: "*Flower Drum Song* will be around for a long time," wrote *Variety's* Hobe Morrison. Calling it "a beautiful show ... an unusual, lively and appealing plot," he seemed sure it was destined to produce a best-selling original cast album, be made into a popular film, and enjoy a healthy national tour.[13]

"A smash musical hit," declared the *Associated Press*.[14] "Not only a hit. It is a joy," wrote John Beaufort in *The Christian Science Monitor*.[15]

And a joyfully long run appeared likely. The box office was booming. A weekly operating profit of $13,000 was rolling in. Sellout crows were the rule. Even after the advance party bookings had been played to, continued mail order and walk up window trade sales "boosted the advance back to $1,200,000," reported *Variety*. And the cast album was selling on a par with previous R & H hits.

Celebs flocked to see the show. The media lavished major attention all over it. Both *Newsweek* and *Time* magazines devoted front-page stories to the musical's development. *Life* magazine came out with a multi-page photo story, its attendant review amounting to a modified endorsement.[16]

These were heady times for Asian actors, singers and dancers. They could see real stars in their eyes—just look around at other Asians in other shows. They could dream of long-term careers in the theatre. Just look around again: By the following spring there were five shows on the Great White Way in which Asians appeared! The other four were *The World of Suzie Wong, A Majority of One, Rashomon, and Kataki.*

"We waved to each other crossing the street," remembers Wonci Lui fondly—waved on their way to backstage doors into playhouses where audiences waited to be entertained by *them.*

One night they were feted by Princess Grace. "Everybody was looking at her rather than the show," recalls Arabella Hong.

Another night, Hong's idol, Lily Pons, who was spotted out in the audience, sent a courier backstage during intermission with a message of praise for Hong. After the performance, to Arabella's elation, there outside her dressing room door stood the Great One herself. "The biggest, most astounding experience. It was like Caruso coming to you. She had red hair and she was saying such lovely things—'Oh, you were wonderful!' A moment I'd never forget in my life."

They proceeded to break one house record after another.

Dancer Patrick Adiarte, as Wang San, delivered edgy, youthful flair (Photofest).

Umeki and Suzuki were two big reasons why. Another was Patrick Adiarte, a budding star in his own right who had captured the first-night notice of Walter Kerr, quick to spot and describe remarkable star turns. The young hoofer, wrote Kerr, called "gleeful attention to himself every time he is permitted to join a couple of the younger girls in an impromptu spirit."

"What a talent," marvels Arabella Hong. "All of them felt he was a super talent."

"We knew he was somebody," remarks Baayork Lee. "We saw him as a star."

During the show, Gene Kelly invited Adiarte to participate in a TV program on Omnibus, "Dancing Is a Man's Game." "It was exciting," says Adiarte. "I just gave it all I had."

Before show time every night and every matinee, he paced back and forth, his nerves jangling. "I get crazy just before the curtain goes up."

And after his last number, "The Other Generation," the kid felt a great relief, his work done for the night. Time to relax and be — in real life — the semi-rebellious youngster he portrayed on the stage in that generationally conflicted Chinese American household.

The cast got along fairly well, with a minimum of the cliquish behavior that can make backstage life miserable, unfriendly, and deliberately forgotten once a show is over. "This was the first show for a lot of people," says Adiarte. "These were very innocent Asians. Not showbiz type. No stab-in-the back. Everybody was sort of wide-eyed. Miyoshi was wonderful, she was so nice to me, and Keye Luke was, too. Everybody was like Miyoshi's character."

Miyoshi and Arabella went out to dinner a lot. Remembers Hong, "She'd yell upstairs to my room — ELLABARA!"

Hong was impressed with Umeki's sophistication and with Suzuki's intellectual bent.

Pat Suzuki loved the sweet civility of it all. "It wasn't until I got out to do summer stock that I realized there was anything like competitive. It just never occurred to me that there wouldn't be a collective goal."

She and Ed Kenney became fast friends backstage. "He could do Hawaiian dancing. One time he showed me his nightclub act, and I couldn't believe it. He could shake his buns. Oh, that kid was gorgeous. He would come into my dressing room and he'd say, 'What are you wearing tonight?' And he'd pick my cologne bottle and shake it, and douse it behind his ears."

To this day, Baayork Lee feels deeply indebted to the show's brassiest star: "Thank God in 1958 there was a Pat Suzuki, who was the new girl on the block, who was fashionable, who sang jazz, and she really put us on the map in terms of bringing us into the twentieth century. It was Pat Suzuki who had her straggly bangs with a long pony tail, and she was brassy. Everybody looked up to her character. She was strong, and there was the contrast. Rodgers and Hammerstein knew what they were doing, because they showed Mei Li as the submissive one. Whatever Wang Ta wanted and whatever her father wanted, she obeyed. And then there was this stripper, Linda Low, and she was doing whatever she wanted. She was a liberated woman."

Midway through the New York run, after Larry Blyden departed the cast and Jack Soo took over in his place, in came Larry Leung to assume the role of Frankie Wing vacated by Soo. Leung was a veteran of San Francisco's Forbidden City, where he and his wife, Trudie, had performed their musical comedy duo as they had at the Palace and on the Ed Sullivan show.

Shaking off old-world restraint, Pat Suzuki as Linda Low goes into her strip during "Grant Avenue." (Springer/Photofest)

With Leung some nights came his three-year old daughter, Jodi. The little one toddled in the wings, all ears and eyes, when a certain lady on the stage belted out "Grant Avenue" or "I Enjoy Being a Girl."

"I remember being backstage as a little kid, and watching Pat Suzuki do it on Broadway," exudes Jodi (now Jodi Long). "Cool? She was great! She was an amazing performer and I just was completely.... I wanted to grow up and be her, and be that 'I Enjoy Being a Girl.' So I knew all the words to all the songs.... She's a teeny little person, but when you're three or four years old, you just think this person is so great. So big. Just an amazing performer, and she still is."

Juanita Hall, self-appointed stage mother, "would kind of police everybody," in the words of Arabella Hong. Hall could be overbearing at times, especially while standing in the balcony shouting down to her fellow cast members, "You're late!"

"She would cuss you out," says Hong, "and invite you to dinner the next day."

Baayork Lee packed ambition into her 4' 10" frame. She learned all the dances in the show, "just in case somebody broke their leg or got sick. I was gonna be ready."

By accident, Baayork got her chance to go on when Miyoshi Umeki and Anita Ellis both called in sick. Cely Carrillo, the understudy for both roles, had to go on for Umeki. So who to cover for Ellis, who sang the naughty "Fan Tan Fannie" in the nightclub scene? The chore fell by strange default to Lee, barely in her teens. She had never walked in a pair of high heels, which the part called for. Actually too young to be performing in such a bawdy number (though in the scene itself she had all along been appearing as a club patron seated at the far edge of the stage), incredibly, Lee went on anyway. They put her in a pair of heels and had her walk around for a bit. "They were desperate. I was terrified. I wasn't a singer."

Lee wore a long dress, went on and got through "Fan Tan Fannie."

Arabella Hong's continued encounters with Richard Rodgers were amicably businesslike. How demanding was he?

"Oh, yes, if you made a quarter note into an eighth note, you'd be corrected afterwards. He did think he was a better composer than me."

"He was never tough," she points out. "He was very explicit when he didn't like something."

One night during "Love Look Away," Hong tripped out on the apron and slipped into a microphone hole. "All of a sudden, I saw the orchestra coming at me!"

Unable to get back on her feet while singing, she sat there on the floor and finished the song, her arms raised high.

"The lights went out. I got up like a butcher woman."

Back in her dressing room three flights up, Hong was approached by an excited chorus guy. "What did you do? They are still clapping!"

"I fell down."

"Why don't you do that all the time?"

Hong's show-stopping turn left a permanent scar on her leg.

During intermission, conductor Salvatore Dell'Isola, passing on the stairwell, noted with a smile, "You missed one beat."

Came the Tony nominations, and with them more reason to dream of a long, long run matching maybe that of *Oklahoma!* In the actor categories, Umeki and Blyden were up for Tonys. Rodgers and Hammerstein were nominated for Best Musical, Carol Haney for choreography, Irene Sharaff for costumes, and Salvatore Dell'Isola for conducting.

Flower Drum Song would be in competition for Tony fame with only a couple of other new musicals of note that unprolific season — *Redhead* and *Destry Rides Again.* Several other new shows which had hit the boards during the same period had either closed early or were about to for lack of interest. These included the 56-performance turkey *Whoop Up*—not quite as unsuccessful as *Juno*, which called it a run after 16 curtains; the listless *First Impressions*, good for 84 showings; and Walter Kerr's *Goldilocks*, which fell to the bears after 161 stagings. Meanwhile, *Destry Rides Again* was galloping ahead towards a respectable though profitless 424-performance outing at the Imperial.

When the Tony Awards were handed out in 1959, the disdain of Tynan and his ilk prevailed. *Flower Drum Song* received only one award—for Dell'Isola's pit conducting. *Redhead* managed to land a slate of Tonys, including the one for best score (both *Flower's* and *Destry's* were arguably superior), even though *Redhead's* reviews were only slightly better than *Flower's* and its run was nearly 150 performances shorter.

In the short term, the Tony snubs appeared not to have subtracted a single patron from the Rodgers and Hammerstein comeback. The musical continued to draw full houses. Then came another December, not quite like the first December. Attendance started to slide, not ominously. Into the following spring, the turnouts varied from 70 percent capacity to turnaways. Nothing to apologize for. How many seats, in truth, does a musical need to fill on average in order to pay its weekly operating nut and hold out for better days? As an unscientific rule of thumb, about 70 percent. Maybe 75 to 80 percent in cases where the nut is unusually high. Rarely did Dick and Oscar's latest opus draw less than 70 percent, a figure that many shows today regularly tolerate — as long as they can occasionally pull in larger crowds. The week when *Flower Drum Song* exited the St. James, the take amounted to about 80 percent.

Summer, the worst time at the box office, loomed. The heat is said to drive prospective customers into swimming pools or under large park umbrellas, if not miles out of town to cooler escapes.

Then, too, all around *Flower Drum Song* were other shows better fancied by the Big Seven. When *Redhead* had come to town in February 1959, John Chapman chirped, "Now we have four tip top musicals—*My Fair Lady, West Side Story, The Music Man* and *Redhead*."[17] *Gypsy*, another show deemed "tip top," landed in the same neighborhood that May.

And Dick and Oscar were now competing against — and being compared to— a new breed of musical play, exemplified by *West Side Story*, a show composed and scripted by younger voices eager to break free of happy talk and predictable romantic bliss, to push the form to a higher level of sophistication, just as Dick and Oscar had done during the prior decade.

And so what they had to offer the public started to look in contrast increasingly old hat — much like the next and last musical they would write together, *The Sound of Music.*

Still, *Flower Drum Song's* inaugural New York run topped all the other musicals which had opened the same season, and it would achieve the best box office record of all the plays utilizing Asian actors, realizing a profit of $125,000 on a $360,000 investment. By the time that *A Majority of One* closed, in June of 1960, racking up a total of 556 performances, the New York stage was once again barren of Asian-themed fare. They had all come to town with high hopes. They had lived out their brief moment in the neon sun.

Mei Li's little show gave its last performance at the St. James on May 7, 1960, then headed up to Detroit to begin a national tour. Some of the original cast members, like the now-pregnant Pat Suzuki, stayed behind. Others, like Ed Kenney, Keye Luke and Juanita Hall, kept going, grateful to keep alive a dream which might soon enough die. Out to the hinterlands they traveled, away from the maddening gaze of Broadway where every ticket holder is a critic in his own mind, where too many suffer Kenneth Tynan complexes.

In musical theatre it is an axiom both vexing and ever-tantalizing that every new *production* in effect creates a different-*looking*, different-*sounding* musical. With an altered cast and crew, and with fresh direction by default, a number of changes were about to take place that would turn *Flower Drum Song* into an arguably different — and better — show.

8

On the Road to
Fractious Maturity

Heading westward for Detroit with high hopes and eager new faces, the road company of *Flower Drum Song* embarked on a long journey that would take it into unforeseen good fortune — and trouble. Leaving New York to test its luck in cities both big and small, gone from its marquee were the biggest names — Umeki and Suzuki, Hong and Adiarte. Replacing them were, respectively, Cely Carrillo (who had understudied for Umeki in New York), Elaine Dunn, Suzanne Lake, and 17-year-old Gene Castle, another mover and shaker.

Four of the New York leads stayed on with the show: Keye Luke, Ed Kenney, Juanita Hall and Jack Soo. Soo retained the role of Sammy Fong, which he had inherited after Larry Blyden vacated the part midway through the original run. Soo's assumption of this character, by all accounts, amounted to the most valuable cast change, for it gave a clearly Asian role to a mischievous Asian face and personality. David Lober, who took over as dance captain, considered the switch a welcome improvement. "His character is in a sense the core of the show. It and the Pat Suzuki character created the dramatic tension around which the romantic leads revolved. He was Oriental (what a concept), and a gifted comedian, neither of which was Larry Blyden. Larry was very good in other things."

Other replacements may have helped, may have hindered. Chao-Li Chi was offered the role of Dr. Li, the part he had originally been cast to play in New York until Gene Kelly decided that his and Miyoshi Umeki's facial structures looked ill-matched. No fan of Miyoshi's "saccharine phoniness," Chi found Carrillo, against whom he now played and whose face he evidently better matched, a more genuine presence. "Well, first of all, Miyoshi was out, and that I considered a great improvement. Cely Carrillo and me made two human beings instead of a caricature. The main part got more empathy from the audience than Miyoshi could possibly do."

Another thing that helped was how well the two actors got along personally. "We had a very good relationship," says Chi. "I can take her as my daughter. I enjoyed watching her, even though she had no choreography to do. I felt very warm with her."

Lober saw things differently from his dance captain's seat in the audience where he studied the production numbers and took notes for post-performance corrections. In terms of acting ability he considered the okay Cely to be "no Miyoshi." Nor was Lober happy with the exit of Arabella Hong, "a far better singer

Discovered in San Francisco's Forbidden City night club, comedian Jack Soo assumed the role of Sammy Fong when Blyden left the show during the New York run (Photofest).

and actress than her replacement, Suzanne Lake."

There was more agreement on Elaine Dunn's reading of the Linda Low character. Chi does not feel she had quite "the energy and drive" of Suzuki. Lober concurs: "Pat Suzuki had a natural raw vulgarity, and a higher voltage that suited the role well."

Another source of change which would give the show a new face and a new beat was David Lober himself, who exerted, by default or design, strong influence. And without Joe Fields, Dick Rodgers or the late Oscar Hammerstein around to meddle in things, secondary voices, including general stage manager Ted Hammerstein, assumed more power. Lober, assigned to keep the dancers on their toes, did not consider himself Carol Haney's "assistant," as he was listed in program handbills on the road; rather, as dance captain "for the show." And, on the side, he had ample unofficial opportunity, should he choose to play his hand, to influence principals as well.

So many things about a musical can gradually, then suddenly change as it heads out to the hinterlands and others take over — especially when major cast changes occur. Indeed, the farther away it goes from New York, the more free it is to wander away from its original staging patterns — or to willfully reinvent itself into different shapes, rhythms and sounds. Some changes to a show happen naturally through the course of time. Away from the spotlight of its producers, a musical unwatched will evolve in a thousand subtle ways. And by many accounts as well as an examination of some on-the-road reviews, the show that David Lober now monitored was about to do just that.

Egos were another source of conflict and change. Juanita Hall represented the closest living link to the musical's legendary creators. She had nearly starred in *South Pacific* playing Bloody Mary, and not just in the original stage version but in the 1958 film. Hall had opened in *Drum*; she sold one of its brightest numbers, "Chop Suey." By road audiences she would naturally be embraced as the one and only Juanita Hall from the New York cast.

Among other strong-willed figures with the company there was Chao-Li Chi, one of several who had felt somewhat betrayed by the lightweight product Dick and Oscar had delivered; David Lober, seasoned musical theatre veteran, who had worked, in his opinion, on better shows and who did not suffer fools gladly — especially incompetent company managers like Teddy Hammerstein, a cousin of the late Oscar. Hammerstein, according to several of those present, rubbed many cast members the wrong way. In Lober's estimation, "without nepotism, he would never have had a job."

All four souls — Chi, Hall, Lober and Hammerstein — seem to have been emboldened by their enhanced status: Hall, as de facto touring celebrity; Hammerstein, as production stage manager; Chi, in a larger role; and Lober, with more functioning authority as a virtual director of sorts. Altogether, these and other forces were soon to influence the show in numerous ways as it moved down the road and adjusted to each new venue. Like every musical before and after it, *Flower Drum Song* would slowly evolve through the shifting nuances resulting from new actors filling in for sick or departing ones, and from each new set of notes given the cast after a performance critically monitored by a frustrated stage manager wishing to show off — or by a dance captain merely trying to do a good job.

The four strong-willed souls embarked on an unforeseen collision course when they took the train up to Detroit to commence the road tour. Without much note, on May 11, 1961, they opened at the huge, 2,700-seat Riviera theatre in Detroit for an engagement of three weeks and one day. Ominously, they failed to fill the Riviera's seats, averaging houses of only

60 percent. Where in New York the maximum total weekly take could be $63,752, here, with 1,085 more chairs, it was exactly $100,000.

Then came the first of a series of nasty internal squabbles: On the last day in Detroit, all 22 theatres in New York City were thrown into pitch darkness when the actors went out on strike against the producers for better pensions and medical benefits. The incident sent sympathetic shock waves through the *Flower Drum Song* company, whose members belonged to the same union. Their initial reaction was to lend an expression of support by circulating a petition. Remembers Chi, who was one of its proponents along with Khigh Dhiegh and two others, "We would gather the signatures of the entire cast and send it back to New York to support the actors."

As they headed West to open four days later in Los Angeles, the action threw an ugly wedge between various members of the cast, many of them newcomers to the profession and easily intimidated by veterans like Juanita Hall, who exploded when she heard of the petition drive. A pro–Rodgers and Hammerstein, pro-management fanatic, Hall went to work against her fellow actors. "Juanita came around and threatened every chorus member," as Chi tells it. "She said, 'If you sign this thing, you'll never work in your life again!'"

Chi's friend and fellow company member Khigh Dhiegh (a second African American in the cast, who essayed the minor role of Dr. Lu Fong and understudied for Chi), got into a "huge fight" over the issue with Ted Hammerstein, described by Chi as "the demented cousin of Oscar Hammerstein. Teddy is short, stunted. He obviously existed only in the shadow of his cousin and he is full of a lot of little mean streaks, so of course he supported the efforts of Juanita Hall."

Most of those initially in favor of signing and sending the petition withdrew their names out of fear.

"I didn't withdraw," says Chi. "Khigh didn't, and a handful didn't. So it wasn't a cast telegram."

Chi does not recall, however, if the petition was actually sent.

This only worsened the mounting tensions between Ted Hammerstein's dominating bluster and the likes of Chi, who refused to be intimidated. Chi believed that he and a few of his like-minded cohorts were, as a direct result, blacklisted by Hammerstein.

At the outset of the actors' strike, *Flower Drum Song* was one of eight Equity shows on the road still in operation.

Dedicated David Lober continued monitoring the dancers and pushing them to sharpen and tighten their routines. Of Russian blood, Lober had danced on Broadway in a number of musicals, beginning in 1944 with *Bloomer*

Girl. He had witnessed the rise of the dancer-director in the form of Jerome Robbins, and he had developed a high regard for quality musicals.

This latest tuner from R & H, in Lober's opinion, was not one of them. He regarded the commercially viable show as a little bit above average. "It always felt like a pretty mediocre show," says he, "except for some of the music and pieces of the dancing."

And still, while on the road Lober did everything he could within the purview of his authority to give it more depth, dazzle, and thrust.

"As dance captain, I gave notes to all the dancers and put in any replacements. I was assiduous in giving notes, probably to a degree of resentment. But I kept the dancers sharp and gave suggestions for interpretation."

Lober also worked closely with a couple of lead actresses. "Elaine Dunn was in *John Murray Anderson's Almanac* with my ex-wife, so I knew her somewhat. I worked with her closely, and as assiduously as I worked with the dancers. She was very receptive for most of the time I was there.... We sharpened her performance a great deal and, not surprisingly, I thought she did a good job."

He also "coached and worked with" Lucretia Gold, who had taken over the minor role of Liu Ma.

These directorial excursions likely did not endear Lober to his boss, Ted Hammerstein, who himself was not anyone's favorite to be around, particularly not if you were young and female and of Asian ancestry. Hammerstein became known for making propositions in "crude Yiddishisms," in the words of David Lober. And Alvin Ing remembers him as "a leech and a terrible stage manager. I think he only got the job because he was a cousin of Oscar Hammerstein's." There were "ugly stories," recalls Ing, about Hammerstein's coercive ways with women.

Though riven with internal strife, the show moved rapidly west to Los Angeles, opening there on June 6 at the Philharmonic Auditorium to a glamorous tinseltown reception complete with three visiting princesses from Scandinavia — one each from Sweden, Norway and Denmark. They had first been out to Disneyland. Now, they were in the audience, helping to give the show a royal L.A. welcome.

Writing for *The Los Angeles Times*, Cecil Smith noted that, with the New York actors' strike still unsettled, only seven major theatrical shows were playing U.S. cities, and that two of them were currently in town (the other being *The Music Man*, just across the street at the Biltmore). This gave the movie capital a rare distinction, mused Smith: "It is that Los Angeles, usually bereft of major theatre, should for once have a corner on the market."[1]

Never to be repeated.

Once the three princesses were seated and the other show — that one up there on the stage — got underway, "the audience lost itself with great delight," reported critic Smith, registering a qualified endorsement. He lauded the reliably amusing production. If not top drawer R & H, wrote Smith, "still, the songs are enormously singable, the plot bounces along merrily, the settings are bright and gay and colorful. What could even a princess want?"

Of similar mind was Harrison Carroll at the *Los Angeles Evening Herald Express*, while the man over at the *Los Angeles Examiner*, Patterson Greene, dismissed such restraint: "Perhaps the boys back there by the Hudson had sung the praises of Rodgers and Hammerstein so long that they just didn't have enough breath to give this one its due," he reported. "It's a swinging, ringing, singing show, twinkling with smart lines and civilized lyrics, blooming with gracious tunes and veering on occasion to a rousing musical beat that Rodgers hasn't used in many a year."

Greene took full satisfaction in Jack Soo's "delightfully delusional" reading of Sammy Fong; in the dance numbers that "time and again had Wednesday night's opening audience at the Philharmonic in an uproar;" and in Elaine Dunn's delivery: "I am sorry not to have seen Pat Suzuki, who created the role ... but if I had seen her, I should have missed Elaine Dunn, and brothers and sisters, that would have been a calamity. She is sex in precipitation."

Other road replacements charmed Greene. He found Carrillo "bewitching," and he had more praise yet for Jack Soo—"as enjoyable a reprobate as the stage has presented to us, and he accounts for much of the joy of the evening." He loved Gene Castle, "so flawlessly brash that only for the writers' strike, the studios would surely have signed him before the evening was over."[2]

The show was off to a bullish beginning, and surging crowds jammed the L.A. box office to snatch up what few tickets remained for the first weeks of the run, largely sold out in advance to a huge roster of season subscription ticket holders. And after all the subscribers took their turns to see the show, it still packed the house with walk-up window trade. Though technically the box office could handled a maximum of $82,000 weekly, one week they hauled in $83,300.

And this was only a taste of the record-breaking, roof-shattering reception which awaited the company up north in a place perennially in love with itself called San Francisco. On the night of August first, less than a mile from the exotic quarter where it had all began when C.Y. Lee sat down to write a novel about life along Grant Avenue, the Chinese Mission Girls' Drum Corps from St. Mary's paraded up Geary Street through the theatre district to add color and pomp to the opening night festivities. The in-crowd folks of the city, many coming from ritzy dinner parties, were out in their finest garb to be seen and noted and photographed on their way to a hit musical comedy born out of one of their own postcard neighborhoods.

"We all love our city," conceded the *News-Call Bulletin's* drama editor, Emilia Hodel, "and our favorite sport, indoor, outdoor and anywhere, is to listen to other people tell us how wonderful our town is."[3]

Inside the foyer of the Curran Theatre, C.Y. Lee gave out autographs to a crush of ogling admirers as the girls' band marched in. Mayor Christopher delivered a welcoming speech and toasted the Pacific Festival, another local event soon to unfold in the city.

Inside the house minutes before curtain time, Mr. Lee was introduced to a cheering audience. Joe Fields, sitting unobtrusively in his seat, was also pointed out for a local toast — once a searching spotlight could find him.

Finally, the house lights dimmed. A welcome hush swept over the audience. The show began. And what a celebratory reception. The musical rocked like it never before had and likely never would again. In the words of Hodel, "The happy ticket holders tried to stop the show a couple of times with enthusiastic applause, but Robert Stanley, musical director, with an eye to running time and an ear to 'pace,' kept the show moving right along."[4]

Gene Castle managed to trump the conductor's impatience with audience interference, as recounted by another seduced critic, the *San Francisco Examiner's* Charles Einstein: "The 14-year-old dancing sensation stopped the show completely twice. If John Barrymore had been on the same stage, the kid would be recovering from wounds in Mount Zion this morning."

Although Einstein agreed with the nagging New York dissenters who had complained of the show "being old stuff for Rodgers and Hammerstein," he countered that such gripes mattered little, because "they didn't see the cast that San Francisco saw last night. This was so much of the magic! ... If it's true that imitation is the surest form of flattery, then maybe self-imitation works just as well. This is a big one."[5]

Across the bay in a smaller city famed for the absence of a "there there," *Oakland Tribune* critic Theresa Loeb Cone, feeling no duty to cheerlead for somebody else's hometown parade, struck a more probing note. Here was an enterprise, she grumbled, "which has little by way of witty dialogue, outstanding songs or vigorous choreography." Here was also an enterprise, she relented, which cast a certain easy-to-take spell. Well, there were those sets and the costumes and a "few personalities so engaging that the viewer gets a far more favorable impression of the total show than its book, lyrics or music actually merit."

Ms. Cone had seen and reviewed for her paper, not kindly, the Broadway version. In comparison, this touring edition struck her as "far superior to the New York staging." As Cone saw things on the San Francisco stage, every single cast change marked a visible improvement. So, too, did the "tightened up and smoothed out" staging; Cone wrote that the responsible party "deserves hearty applause." That person might have been David Lober.

From ambivalence to veiled praise went Cone, ending up on the side of rouse: "If San Francisco's Chinatown is glowing with extra pride during the next few weeks of the show's engagement, it will be understandable."[6]

The city by the Golden Gate gave its hometown-inspired hit a sensational run. Unprecedented crowds broke one house record after another. And if some of the performances felt more like a joyful church-sponsored talent show than a professional touring company, the lucky audiences who attended them may well have enjoyed the most spirited version of the musical that the world would ever witness.

David Lober warmly recalls those high-flying nights by the bay, saying that the show was improved by "playing San Francisco itself, since many in the cast were from there originally, besides its being about Chinatown in SF. Grant Avenue indeed! There was more motivation to perform well in that city."

Summing up for the *San Francisco Chronicle*, Paine Knickerbocker echoed to a thoughtful degree what Walter Kerr had understood and appreciated on opening night back in New York: "It is a wonderful combination of soft sentiment and sparkle."[7]

Post opening night, cast and local Chinese dignitaries adjourned, along with C.Y. Lee, to Kan's in Chinatown for a lively bash.

Those feverish nights of hometown pride and passion were not to last. Soon after the San Francisco stop, the magic began to lose its force as the tour continued and backstage tensions worsened. "It was more troublesome because of Teddy's mismanagement," explains Chi. By the time, shortly after departing California, that they reached the music hall at the Dallas County fairgrounds, the friction between Ted Hammerstein and David Lober was obvious. And Hammerstein, in Chi's recollection, still resented the actors who had supported the New York strike. The mood turned so sullen and threatening that Chi and his friend and understudy, Khigh Dhiegh, became paranoid, fearing that some sort of retaliation was in the works. And being in "Big D" itself only added to their fears.

"Hammerstein couldn't do anything to me. He didn't like Khigh Dhiegh because Khigh Dhiegh was black. In Dallas, the situation became very dangerous, so I bought a pistol and I never allowed my friend Khigh Dhiegh to go back to the hotel alone. I accompanied him all the time, because he had a feeling that he would be beaten up in Dallas. Dallas is that kind of a town."

Chi felt convinced that Hammerstein wanted Dhiegh out of the cast. "But Khigh is a seasoned actor, a long-time union member and he didn't like that Khigh Dhiegh knew every rule."

David Lober, too, was sinking deeper in the vortex of his own problems with Ted Hammerstein, whom he considered "affable but incompetent," and company manager Maurice Winters. Of late, Hammerstein and Winters had been capriciously implementing a number of irritating new policies. "They were flaky and kept making different rules," says Lober, "which didn't include them, and then they started to try to be disciplinarians, and I wasn't about to follow their particular directions."

Another factor that added to the bad blood between the two was Lober's quasi-directorial attitude, assumed to keep the dancers in tip-top form and the show moving crisply on beat. Hammerstein may have felt a tad upstaged. Nor was Lober about to dilute his duties in order to placate a superior whom he hardly respected. The escalating tensions came to a head in Dallas—ironically, after Carol Haney and others from the New York production staff had come out to take a look at things, and expressed nothing but pleasure with the dance captain. "I was praised by all for the condition of the show," recalls Lober.

Then, shortly after Haney and colleagues left Dallas, Lober was fired. Ted Hammerstein gave him — and Khigh Dhiegh — the heave-ho.

As for Dhiegh, Chi speaks of his friend being called on the carpet for some trivial infractions such as blackening his teeth or "unprofessional stunts." The allegations were never proven, and when Chi helped Dhiegh bring the matter before Actors Equity in New York following the national tour, "we won our case, and Khigh Dhiegh got his back pay from the time he was fired to the end of the tour."

Lober's treatment by Actors Equity, with whom he, too, filed a wrongful termination complaint, left him disillusioned with the very union which, only months earlier, had won its strike against the producers. "Somebody in Equity said they couldn't possibly make a negative judgment against Richard Rodgers.... I thought that Equity acted very badly, making such a statement and asking us to bind ourselves to arbitration."

Which they did.

Without Lober's sitting out in the seats and taking notes, the show moved on to a nearly six-month engagement in Chicago. Greeted by four discouraging notices, lukewarm at best, it still did satisfactory business overall, filling up an average of 71 percent of the seats. *Variety*, in a year-end report on the Windy City season, figured that the show had "departed prematurely"[8] when it could have prolonged a still-profitable run. Of three musicals to play Chicago that year — the other two being *Once Upon a Mattress* and the Pulitzer prize–winning *Fiorello!* — Dick and Oscar's oriental delight easily ruled at the ticket windows.

They were now traveling to midsized venues, to Des Moines and Omaha, to St. Paul and Milwaukee and Rochester, and the business was good enough.

"Most cities welcomed us with open arms," says Alvin Ing, who had joined the show during the San Francisco engagement after he closed in Los Angeles with *The World of Suzie Wong*.

"Well," reflects Chi with a sigh, "People laughed and people had a good time, and didn't learn anything."

Each new stop along the road posed a different set of technical and human challenges. They adapted to each new theatre they played and recast minor parts as needed. Even so, unexpected problems continued to bedevil cast and crew. When the company arrived at the Canadian border to enter Toronto, immigration agents were waiting to check passports. The show came close not to crossing. Both Cely Carrillo and Chao-Li Chi were working with temporary visitor permits; had they ventured north, they would have not been permitted to return to the states, but automatically deported to the Philippines and China, respectively. Carrillo's understudy, Virginia Malvar, another Filipino, had the same problem.

Who, then, could play the Mei Li role? Hurriedly, Hammerstein's staff scrambled to secure a temporary stand-in. They imported Joy Kim, who was then appearing as Mei Li in a touring tent-show, straw-hat production of the show under the direction of James Hammerstein. Kim got to play her role in a first-class production in another country. Once across the border, they were a smash in a two-week Toronto engagement. Afterwards, she returned to the sawdust arena. As for Chi, held back in the states, his understudy, Wyley Hancock, took over.

The show enjoyed smashing business in a two-week Toronto date.

Ted Hammerstein told a correspondent from *Variety* what a tough time he was having, constantly on the lookout for Asian dancers in each town. He was routinely contacting local dance schools. During the Chicago date, he had signed two Japanese-born girls just finishing up their high school exams — Connie Sanchez and Sharon Konishi; the latter, at 17 years old, was the youngest in the company. In San Francisco, a Tokyo girl,

Yoschiko Kutzutani, in the city as an exchange student, had auditioned and been cast in the chorus. During the Canadian stop, Hammerstein recruited a local girl, Shirley May, to sing and dance.[9]

Everything — and even anything — to keep this show on the road.

Crossing back into the states, they played Pittsburgh. A little later they were opening in Philadelphia, where they were acclaimed by three boffo notices and did more good-enough business. They barely broke even in Baltimore, did okay up in Hartford. And finally the last stand was at hand:

Cleveland. That's where, on October 14, 1961, it all ended. That's where the very last production of the 22-city national touring company of *Flower Drum Song* was seen. The New York run had lasted for 17 months and six days; the road tour was shorter by only three days; a London run at the Palace Theatre, which closed April 21 of the same year, had lasted for thirteen months and five days— despite generally dismissive notices. None of the leads from the New York company appeared on the West End, although the supporting role of Wang San was played by original Broadway cast member George Minami, Jr.

At this point in its infancy, who could predict what sort of future lay ahead for this new Rodgers and Hammerstein hit which many loved and others disdained? Within five, maybe ten years at the most, the way things went for successful R & H shows, *Drum* would likely be back on Broadway in its first revival. Already, some civic light opera groups around the country had either mounted their own locally cast productions or were planning to in the near future. The cast album was a winner, and a film version, about to be released, promised to bring the new tuner to millions of moviegoers nationwide, vastly expanding the prospective audience for future productions of the show near and far — whether under tents or on the grandest of stages.

And with luck, the movie would achieve what movie versions of hit stage musicals rarely achieve. And the sky would not come tumbling down on Mei Li and her fragile little songs about the simple wonders of life.

9

Hollywood Suey

To the soundstages of Hollywood — the most grueling challenge any musical will ever face — *Flower Drum Song* next went. Joe Fields signed a contract to sketch out a screenplay aimed at capitalizing on big screen developments. He had plans to make the work more dramatic — judging by what he told Arabella Hong, whom he hoped would recreate her role of Helen Chao.

"Oh, we're going to rewrite the part," promised Fields. "It will be a much better part!"

In exactly what manner, it was never made known. Possibly Fields envisioned portraying Helen Chao's suicide on the screen as it was depicted in the novel. In fact, however, the only marked change he made was to the ballet, turning its focus away from Wang Ta and onto Chao. Other than this, Fields, a comedy writer by trade, stuck to his lightweight approach.

And Hong stuck to her approaching motherhood. Eight months pregnant, while she was lying down one day she felt her daughter inside "flipping over," in effect, telling her to leave the movie alone. "So I had my own flower drum song."

Fields adhered to the story that he and Hammerstein had developed, although he introduced the characters and their situations very differently. So, too, when he laid out the score, were the songs reshuffled like a deck of cards. In overall tone, he opened the work up through the prism of stylized ersatz '50s movie musical production numbers. One song was filtered through a '50s beatnik mindset. Three others were reorchestrated to include waltz tempos during instrumental passages. And by the time that director Henry Koster started shooting at Universal, the strange celluloid makeover wrought a sexier set of characters and situations.

Ironically, this approach tended to coarsen the subtler Asian charms of the original. And without now-deceased Oscar Hammerstein to counter the more egregious liberties taken, the play's visual context morphed from quaint old exotic Chinatown to a kind of orientalized Avon-calling fashion show for the masses of middle American. The musical ended up looking and sounding more like *Pillow Talk* than *Gigi* or *Brigadoon*— or *Flower Drum Song*.

Fields had scripted only a couple of minor song and dance flicks, while the Hollywood portfolio of producer Ross Hunter was totally tuneless. However, director Henry Koster (*Harvey, The Robe*) had helmed several winning movie musicals.

To their credit, Fields and Hunter did enlist a top-notch veteran choreographer in Hermes Pan, who had worked on many of Fred Astaire's films and who could be counted on to implant a degree of footwork pizzaz into the proceedings. Young Patrick Adiarte, cast to recreate his Broadway role of Wang San, was excited over the chance to work with Pan, though at first it did not appear that such a thing would happen. Adiarte called his first meeting with Pan "the worst audition I ever had."

"What do you want to do?" asked Pan, waiting.

To which, dumbfounded, Adiarte replied, "What are you going to show me?"

Pan was not one to dictate. Adiarte was on his own. Inspiration did not set him into graceful motion that day.

"I was falling all over."

When filming began, the young Filipino hoofer wasn't even called upon to rehearse the choreographed sections. "Somehow, he thought I couldn't dance."

By mistake, Patrick was placed, nonetheless, into one of the numbers, in which, more relaxed, his native talents snared Pan's instant attention. "They put me in one number, then they put me in two, and then they liked me and they said, 'You know what? We're gonna create another number for you.'"

That number was a solo carved out for the teenage dynamo during a truncated version of "The Other Generation."

As remembered by Adiarte, "the very shy, very quiet" Hermes Pan would sit around and watch what he could do. "He let me fool around. He took what he saw that I could do and he choreographed around me. He didn't give me stuff. He got an idea of what I did best, and he tried to work around that somehow."

Working with Pan was like being back in *The King and I*, working for his idol: "He is like Jerome Robbins to me."

If Adiarte felt the illusory magic of a very good thing going up before the cameras, he was too young to know of the abysmal track record for Broadway hits being revised beyond recognition on the huge soundstages out on Melrose Avenue or in Culver City. During the 1930s, master show-man Busby Berkeley choreographed a slew of girl-laden film extravagan-zas, offering depression-era audiences one dazzling escapist blockbuster after another, among them *Forty Second Street* and *Gold Diggers of 1935*. Fred Astaire and Ginger Rogers danced a glorious path through nine movies during the same period. The silly but affecting rags-to-riches tales kept fragile American dreams alive during the nation's darkest hours.

Into the forties and fifties sailed the new epic movie musical — at its best when originally conceived *for the screen* and set in the world of enter-tainment. Ask somebody to name a favorite *movie* musical. Chances are, they will name something like (yes, you've already named it) *Singin' in the Rain*, or another one of several gems (*Holiday Inn; The Band Wagon*) penned expressly for the screen featuring hit songs from old Broadway shows.

Throughout the same period, less lucky were the "smash" musicals that had opened on New York boards and ended up in back-lot waste bas-kets, recycled to death before anybody shouted the first "Take!" From proscenium to projected image, the bulk of them went down in infamy, turned into nondescript fluff by wrong-headed hacks or sadistic produc-ers or stupidly ambitious directors. The list is long, the reasons many.

One fact is inarguable: The journey from stage to screen is fraught with unforeseen pitfalls, not the least being the nearly impossible opera-tion, once a stage libretto has been dissembled, of putting it back together into a viable motion-picture format that will retain the innate chemistry of the original. Since the mere static filming of a Broadway show — three or four cameras rolling from fixed positions in a theatre — rarely, if ever, will please ticket-buying types, then the problem each time becomes how to make the thing work in a different medium. Most of all, how to make it look like a real movie and not a stage show being performed in front of painted sets.

Invariably, because moviegoers expect movies to simulate reality, the panning camera's closeup magnifications can have the unintended effect of making a stage musical, artificial by nature, look more artificial. Films like *Guys and Dolls*, the *Pajama Game, Finian's Rainbow, A Chorus Line*, and, more recently, *The Fantasticks* and *The Phantom of the Opera*, are rat-tled off by the disillusioned as examples of messed-up conversions. The camera's eye gives audiences a panoramic view of selected realism. In the atypically successful film version of *Oklahoma!* what we see is not a stage, but the real world.

Stage shows play to the imagination. They are theatrical. Inside a playhouse, patrons instinctively make allowances for drops and props, flats and footlights—allowances they will not so readily grant the images on a flickering screen. So ... how to dispense with that in-the-theatre artifice without losing the work's essence? In translation, many musicals simply do not survive, even the ones handled by the best of directors with the best of intentions. It is a hellishly tricky process.

Defying the odds, Dick and Oscar fared much better at the movies than most of their stage colleagues. The first four of their works to make it to the screen—*Oklahoma!*, *Carousel*, *The King and I*, and *South Pacific*—all made plenty of money and pleased plenty of moviegoers. These were the days when the R & H brand of romance was a sure ticket.

Even then, however, every one of their musicals lost a certain something in the sugar-coated screen translations. The lushly orchestrated soundtracks; the soaring dance numbers that fill the big screen from right to left; more important, the editing that removed darker numbers—all of these factors combined to canonize the sweetness and charm of R & H in subtly unflattering ways. And the added saccharine only gave an emerging school of critics more ammunition.

The omission of selected songs from the original versions had to have been approved by Dick and Oscar. Most of the deleted material supplied worldly counterpoint to all the happy talk. From *Oklahoma!*, in a move that now seems artistically criminal, they dropped Jud Fry's soliloquy, "A Lonely Room," which brilliantly gives singing voice to the misfit farmhand's harrowing sense of social and romantic isolation. From *Oklahoma!* too, the gutsy, rip-roaring lament against forced marriage, "It's a Scandal! It's a Outrage!" was left out. Another outrage.

From *The King and I*, they dropped Anna's testy anti-valentine to the misogynist King, the very funny and sarcastic "Shall I Tell You What I Think of You?" *Carousel* fared better; only one of its numbers, "The Highest Judge of All," fell to the cutting room floor.

Likely because *South Pacific's* Broadway director Josh Logan also helmed the movie version, that show did not suffer a single cut. To the contrary, a lovely little refrain, "My Girl Back Home," which had been dropped out of town, was reinstated with a revised lyric, at the urging of Logan, who understandably loved the song.

In years to come, similar butchery would befall *The Sound of Music*. It lost the stage version's two most sophisticated ditties, "How Can Love Survive" and "No Way to Stop It"—neither of which has anything to say about any lark out there learning to pray. These dreadful slights made the film that much more compulsively cheerful, giving movie patrons who had never seen the original show a far more idyllic vision of an upbeat R & H universe.

What might they drop from *Flower Drum Song*? The closest thing to a dark moment in verse was the brooding "Love Look Away," which they were not about to drop. Reiko Sato, cast to play Helen Chao, did not actually sing the song; she lip-synced it to the voice of Marilyn Horne.

Compared to the their predecessor shows, Dick and Oscar's score for *Drum* contained a number of "hip" elements from bawdy jazz to '50s rock and roll — enough to tempt and confuse a second-rate director with scarce regard for the original work. And on this project, Henry Koster seems to have fit this loathsome category. For, in truth, those hip moments in the stage version were only nods in passing to the contemporary scene. In the hands of Hunter and Koster, *Flower Drum Song* was inflated into a disjointed panorama of pedestrian fifties cliches.

How to count the missteps? To start at the very beginning, as Oscar Hammerstein would say: Casting, or the lack of. James Shigeta and Benson Fong, paired to play the eldest son and his father, respectively, come off like a community theatre duo in a town bereft of Asian-faced talent. Fong looked not much older than Shigeta, and his mannerisms were amateurishly stiff.

Another lingering disappointment would be the absence of the unpursued Pat Suzuki. Instead, the non-singing Nancy Kwan, fresh from playing a bar waitress in *The World of Suzie Wong*, was offered the role. She had the looks that Suzuki did not. She could dance, which Suzuki, so it is said, could not. Kwan's pouty semi–bad girl persona suited the film's descent into cosmetic bubble gum. The way that Kwan was directed to imitate a typically jaded '50s sex kitten, she hardly looked Asian at all.

When they were in a casting frame of mind, Hunter and Koster and the gang made a trip up to San Francisco to check out the local talent at Forbidden City, by then in its final days of operation. Ivy Tam, who now danced in the floor show, was told that they would be looking at her — maybe for a part. She was never formally auditioned. Neither was anybody else. Tam does remember enjoying, with husband Charlie at her side, a wry evening of chat over drinks with Hunter and his tinseltown cronies. Hunter had grown savvy to the club's penchant for hiring Filipinos and Japanese to the point of paranoia.

"You don't look too Chinese," said he to Ivy. "Are you sure you're pure Chinese?"

Answered Ivy, "I think so. My mother is Chinese. My father is Chinese. So I have to be Chinese!"

They all laughed.

Hunter took a closer look. "Are you sure you don't have a little French?"

And so went the small talk. Tam was later offered, and rejected, a bit part.[1]

Tam recalls that Hunter cast a few showgirls from the club. Interestingly, he also signed film actress Anna May Wong to play the role of Sammy Fong's mother, but Wong fell ill before filming began and died soon after.

Jack Soo was cast to play Sammy Fong, the role he had perfected to the delight of numerous critics on the national road tour. Which brings up another nagging problem that can surface when stage actors turn to screen acting: the many closeup shots awarded Soo and Umeki made each a less appealing presence in this long, long cinematic slog. Soo's style of mugging, which projected well enough from a stage, did not wear as well in front of a camera. A gifted comedian, he nevertheless seems to be sleep-walking through his paces for Koster. Too often he looks trapped by the camera's fixation. Umeki's, too, suffered from too many prolonged close-ups; her chronic sweetness and submissive mannerisms grow tiresome well before the end credits roll.

To Soo, however, goes credit for one of the film's few highlights. And a hilarious one at that. It occurs at the nightclub scene during Linda Low's strip number. Soo is seated next to Wang Chi-yang at a table while Low begins to peel. Soo's gloating deadpan glare in Wang's direction — as if to say "So, ah — how does your son's fiancée look to you now?" — is priceless. It is the perfect sendup to the father's hasty retreat, coughing up a storm of disapproval as he exits Mr. Fong's crude Celestial Bar.

The princely moment shares high honors with two others: Shigeta's tender rendition of "You Are Beautiful" and the marvelous over-the-top "Chop Suey" — although the latter takes fun to tasteless extremes by turning the song at one point into a square dance complete with bogus Asian-accented caller. In the stage version, "Chop Suey" is a rousing cha-cha rocker swinging cleanly to a particular beat of the day. By the time it made it to Universal Studios, from hip to barn it went. Even so, it serves as a rousing good toast to the crazy quilt of American culture. In it, best of all, Patrick Adiarte is as quick-footed and flamboyantly engaging as one could be in those times; indeed, he is subconsciously ahead of his time. His spins are as terrific and visceral as a champion skater's. The star power is there almost by accident. And therein lay a key to some kind of a different movie musical which, in more gifted or daring hands, this one might have been.

It wasn't. It wasn't. Beyond a lush abstract panorama of opening title watercolors— delicately rendered with childlike innocence by San Francisco artist Dong Kingman — the rest of this yawning flick is rather like a pre–John Waters picnic for bad movie-musical voyeurs. Much of Rodgers' fine music was drained of its primal energy in the director's push to make things sound fifties-cool. "Like a God," the score's most exhilarating piece of music, is rendered near-useless in a North Beach poets' coffee house, where its first lines are spoken by a beatnik in a stilted soporific manner. "The Other Generation" is sung minus its most exciting section — the verse. "Don't Marry Me" is performed by Soo and Umeki, sans the charming soft-shoe interlude that made it so irresistible on the stage.

Nancy Kwan's "I Enjoy Being a Girl" lacks the earthy gusto of Pat Suzuki's liberating front-door delivery, belted out high on a hill overlooking San Francisco Bay. Here, removing the song even farther from the visceral authenticity of the stage show, Kwan, another lip-syncing non-singer in this exceedingly manufactured film, is supported by unseen vocalist B. J. Baker. And in her blase kitty-cat rendition, complete with teasing gestures, the number is not so much a song as just another synthetic prop of feminine self-indulgence, like her chiffon-white boudoir and negligee. Competing for her attentions are the wall-high vanity mirrors in her bedroom — mirrors that, in the end, give off images of Kwan in various fashions. Inside the set-bound film (even "Grant Avenue" was filmed on a soundstage), "Girl" sings itself to sleep in a void of white lace.

The movie reaches the nadir of awfulness when it gets down to jazzing up "Sunday." As originally staged by Gene Kelly, the number was an infectious soft shoe of the sort that can float across a dreamy stage. On the leaden Universal lot, "Sunday" goes from generic to polyester into a very strange night. Enter Jack Soo in orange pajamas, sharing with Nancy Kwan a soulless vision of how it will feel on the seventh day of the week once they are married. They are forced to entertain a silly couple who drop by with social pretensions. Out of a huge television jump a cowboy and Indian in reaction to their being shot at by a young boy in orange, presumably the son of the weirdly domesticated Mr. and Mrs. Sammy Fong. The ancillary dances call to mind an outdoor fling designed by Agnes de Mille à la *Oklahoma!* The oddball set looks like a cross between a Christian Dior joker-is-wild fashion show and a modernist Chinese car wash.

"Sunday," Ross Hunter style, makes one long for any other day of the week, and a day preferably away from the set of Henry Koster's *Flower Drum Song*.

The only example of Joseph Fields' having given the Helen Chao character more dramatic attention is in the ballet, whose storyline he turns on its head, causing further damage to his antiseptic script. As performed on Broadway, the ballet depicted Wang Ta torn between his two love interests — Linda Low and Mei Li — and succumbing, on the rebound, to the grasping arms of Chao. The film redirects the focus onto Chao: She slips helplessly underwater, there to be menacingly pursued by a chain of lech-

Lost in Hollywood, Nancy Kwan (left) and Jack Soo (on the floor) appear in "Sunday" in the 1961 movie version of *Flower Drum Song* (Photofest).

erous men, and to be saved at the last minute by Wang Ta, whom she then seduces.

Finally, another contributing hack was editor Milton Carruth, who took thirteen minutes longer than two prolonged hours to tell a story deemed excessively wordy by even those who liked the film.

It is tempting to wonder how different the finished product, shot in Panavision, might have been had someone with the sensitivity of, say, a Vincente Minnelli directed the enterprise; had the casting been markedly better; had the finer qualities of the stage work been brought more subtly to the screen. Had it been an MGM movie.

When the film was released — less than a month after the close of the national Broadway road tour — millions of Americans were exposed to a bizarre pastiche of limping mediocrity which would in future years come to stand for the stage musical it so crassly misrepresented. Yet many film critics were tolerant when *Flower Drum Song* first hit the screens. From *The New York Times* came an easy pass from Bosley Crowther: "... fairly blossoms anew on the vast Panavision color panel ... nothing subtle or fragile ... gaudy and gaggy and quite melodic. Along those lines, it is quite a show."

Paul V. Beckley of *The New York Herald Tribune* described it as "corn, picked a little late and cooked a little slow but salted and peppered and shiny with butter."

Other critics saw nothing to cheer about: "It's still preposterous and still occasionally tuneful and pretty," reported the *New Yorker's* Brendan Gill; "phony Chinese apothegms flower like tiger-bone wine, and the settings are every bit as authentic as Fu Manchu."[2]

In an unforgiving mood, *Variety* saw an oriental turkey, noting that the work's "fundamental charm, grace and novelty" in Ross Hunter's translation had been "overwhelmed by the sheer opulence and glamour ... curiously unaffecting, unstable and rather undistinguished."[3]

Worse still, this Hunter-Koster botch job gave critics of the stage show — and of R & H in general — further reason to feel vindicated and to remain hyper-skeptical about all things from Happy Talk, past, present and future. As well, the movie helped to push fence sitters over into the anti–*Drum* camp, and they began closing ranks. A sad residual history of critical disdain based on a celluloid crime was born.

Too, average moviegoers did not flock to this film in droves. History would also write, correctly, that it was the first and only Hollywood adaptation of a Rodgers and Hammerstein show to lose money at the box office.

So, reduced to drivel on a screen often unfriendly to New York stage hits, the show's wavering destiny took a turn for the worse, and everyone in the original cast who had first brought it to a largely adoring world had — and still has — ample reason to feel embarrassed.

Pat Adiarte calls the movie "a little strange. I loved the stage. I was brought up on the stage. To me, the stage is the best. It's very difficult when you translate, because you always want to do more with the movie than you do for a stage because it's sort of limited by the scenery."

Alvin Ing puts things into historical perspective: "You can count on one hand the musicals that were better on the screen than they were on the stage." Of many disappointments with the film, Ing rues the absence of Keye Luke, who "had a kind of solidity about him that I respected and enjoyed."

David Lober does not hold back on this one: "They made a terrible musical and film out of it."

Unfortunately, too, *this* was the version of *Flower Drum Song* which the academics and latter-day theatre critics would judge when they got around to analyzing the musical. For example, it would be cited as evidence of how "white" American writers ignorantly stereotyped Chinese people and life in San Francisco's Chinatown. In his book *Orientals: Asian Americans in Popular Culture*, author Robert G. Lee recently (and justly) took the film to task for shunning one of the most affecting and important themes of C. Y. Lee's novel: "the interrogation of racial exclusion"— in other words, the lack of work for the young educated Chinese American male.[4]

In the stage version, Hammerstein and Fields did give this theme respectful if minor attention in a scene between Linda Low and Wang Ta, wherein Ta asks Low to define her ambitions, and in reply she shares a desire to excel at her "gender." In turn, Linda asks Ta about his ambitions.

"Well," he answers, "it is difficult for a Chinese, even with a college degree, to find employment. I think I will study law, because then I won't have to look for a job for another three years."[5]

On screen, Wang Ta, about to graduate, comes off as something of a lazy rich kid, skipping any mention of the employment discrimination problem in his reference to law school.

Robert Lee takes umbrage with the sight of so many Asian-Americans in a "Chinatown park" dressed as "middle-class white Americans of the period."[6] He seems to have confused Union Square, where the scene appears to have been shot, with another park. Even then, the idea that local Asians should not be dressed as middle class Americans is a puzzling assertion.

Lee might have saved his ire for the sarcastic remark made during the same scene by a Chinese American policeman. Handed a slip of paper by Mei Li, who is asking for street directions to Madam Fong's house, he glances it over, rolls his eyes impatiently, and cracks, "I guess I should have taken lessons in Chinese!" This elicits laughter from the locals, many of them Chinese, who have gathered around to hear Mei Li and her father sing their songs. We, looking in, are left to gawk at how stupidly insensitive Joe Fields could be without the counter-intelligence of an Oscar Hammerstein around. Another of many examples of wretched taste not imported from the more discreet stage version.

Robert Lee quotes a *New Yorker* scribe blaming a pair of white writers for the clichéd portrayal of a native Chinese girl being taught how to kiss by an American: "It seems to have worried neither Mr. Rodgers nor Mr. Hammerstein very much that the behavior of war-torn Pacific Islanders and nineteenth century Siamese might be slightly different from that of Chinese residents of present-day California, where *Flower Drum Song* is fictionally sung."[7]

Not so. Those white writers were quoting directly from the novel that supported their libretto. In it, Mei Li, in a warmly flirtatious scene with Wang Ta, is told, "Perhaps you are the only person on American soil who does not know what a kiss is. Well, let me explain it to you." The jokes that follow about "half done" kisses and "well done kisses" were taken nearly verbatim from C.Y. Lee's narrative.[8]

If the film is not very good, it might still be good for somebody's arching thesis. Robert Lee was sufficiently antagonized by Linda Low's I-Am-Girl-Hear-Me-Purr anthem to argue, "'I Enjoy Being a Girl' is uncompromisingly — and, to its presumed audience, reassuringly — heterosexual. Linda Low's sexuality is contained and domesticated by its transformation into consumption. The song fetishizes the female body, which the Barbie doll (a new hit on the toy market that year) was making into a new vehicle of consumption."

Mostly, Mr. Lee likes to liken the *film* musical to another movie, *Sayonara*, for both, in his view, "celebrate American liberalness. In these films ethnic assimilation is the vehicle through which the social identities of race, class, sex and nationality can be displaced by the embrace of the modern.... In both cases, the domestication of exotic sexuality recreates the Oriental woman as a naturalized woman, ready to assume the mantle of mother of a new American empire."[9]

And maybe even a new American musical. Younger generations of scholars and theatre writers, among them a rising class of Chinese American students and professors, would see whatever they wanted to see in *Flower Drum Song* whenever they rented the video or watched it on the tube. And through their probing skepticism, it would evolve over the years into a huge oriental ink blot test to be argued over, dissected and reinterpreted.

It would also provide carefree pleasure to any number of Asians, some secretly tolerating it in the privacy of their homes with one slightly ambivalent finger resting on a TV remote control.

"From a more culturally aware-angry-Asian-Man-Guy-Aok perspective," argued another Lee — Joanna W. — during a retrospective presentation in 2002 at the San Francisco Asian American Film Festival, "*Flower Drum Song* is chock full of egregious racial slights.... And of course, the fact that it's written and directed by two white men for a Hollywood audience certainly limits its validity as a genuinely Asian American production." For Lee, the initial experience of watching an All-Asian cast "with and without accents and Mandarin-collared shirts" was "amusing and horrifying at the same time."

Admitting, nevertheless, that "to be honest, the film is simply a lot of fun," Ms. Lee recalled growing up in Chinatown in the 1950s and 1960s when her mother and siblings were "huge fans of the musical." With all of her reservations, she confessed a surprising affection for the film, unable in conclusion to resist its portrait, however limited, of actual Asian Americans participating as "prominent and legitimate American citizens ... a rare treat — progressive by even today's standards."[10]

Interestingly, though, when Ms. Lee spoke of her family's laughing at the "ridiculous asthmatic patriarch stereotype," she apparently did not acknowledge how the coughing spasms of that asthmatic — Master Wang Chi-yang — are more flagrantly portrayed in the novel, itself the work not of a white man but of yet another Lee and one of Ms. Lee's fellow Chinese Americans.

10

Obstacle of Changing Weather:
Actors and Activists

Beyond the flattering lights of Broadway, Mei Li's little show got bumped around and misunderstood a lot when amateur and civic light opera groups around the country took their turns presenting it to the public. Their oddly divergent productions would continue splitting the critics for the next twenty-five years until, ironically, this penultimate opus from Rodgers and Hammerstein became their most controversial. Indeed, it is one of few musicals—if not the only one *ever*—to be the object of a virtual boycott. Dick and Oscar: Pollyanna racists worth a protest?

The show's checkered production record and the careless tendency of some to mischaracterize and denigrate its original New York run had left a trail of theatre aficionados and historians with divided attitudes. Two lingering problems—the dearth of Asian actors and the show's tricky split personality (discreet to bawdy)—made it one of the most difficult properties to mount, especially at the hands of timid, politically worrisome directors.

It was never an easy show to put on the boards. On the one hand, its story and characters form a light-hearted tale easily buried under a director's heavy hand or a cast too inclined to be overly theatrical. On the other, with too sensitive an approach to the work's subtler nuances, a production might fail to achieve lift-off lacking the power normally supplied by such figures as Linda Low and Sammy Fong. And that's assuming a sufficient number of adequately talented Asian performers show up for auditions. Where, oh where, to find them? Around New York, San Francisco and maybe Los Angeles. Elsewhere, the makeup artists often worked overtime applying slanted eyebrows and black dye-jobs to occidental standins.

In 1985, *Flower Drum Song* was produced at New Jersey's summer repertory Surflight Theatre (where 12 shows a season were presented, each running seven consecutive nights). Theatre head Scott Henderson, in a downbeat assessment, remembers the show going over so poorly that it was never done again. Backstage on a Wall of Shame bulletin board where fliers and personal notes poke fun at floperamas, somebody tacked up a sign that read FLOWER DUMB SONG.[1] Was it the show or maybe the actors? Script or sets and costumes? Musical director Dean Crocker, referencing a "tiny stage" and a two- or three-piece orchestra, said, "I think it went okay — if cheap production values and a half-dead cast and crew ever are okay."

Any musical will fly or fumble on a myriad of elements. Without the right cast, few make much of an impression.

The musical's life out in the hinterlands began on a promising note. In fact, the first groups who took it on (while the national touring company was *still* in progress) drew cheering, turnstile-spinning crowds and broke many house records. Exhibit A: In the summer of 1961, the San Diego Civic Light Opera's Starlight Theatre, whose shows went up on the huge 4,324-seat Balboa Park Bowl, decided to skip the search for a quasi–Asian cast. Instead, they settled for anybody who could act and who seemed to fit the parts. Slanted eyebrows would have to do. "None of us had seen the show," says Ole Kittleson, then a young all–American blond cast to play Wang Ta. "With or without Asians, it was going to be produced."

Produced it was, with 90 percent of the faces belonging to Caucasians. Kittleson's hair was spray-tinted black, his eyes altered by epicanthic folds which did not last beyond publicity photos.

The show they presented caused a box-office stampede. "Ticket sales went through the roof," recounts Kittleson. "They were selling seats on the steps for fifty cents."

Its "gentleness of spirit," as the actor puts it, worked wonders on audiences. Jean Hedger, reviewing for the *San Diego Union Tribune*, spotted the quality: "The gently and exactly stated musical of two Chinese generations never shouts at the top of its voice. A fine book and the music of Rodgers and Hammerstein combine to make one of the best productions of the decade."[2]

"We are breaking attendance records of 16 years," stated Starlight president Earl Cantos to the *Union Tribune*. "Last Sunday night, Balboa Park Bowl was filled to capacity and 550 surplus patrons had to be seated in the aisle."[3]

Linda Low and company proved to be the Starlight's biggest hit in its fifteen-year history, and so the show was brought back to Balboa Park five years later. Had they duplicated their original concepts, they might have achieved another milestone. Instead, they made a number of changes which worked against the *Drum's* special qualities. Parts of the production were sent out over the audience on huge ramps. Half the cast was new, and still predominately white. Now, this resourceful troupe was employing gender-blind casting as well, turning Wang Ta's brother, Wang San, into his sister, Wang San, played by one Cathy Ordona. And the critics were disappointed by another change: The new actress who played Linda Low was not up to belting out Low's showstoppers. Overall, a somewhat muddled result.

Ole Kittleson, brought back to play Wang Ta, thought the horse-show ramp was alienating. On it he had to sing "Like God." On it, too, Mei Li had to sing the quietly pensive "I Am Going to Like It Here." Although audiences came out in large numbers, Kittleson felt a lack of something: "It was not the joyous production to me that it had been the first time. You can't go home again."

Not when home is no longer there.

One local scribe, Reggie Morin, got up the nerve to say in print what he had all along felt about the libretto. Careful to compliment all of San Diego's familiar "ingratiating" players in a *San Diego Evening Tribune* piece, Morin let go with his "hate" for the "dreadful book which, yes, like the old cliche about Chinese food, leaves you empty almost immediately after you've sat down to enjoy it." As if competing with Kenneth Tynan, Morin put up a good match: "It is blender pureed-pre-masticated Cantonese pap. And the score, which sounds affable enough in recordings, doesn't really do anything to freshen up the unending succession of boxy interiors.... *Flower Drum Song* creates as much soggy myth about orientals as other fictions do about Negroes, Jews or, for that matter, Englishmen."[4]

Nevertheless, audiences in a few other cities likewise turned out in abundance when their respective light opera companies ran the show across their boards and set more house records. The musical seemed destined to enjoy a thriving career in regional playhouses.

When the show was first staged by the St. Louis Municipal Opera, also during the summer of 1961, Myles Standish, critiquing for the *Post Dispatch*, echoed what other tempered road reviewers had been writing: "Delightful.... It isn't up to the famous team's major works, but it is a good show. It is a lively and colorful piece with a pleasant score, a lot of humor and a wistful note here and there as it contrasts the modern and westernized younger generations in San Francisco's Chinatown with the older tradition-bound Chinese."

Savvy (or tolerant), as only a few were, to the musical's dual personality, Standish credited the authors for taking a correct approach in veering clear of pathos. The book, he wrote, "does not remain long on the serious line, perhaps fortunately, as it isn't too deep in that direction. But it provides many diverting moments."[5]

Those diverting moments kept the cash registers ringing in St. Louis. *Flower Drum Song*'s ticket sales easily topped the previous season's closer, *Redhead*. All of which was incentive to bring the show back four years later. On opening night in 1965, it drew the largest crowd ever for a first performance. Reviewing once more for his paper, Standish felt much the same, reaffirming his initial impression: "The book ... seems undecided for a while between a serious approach and one in the lighter vein.... Fortunately, the lighter approach wins out as there isn't enough stature to the book to support dramatic tensions."[6]

Members of the original cast were now showing up in various regional productions. Jack Soo played Sammy Fong in St. Louis; Standish described him as a sort of "oriental Robert Mitchum." And Alvin Ing, who had understudied for Wang Ta on the national tour, finally got to own the part in St. Louis, where he earned kudos from Standish.

When the show returned to San Francisco in 1963 in the form of a dinner theatre production at the Sheraton Palace Hotel with Jack Soo and Elaine Dunn headlining, the veteran players lent an air of seasoned luster. Writing for the *San Francisco Chronicle*, Paine Knickerbocker found Jack Soo "in marvelous form. His timing is precise, his clowning has a wonderful air of harassed rascality and he occupies the small stage artfully."

The scaled-down edition seemed to flatter the show's more intimate nature, in Knickerbocker's opinion: "Its appealing melodies and tough and tender comedy are both appropriate and delightful as a part of the celebration of the Chinese New Year."[7]

In agreement was the *San Francisco News Call-Bulletin*'s Pat Speegle, noting, "There is a certain fragility to this exceedingly successful musical and it takes a performance in the round to emphasize this quality."[8]

Over at the *Examiner*, Stanley Eichelbaum saw only pandering contrivance: "This late in the extraordinary career of *Flower Drum Song*, I am scarcely foolhardy enough to fight its phony Chinese, its unbelievably simple-minded book and its improvised Rodgers and Hammerstein score. The musical's tremendous popularity in more than four years has surely disparaged every irate critic's rap, including the one who aptly described it as 'the world of woozy song.'"

Fairly, he concluded, "Yet this is an ingratiating, talented and buoyant crew, headed by that superbly entertaining master of deadpan, Jack Soo, a frog-voiced Jap comic who seems even funnier as Sammy Fong ... than he did when we saw him at the Curran.... The show really bounces."[9]

Helping to drum up opening-night publicity during a makeup session in her dressing room, petite Elaine Dunn, of Russian and Polish ancestry, let a fashion writer watch a makeup artist transform her face. During the hour-long process, Dunn took questions and offered answers about how "oriental eyes" are applied. "Mascara, a false straight eyelash on the outer half of the eye, a touch of rouge high on the cheekbone, a gently curved eyebrow and 'I've had people ask me if I were Oriental.'"[10]

One year later and the show was almost back in San Francisco—to open the new 2,500-seat Hyatt Music Theatre a few miles south in Burlingame. And just in case patronage might lag a little, none other than the original Linda Low—Pat Suzuki herself—was making her first Bay Area appearance in the role. It was a casting move well engineered to assure a full-circle audience in this new theatre-in-the-round auditorium.

The *Examiner's* put-upon critic, Stanley Eichelbaum, again assumed an impatient post on the aisle, ready to pit his personal disdain for the show against audience reception. And once again, the mob won out. "It was immediately obvious," he wrote, "that this centrally staged *Flower Drum Song* went straight to the opening-nighters' hearts, though Rodgers and Hammerstein's frou-frou left me, as always, quite unmoved, despite the dynamic presence of Pat Suzuki.... Miss Suzuki's energy, electric smile and big purring, velveteen voice did wonders for the evening."

Another compensating pleasure was the choreography of Gildo Di Nunzio, "the most imaginative element of the show," which helped allay Eichelbaum's gripe with "too many leaden stretches in Yuki Shimoda's staging, which barely succeeded in distracting one's attention from the musical's insulting satire of San Francisco's Chinatown."[11]

Eichelbaum may be counted among the first critics to charge the show with ethnic insensitivity. And in that charge, a first warning of trouble rang out.

Setting eyes on the show for his third reviewing stint, the *Chronicle's* Paine Knickerbocker, in a revisionist frame of mind, likened its in-the-round spread to "one of those USA shows which during World War II were designed to cheer the boys in the remote camps.... Because it was assumed that almost anything would prove a welcome diversion." And into the Kenneth Tynan camp he strayed, no longer a fan. "This is a carelessly cast production, earnestly presented by a hard-working group who are usually unable to build up any momentum, whose voices cannot be heard, whose dancing efforts are hampered by the limits of the stage. When one appreciates that *Flower Drum Song* is allegedly set in a city merely 20 miles to the north, the audacity of Rodgers' assessment of his audience's provincialism is awe-inspiring."[12]

Outright critical dismay was beginning to trump congenial deference to a commercial charmer. The professional evaluators were grappling with a paradox inherent in all too many successful song and dance amusements: They are just that. Never mind, for a long disillusioning moment, the touted critical importance of the libretto. *Flower Drum Song* would not be the first enterprise charged with the sin of an underwritten book stocked with show-saving tunes, jokes, legs and clowns. Not the first by a hundred or more musicals known for getting by, time and again, on standardized ingredients recycled for box office insurance.

There was a distinct, potentially controversial difference to this particular property, however, which time would only magnify: The "Chinese" idiosyncracies of its characters— true to life or not — were destined to offend certain Asian Americans and their sympathizers somehow, somewhere, sometime. And that time came when the show ran into the residual cultural wars of the 1960s in the wake of the civil rights movements and the attendant political upheavals which had swept America. Out of the sixties marched a new breed of student, emboldened by protest against the war in Vietnam and a growing demand of all "oppressed" minority classes for a greater voice. Came ethnic studies classes in major colleges and universities. Minority racial groups were no longer willing to accept the histories crafted and taught by white professors using textbooks penned by white scholars. Each group clamored to tell its own story. African Americans would write African American history. As would Hispanics, and Indians, and Asians.

Some of the most outspoken students operated at San Francisco State College (since renamed University). Chinese undergraduates, too, joined the battle cry against white control. In their 1974 study, *Longtime Californ': A Documentary Study of An American Chinatown*, Victor G. and Brett de Bary Nee wrote of "the development of youth rebellion and the exploding crime rate among Chinatown teenagers, and the recent arrival to the community of radical students from nearby university campuses who had held public rallies and demonstrated.... Buoyed by the rising tide of minority rights movements among other racial groups, ethnic consciousness was at a high peak in Chinatown and references to exploitation and racial discrimination against American Chinese came up in conversations with a high degree of frequency."[13]

The older so-called "white boys' club" which had dominated politics was losing ground to the emerging alliances of diverse ethnic coalitions, resolved to speak and write for themselves and to recast their respective histories and traditions according to their own perspectives. One of their primary aims was to stress positive cultural aspects and achievements— sometimes at the expense of truth. Self-esteem was at stake. And in the distorted extreme, a new historical revisionism was allowed to flourish, which elevated controversial figures like Black Panther founder Huey P. Newton beyond sobering, unacknowledged realities.[14]

Chinese Americans, a group that had suffered hostile and violent discrimination in years past, had a strong incentive to project a more modern American image — anything to negate lingering public perceptions about quaint ancient traditions and familial patterns still thought to be practiced in Chinese neighborhoods. University-sanctioned efforts to recast Chinese American history in a better, arguably more comprehensive light inspired Chinese American students and writers to assert themselves through the activist 1970s. If they had been raised to conceal their deepest feelings— well, not so anymore, young college-educated thinker!

By 1983, when Mei Li's little musical came back to San Francisco, the local Chinese American intelligentsia were in no mood to be offended by a show which many believed made fun of and caricatured their forebears along Grant Avenue. All they could see were racially offensive "stereotypes" about to strut a stage in front of ignorant white audiences who needed to be set straight once and for all. A number of local activists within the Chinese American community vowed not to sit back and let the show proceed without a good intellectualized protest. This resulted in an incredibly bizarre kowtow to political correctness.

Flower Drum Song was to be produced by David Plotkin and George Costomiris as the second offering in their debut season at the Palace of Fine Arts theatre in the Marina district. Most of the personnel failed to anticipate all the flak they were about to take, although the man they hired to direct the show, Fred Van Patten, did. After reading the script, Van Patten feared that "the drama might extend considerably beyond the stage." He spotted things about it which would "certainly be sensitive to the burgeoning consciousness of the Asian community."[15]

Just as Van Patten had expected, a furor erupted over news of the auditions. A gingerly-composed press release, designed to counter expected resistance, had announced that the show, slated to open April 7, would be set in the 1930s, and that it would possess "a greater sensitivity toward the Chinese immigration problems at that time."[16]

The producers and the director purposely moved the time frame of the show back by twenty-five years, presumably to make the characters and the old-world themes appear more plausible in the regressive context. They engaged Chen Ling-Ehr, a "cultural advisor," to help weed out offensive lines of dialogue. By telegraphing in advance their insecurities with the script, the producers opened themselves up to all manner of assaults by uppity students eager to practice their newfound freedom of expression. Freshly credentialed scholars banged out letters of protest and shared anger with colleagues. The local community had a field day with anti–*Drum* hysteria.

The pre-show script overhaul featured the interpolation of a radio scene in which Mei Li listens to "an ominous radio broadcast warning its listeners of the peril of Asians— particularly Chinese who are making their way into the country and threatening the vitality of the United States."[17]

They subtracted on, and on … "What we've done is cut things in the show that Asians said to make white people laugh," explained Van Patten to *San Francisco Examiner* columnist Dwight Chapin.[18]

During tryouts, a large number of Asian American actors purport-edly either stayed away or kept the directors on edge — this after the producer circulated audition fliers in mid–February promising a sancti-fied version of the original Broadway libretto. "All songs, dialogue and plot devices which even hint of racism are being cut from this produc-tion."[19]

And still, prominent figures with two local Asian theatre companies took aim, shooting off letters of resentment and threatening to boycott the show. As reported in *Asian Week*, Forrest Gok, public relations director for Paper Angeles Productions, had written producer Plotkin, "The play panders to those who accept outdated and insulting ethnic images and is an unfortunate choice of material to be produced in San Francisco where there is such a large Asian population…. It is a momentous error in judg-ment for you to promote this anachronism. It could just as well have been *Uncle Tom's Cabin* or *Cabin in The Sky.*"[20]

Dennis Kinoshita-Myers, director of the Asian-American Theatre Company, voiced his group's displeasure: "Were going to put something together that would ask people not to see it."[21]

Meanwhile, the producers were genuflecting right and left, up and down, in and out of Chinatown, to every self-proclaimed Asian victim of a white-man insult. They made cuts at the slightest hint of anxiety. This they did for at least two actors, to whose every reservation, it appeared, they groveled with script scissors at the ready and gratuitous apologies for unintended slights.

"Chop Suey" was removed. Out came the line about all white men looking alike. Never mind that it repeated a crack in the novel made by Wang Chi-yang that "all foreigners look alike."[22] Out, too, went the joke about laundry work. Drama critic Stanley Eichelbaum, who had long argued for its removal, should have something to cheer about.

Hong Kong actor David Lamm was relieved to inform a reporter from *East-West* that all of his suggestions had been "seriously considered by the director.... From the first day, Fred told us that if we had trouble with a line, my own or others,' we would cut it or make minor alterations."

Lamm spotted Mei Li's sign of birth as being the rabbit, Wang Ta's, the sheep — totally incongruous given their ages as stated in the script. Explained volunteer script editor Lamm, it did "not correspond to the interval between the rabbit and sheep years on the Chinese zodiac."

Inaccuracy rectified.

"Asian-American actors breathe fresh blood into the characters," stressed Lamm. "We're not cardboard characters."

His reservations having been duly addressed, Lamm then defended the play despite any remaining quibbles. "The Broadway version is a lot different than the movie. And this production is closer to the Broadway one.... The play is very valid because of its human relationships."[23]

Filipino actor Michael Ramirez, contracted to play nightclub comedian Frankie Wing, was less forgiving. He claimed that he took the job despite community resistance only because, since he held an Equity card, he enjoyed the luxury of refusing on principle. As Ramirez saw it, without that card in his wallet, he would be like every other struggling actor in San Francisco desperate to appear in a union show in order to qualify for union membership; i.e., he would "have to do the show."

Since he didn't *have to* do the show, he did. And even then, he agreed to take part only after the elimination of all the "racist overtones." What still bothered Ramirez, however, were undeleted scenes which might offend women. "I think the musical is more sexist than racist," he said, pointing to the song "I Enjoy Being a Girl."[24]

Not every practicing Chinese intellectual in the city closed ranks with their offended brothers and sisters. Sheri Tan, covering the issue for *Asian Week*, reported that many critics of the show had not taken the time to read the script. Dennis Kinoshita-Myers was one, admitting, "I didn't fully read the rewrite, but it's said to be less racist, not non-racist. The play still seems to extract the exotica of the Chinese community and make that seem like the norm."[25]

Incredibly — what sort of scholarship was *this?* — Kinoshita-Myers also conceded that he had *never* read the novel.

This drew yet more ire from disgruntled naysayers, prompting Kinoshita-Myers and Mr. Gok in concert to compose a joint letter to *Asian Week*. Argued they: "The musical comedy ... (not the novel by C.Y. Lee) utilizes racist and sexist images of Asian-Americans and no amount of revision can change that basic premise.... We raise questions about our own images and how we are portrayed in the media because, historically, Asian-Americans have been portrayed in a negative, caricatured, offensive manner."[26]

A lively debate among San Francisco's Chinese Americans revealed a healthy aversion to group-think. "I, for one, wonder exactly what is the tempest in the teapot," wrote Chan L. Leong in *Asian Week*. "Oh, oh, I better be careful ... can't be too careful when swimming in a sharkful sea of controversy.... Basically, if one looks at it broadly, *Flower Drum Song* is just another musical comedy with the same old formula: Boy meets girl, boy loses girl, boy regains girl — or with variations therein. In this case, the setting is Chinese."[27]

Leong also affirmed that the show had given good employment and a showcase for Asian talent for several decades.

All the brouhaha had a constructive effect of causing the man behind it all — novelist C.Y. Lee himself — to come out from behind his usual aloof grin and actually defend his work. Up from Los Angeles to attend the opening, Mr. Lee made a rare show of candor in answer to the critics. To one writer who had complained about the character of Mei Li's father, Dr. Li, being too submissive, complete with stooping posture, Lee explained, "It is true that characters in today's theatre do not usually take the overly polite attitude of Dr. Li, but there are still actors and people like that today.... And it is historically accurate to portray some of the Chinese immigrants of that period in such a manner."

The novelist spoke of pigtails, an unwelcome sight to Asian audiences. "But it is a historical fact that Chinese did in fact wear pigtails during a certain period. You can't rewrite history."[28]

In other comments quoted in *Asian Week* one week before the show's opening, Lee addressed the issue of historical and dramatic treatment. "I don't see any problem with [the play]. I don't think there's anything against Chinese-Americans or Asian-Americans in it. The concept of the generation gap is definitely universal.... Perhaps there is a deep-rooted inferiority complex, that's why they raise so many questions and always object to certain things. I've discovered that if I write a story with the Chinese as the 'good people' and the white people as the 'baddies,' it's OK. But if I do it the other way, I'll probably be shot at!"[29]

At the Palace Theatre on opening night, Mr. Lee may well have wished that someone would take a shot at him. At the least, then he would have had an honorable excuse to make an early exit from one of the most weirdly botched productions ever to face a crowd. Dick and Oscar, had they been there, would likely have headed straight for the Golden Gate Bridge, famed as a jumping-off point into self-willed oblivion. Critic Nancy Scott probably would have joined them. Reviewing that sodden night for the *San Francisco Examiner* (presumably her colleague, Mr. Eichelbaum, could no longer face this particular music), Scott wished in print for "a small earthquake" to hasten her own escape, so tyrannized was she by the ailing affair. "You heard people say, they were so embarrassed they wished the earth would open up and swallow them."

By the time that "Fan Tan Fannie" and "Gliding Through My Memories" rumbled across the boards, Ms. Scott decided, as recounted in her one-star review, that "a quick retreat was more practical than prayer."[30] She fled the politically correct disaster during intermission.

Exactly when C.Y. Lee exited, if in fact he had ever actually *entered*, was not reported. Clearly, his frank remarks had come too late to stave off the artistic damage done to the show.

The *Chronicle's* man, Bernard Weiner, threw a little thoughtful sympathy in contrast, regretting how the citywide protest had kept "a lot of talented local actors from auditioning." Granting that it wasn't one of Dick and Oscar's "best" shows, Weiner wasn't ready to write it off completely: "It certainly deserves better than the all-too-lifeless version being presented here." Weiner cited actors who couldn't sing, singers who couldn't act. He complained of sluggish pacing, inept set changes and missed cues. "In short, there's little snap, crackle or pop on stage."[31]

Carl Maves, reviewing for the *Peninsula Times Tribune*, saw a large stage conspicuously devoid of scenery that looked "as if the story were taking place at 3 A.M. during an influenza epidemic.... It's appallingly third rate."[32]

To the *Asian Week's* Margo Skinner, the show was a listless treatment that "seems remarkably subdued, even for 1932.... One had the feeling that the direction somehow served to tone down the competent Asian cast. Needed: more zing!"[33]

The production did not last out its scheduled three-week run at the Palace.

Across the bay at an *Oakland Tribune* typewriter, Robert Taylor began his post mortem: "Maybe it's just a hopeless assignment to revive. Maybe the memorable ballads deserve to survive at symphony pops concerts, and the rest of the Broadway musical should be stuffed back into the trunk with all the other 'oriental' souvenirs."[34]

Stuffed back into a trunk it went, never to be seen again in the city of its conception.

Once a fragile delight so engaging in the right hands, so not in the wrong—*Flower Drum Song* nearly died that fateful San Francisco spring. And for a long time to come, it looked as if it might never bloom again on any stage anywhere, so effective were its critics in denouncing the show's content and getting the theatre community to accept as gospel Kenneth Tynan's classic epitaph.

Alas, the clumsy remake-a-musical mess they brought to the Palace of Arts Theatre would prove but a harmless prelude to a far more radical revision that lay ahead. Mei Li was about to enter the twilight zone and travel to a place called "Back to Broadway, Whatever It Takes!"

The address: Happy Talk.

11

Darkening the Image

Once the accusations of political incorrectness had marked it as damaged goods, *Flower Drum Song* nearly faded into the vast wilderness of forgotten musicals deemed too old-hat and out-of-step for revival. Another strike against the show was a growing consensus among fans and historians that it fell short of the best of Rodgers and Hammerstein.

"It always had a bad rap," in the view of Ole Kittleson, who believes it deserves a rightful place with the five other R & H hits. With few exceptions, though, regional and community theatre producers who expressed an interest in the show faced the unpleasant prospects of community resistance or snickering reviews. Such was the case for Broadway veterans James and Harriet Schlader, who operate Oakland's Woodminster Summer Musicals just ten miles east of San Francisco, across a bay that separates liberal from conservative — big city dilettante from smaller-town average Joe and Josephine.

Each summer in a large and airy outdoor amphitheater nestled on a redwood-shrouded hillside, the Schladers present three mainstream musicals. For a number of seasons they had wanted to put up *Flower Drum Song*, which they first saw during the national tour in Los Angeles. "We liked it a lot," says Harriet Schlader. For the same number of seasons, they felt a certain intimidation from local Asians, especially those who would be most suitable to play the parts for, ironically, the only American musical ever written about *them*.

"We had planned to produce it earlier than 1993," says Harriet, "but we were discouraged from rumors spread by actors saying it was 'politically insensitive.'"

James and Harriet grew so tired of the same old nebulous complaints that they decided one year to proceed anyway, no matter the flak. They had always kept a low profile in the local media, which rarely reviewed their shows, so in a sense they would be producing the musical in semi-anonymity anyway, out of the radar of at least the San Francisco critics. The entire run might transpire without a single student — or Chinese ethnic studies professor out at San Francisco State University — getting wind of it.

Recalls Harriet Schlader, "Finally, at an audition I pinned a person down and asked him to be very specific" about what people considered objectionable. The best the actor could do was point to the song "Chop Suey," an answer Schlader found remarkably lame. The actor told her that the number "was offensive because it heaped all Asians into one pot."

"What are any of us but chop suey, anyway?" asks Schlader. "And so are the Asians who live here. They need to get with the program."

They got with the Schladers' program, showing up in droves to auditions and getting cast right and left to comprise a majority of the Woodminster cast. Schlader's fears were soon a memory. "They were a joy to work with. The 1993 cast was one of my three favorites. So it was good for us."

James and Harriet followed to the letter, without slicing or dicing, resetting or revising for anybody, the script they were sent from New York. They included the ballet, although minor cuts were made to it for lack of rehearsal time, as remembered by Schlader.

The now-maligned "oriental" musical from R & H proved to be a thriving success in the Oakland hills. No protests. No confrontations with actors wanting this dropped or that reworded. No cultural advisors poring over every line, nor reporters hovering about with a list of racially charged questions. According to Schlader, the production was "very well received, and our Asian audiences remained patrons and we almost cast the entire production with people of Asian extraction and many of them have continued to audition and perform in nontraditional roles for us."

How would she characterize the musical's appeal to her audiences compared to other shows? And how did it fare at the ticket windows?

On a scale of 1 to 5 (1 being the lowest), Harriet gives the attendance figures a 4. "The production was warm and fuzzy, typical of Rodgers and Hammerstein — singable music, poetic lyrics, typical of the lyricist. It was entertaining."

Schlader has little patience with the show's perennial bashers, believing that its critics "are not typical of the taste of the average American who attends a musical, but they are vocal as are the extreme right or left in politics. The silent majority goes to the polls and speaks behind the curtain for Reagan or Bush or *Flower Drum Song*. If there were more *Flower Drum*

Songs there would be better attendance in theaters throughout the country."

Two years before the Woodminster production, Ole Kittleson, artistic director of the San Diego School of Creative and Performing Arts which he co-founded, decided to do the show. He met surprising resistance from his students, who knew little about the unsung work and were obsessed with all things Sondheim. Reluctantly they became involved. Soon, their attitudes brightened. "They loved it," claims Kittleson, whose color-blind casting rivaled a rainbow: Black actor Sharif Booker played Wang Ta against a white Mei Li essayed by Jenny Vaughn. Wang Ta's younger brother, Wang Sa, was handled by an Asian, Paul Pasion. Jon Taylor, a Caucasian, was Sammy Fong. And so on. "Fan Tan Fannie" was sung by African American Pharanda Cole, "Love Look Away" by Caucasian Rose Mattio. Linda Low was handled by a promising young Hispanic performer named Sara Ramirez, who more than ten years later would land a Tony for her performance as the Lady of the Lake in *Monty Python's Spamalot.*

The open-minded Kittleson believes the show to be much more universal than local (as in Chinatown). "I think the fact that the characters are Asian doesn't totally define the musical," states he, arguing that the show's generational conflict transcends ethnic specificity: "You can draw so many parallels with the text of *Flower Drum Song* and *Bye Bye Birdie, Fiddler on the Roof,* and so many other shows where there's a clash of generations or cultures."

Just another Broadway musical?

"It's a show that has so much to it. It's one of those shows that when people leave the theatre, they've been completely charmed. But it was not a great success for them because it was always compared to *The King and I* or *South Pacific.* I think that *Flower Drum Song* certainly belongs in that selection of shows that are their five most special shows."

Not bothered, as many are, by outdated racial stereotypes?

"Give me a break! There are some shows that deserve to be produced. There's nothing about any of the characters that you could find offensive to the race. Linda Low and Sammy Fong are somewhat shady, but they're not murderers or rapists."

The mysterious Asian slights charged to the text of the musical are conveyed vaguely in words, more likely gestures, that never quite form a valid, succinctly articulated complaint. The dissenters may suffer, as C.Y. Lee himself suggested, from veiled inferiority complexes. On the subject, several alumni from the original production have offered their own views.

Baayork Lee: "I don't think anybody thought this was offensive because that's what happened at the time. There were picture brides. That was the truth."

Patrick Adiarte notes how totally he identified with the American-ized ways of Wang San, the character he portrayed on Broadway. "My part was perfect, because that's exactly who I was."

About the show itself, argues Adiarte: "I don't think it was politically offensive, not anything more than *West Side Story* with the Jets and the Sharks. Not all Puerto Ricans are that way. It's just how people were per-ceived, and I don't get upset at that.... I can't think of anything which could even be close to being offensive. They had mail order brides then. Nowa-days, you get a Russian girl, she comes over to the States and she gets divorced and she has a lot of money."

Nor is Adiarte taken back by laundry jokes and their like. "I love racial humor and I think that people should be able to joke about themselves."

Pat Suzuki: "For them to say it was racist is ridiculous. Most people that make that kind of comment have never seen *Flower Drum Song*."

From Arabella Hong: "'Chop Suey' is amusing and entertaining. It's America. The show gave a good representation of the generation gap of the Chinese in America.... My dad was like that, very intellectual, always quoting Confucius, and so forth."

Alvin Ing: "I believed [the characters] because I knew people like that. I knew kids who have come from China, who did act somewhat like Miyoshi, and I knew there were activists who were violently against the show. But my argument to them was—yes, we did have Mei Li and her father and they were kind of stereotypical, but we also had Linda Low and Sammy Fong, who definitely were not stereotypical. So I felt that they didn't have an argument."

Further, he asks, "What are stereotypes? Stereotypes are based on real people. Unfortunately, there are people like that."

David Lober offers a slightly different take on the libretto, stressing how the older characters were purposely "cartoons" intended to provide comedic contrast to the more "real" younger ones. "You couldn't call the contemporary roles—Kenney, Soo, Suzuki—a stereotype. That was the point, the modern against the stereotype."

Nonetheless, the show's fate as problematic, second-drawer Rodgers and Hammerstein seemed sealed.

When it was staged a third time in San Diego by Starlight, in 1981, the reception was decidedly less boffo. Pat Suzuki, that many seasons older, at the urging of a choreographer friend reluctantly took on the role of Madam Liang, which she also did in a Las Vegas production. So the pro-ducers had a bona fide star to hype in newspaper ads—a star who had to compete out on the open Balboa Park stage while perilously low-flying planes traveling to and from a nearby airport blasted across the sky every few minutes. Ronald Banks, appearing in his first musical as Frankie Wing, remembered the experience as being "very nice," the reviews "so-so."

And as disparate as they could be. While Linda Dudley, a *San Diego Evening Tribune* entertainment writer, applauded the show's "warmth ... fairly bubbles with it"[1] and judged the entry "certainly the best of this summer's Starlight season," her counterpart at the *Union Tribune*, Welton Jones, was ill-inclined to beat any drum for this outing. To his eyes and ears, the Starlight staging was an unwelcome reflection of overrated, over-the-hill musical comedies from the

Alvin Ing appeared in both the 1960 national tour and the 2002 Broadway revival of the show (Craig Schwartz/ Mark Taper Forum).

fifties, which he likened to the era's vehicles from Detroit with their "fat tires, extra headlights, festoons of chrome and baroque tail fins." *Flower Drum Song*, wrote critic Jones, was clearly not in the Cadillac class of R & H classics. And the fans who had flocked to Balboa Park to ooo and ahh over it resembled "a convention of Edsel owners."

After carelessly advancing the erroneous charge that the show received "grumpy" reviews when it opened in New York, and then citing numerous examples of hack mediocrity on display in the San Diego revival, Jones concluded, "Don't say you weren't warned."[2]

It would never be done again by Starlight — a company so in love with Rodgers and Hammerstein that it could boast seven productions of *South Pacific* and six each of *Oklahoma, The King and I*, and *The Sound of Music. Carousel*, which they did on four occasions, was last presented in 1990.

The Starlight's current assistant artistic director, Jeanette Thomas, expresses little love for *Flower Drum Song*, fully agreeing with its detractors that the show is outdated and stereotyped — the reason Thomas gives for why the Starlight has not revived the show in over twenty years.[3]

When asked to cite examples of offending stereotypes, Ms. Thomas declined to respond.

"If you look at *West Side Story* or *Oklahoma!*," remarks Pat Adiarte, "a lot of things are dated. It's a hard question."

By now, the Rodgers and Hammerstein office in New York, which controls the licensing of all the R & H musicals wherever they are presented, had started to turn against their Grant Avenue property like parents finally coming around to believe all the false and nasty rumors spread about an errant child.

An accumulation of knocks over the years had reached critical mass. The show's arch detractors, in complaining of a quaint libretto too dated and musty to revive, somehow failed to acknowledge that other R & H musicals had also been subjected to similar criticism. The Brits, in fact, had been toasting *and* roasting Dick and Oscar clear back to *Carousel*, which Harold Hobson of the *London Sunday Times* called "a combination of circus and Sunday School."[4] Of *South Pacific*, John Barber in the *London Daily Express* had written, "Nice show, I thought, yawning. Quite. But only a moderately enchanting evening." Another apostate, Cecil Wilson of the *Daily Mail*, dubbed it "South Soporific." Both *Flower Drum Song* and *The Sound of Music* left the West End judges competing for sarcasm awards.

As the seasons rolled on and music theatre styles changed and evolved, similar charges began to surface in the writings of *American* critics and historians. For example, when *Oklahoma!* returned to Broadway in 1953, John McClain ridiculed its often-revered libretto: "This is not now, and never was, a very stimulating book.... It is lacking in ingenuity and laughs but it is lifted to a high level by the insistent brilliance of the music and the pace of the performance."[5] Writers have treated virtually all the musicals created by Dick and Oscar, save for *The King and I*, with the same sort of varying opinions that marked *Flower Drum Song's* review record. Yet the "mixed" reviews erroneously charged, over and over again, to *Drum's* opening night reception (most recently by author Meryle Secrest)[6] are regularly cited as another reason why this show does not merit revival respect — even though *The Sound of Music* received, on balance, a near-identical critical tally. Let us recap one more time the seven first-night notices *Flower Drum Song* received:

According to *Variety*— one rave, five affirmative and one negative.

According to *Broadway Opening Nights* by Steven Suskin — two raves, four favorable and one mixed.

How to keep alive the sounds of their music when the librettos that showcase those wonderful songs fall farther behind the times? Within the Rodgers and Hammerstein Organization, there are ongoing efforts to keep the shows on as many big boards as frequently as possible. Eager to prove to the world that their heroes are as commercially viable today as they were forty and fifty years ago, the folks at Happy Talk struggle to recast the musicals in darker terms, a move that has led to a number of questionable artistic compromises.

If, indeed, Oscar Hammerstein had specialized in good will and optimism, one could easily assert that the most concentrated dose of this aesthetic was to be found in *Flower Drum Song*. And without an undercurrent of the gravitas that had darkened Dick and Oscar's bigger hits, *Drum* parades naked in its sunny allusions to miracles happening over and over. It was intended to be a musical comedy. So too, as advertised up in Boston during out-of-town tryouts, was *Oklahoma*. Except that *Oklahoma* had the looming threat of Jud Fry hanging over the entire evening, whereas *Drum* had only Helen Chao, confined to a couple of forlorn scenes.

Even *The Sound of Music*, which suffered similar scorn from critics for pushing sentiment to the hilt, did have plenty of gravitas hovering in the wings—the ominous threat of Nazi aggression. Unlike *Music* and the other big shows, *Flower Drum Song* has little darkness in its soul to offset what Ole Kittleson terms its "gentleness of spirit." And now it no longer has even a semblance of support from the R & H office, which appears amenable to recycling certain of their properties to the highest bidders—just as long as it can keep the names Rodgers and Hammerstein on big-city marquees or, especially, in Times Square neon. R & H president Ted Chapin's job, it does not take a rocket scientist to figure out, is to haul in more loot for the estate heirs.

What price residual fame and royalties? The R & H agenda seems skewed toward artistic liberties for favored directors who just might be able to make one of those distant blockbusters a blockbuster once more. However impractical the agenda, forge ahead R & H have, striving to deepen every stream and darken every rainbow. How to remove tons of "treacle" and gratuitous fluff from the properties? How to make R & H freshly relevant to modern times? To a visiting reporter, Chapin talked about "problematical" Rodgers and Hart shows in need of updating—including, incredibly, *Pal Joey*. The implication was that R & H was on the lookout for a new script that would do for this once-heralded masterpiece what two recent returns to the Big Apple had failed to do.[7]

And he spoke fancifully of turning *Pipe Dream* into an adult television cartoon. "I think it would be fabulous as a Muppet special featuring

Miss Piggy." Well, the thought of Miss Piggy as a brothel madam does amuse.

"Bravo!" seconded Mary Rodgers. "You see, we're always here to encourage good ideas."

In a tricky, intensely competitive revival market, Rodgers and Hammerstein are not the kings, not anywhere near the icons they once were during the 1940s and 1950s when they practically owned the town. More often, they are also-rans. There are reasons for this: When they set box office records, they were in perfect harmony with the sentiments of post–World War II America. And their shows celebrated in entertaining fashion mainstream values of romance and citizenship at least outwardly embraced by Americans during the repressive McCarthy era of the fifties.

Nor have Rodgers and Hammerstein's chief compatriots in sentiment, Lerner and Loewe, done much better in return trips to Times Square houses. *My Fair Lady* has never been so fair at the box office on the rebound. Compared to the 2,719 performance run it pulled off in 1956, it went successively downhill ever since: 377 curtains in a 1976 revival; 120 in 1981; 165 in 1992.

The "golden age" of the Broadway musical (generally thought to encompass the years of Rodgers and Hammerstein) is often humbled when put to the follow spots of today: In revival, *Bells Are Ringing* gave up after a paltry 169 shows, *Hello, Dolly!*, after only 42 in 1975 and 116 in 1995. *West Side Story* came back to New York just once, when it held on for 341 showings. *A Chorus Line*, in its time the longest-running musical ever, inexplicably has never returned. Perhaps producers fear exposing previously unchallenged flaws to a new generation of theatregoers?

Of musicals equally well or better received in revival, the all-time champions are two gutsy works penned by John Kander and Fred Ebb, in style and sensibility about as biting and amoral as Dick and Oscar were romantic and believing: *Cabaret*, when it first took the town, lasted for over a thousand shows. In a 1987 return, it fell after only 260, but in a third bid for renewable fame in 1998, it held on for 2,377 performances— a record that only a lucky few new shows achieve. Easily the kings of revival row, Kander and Ebb sent their other slyly cynical stage romp, *Chicago*, back to town in 1996. Amazingly, it is still drawing hefty houses.

The following informally compiled list is meant to give a reasonably accurate idea of how the most successfully revived musicals have done. This list includes titles which have played for a minimum of about 600 performances, the figure arbitrarily chosen to optimistically represent, on the average, a possible break-even point for the investors. Included are all known Broadway revivals of the respective musicals. All of the Rodgers and Hammerstein shows that have been revived at least once are also included, no matter their track records. Following the titles are the dates revived and the number of performances played[8]:

Chicago: 1996 — still running (3,328+)
Cabaret: 1987 — 261
                  1998 — 2,377
Crazy for You (hardly the "revival" it is sometimes termed; actually a new musical using songs by the Gershwins from their *Girl Crazy* and other sources: 1992 —1,622
      Grease: 1994 —1,505
      Guys & Dolls: 1992 —1,143
                  1976 — 239
      Annie Get Your Gun: 1992 —1,045
      Show Boat: 1994 — 947
      Kiss Me Kate: 1999 — 881
      No, No, Nanette: 1971— 861
      Anything Goes: 1987 — 784
      A Funny Thing Happened: 1996 — 715
      The King and I: 1996 — 780
                  1985 —191
                  1977 — 695
      The Music Man: 2000 — 685
      Irene: 1973 — 594

Other Rodgers and Hammerstein shows:

      South Pacific: never revived·
      The Sound of Music: 1998 — 533
      Oklahoma: 1951—100
                  1979 — 293
                  2002 — 388
      Carousel: 1994 — 337

Most puzzling to comprehend is why the Pulitzer-prize winning *South Pacific*— the only work by Dick and Oscar to win unanimous first night critical raves— has *never* been brought back to the big town. It was widely rumored back in the 1980s that the producers of a national touring company starring Robert Goulet tried but were luckless in gaining a licensing agreement from the R & H office to show it in a New York house, which would have constituted a revival. Like *Flower Drum Song*, oddly *South Pacific*, too, has its own modern-day skeptics, people who believe it is now racially quaint and behind the times for today's more hiply integrated society. Yet the Nellie Forbush story has continued to draw fine crowds wherever it is presented. It is the most revived Rodgers and Hammerstein offering at San Diego's Starlight. And as late as 2000, Robert Goulet was touring with yet another first-class production of the show.

If *The King and I* has done so well, why not the other two musicals which also trade to degrees on exotic figures and settings?

If left to his own devices (and, who knows, in time he well might be), the pragmatically driven Ted Chapin would likely take more radical steps to shake up the entire inventory. Anything to keep those wonderful songs being sung. Some will counter that Chapin may only be doing what has been done time and time again to musicals from an earlier period that are said to bear "trivial" or "simple-minded" or "hopelessly outdated" scripts. Increasingly, the rationale seems to be that it is better to rewrite or rework a faulty or outdated book than let languish a first-rate set of songs attached to it.

Mr. Chapin would have observed through 1992 the tremendous success of *Crazy for You*, an oddball hybrid which used five songs from the George and Ira Gershwin 1930 hit *Girl Crazy*, plus another dozen from other Gershwin sources, including two unknowns from a New Jersey warehouse — and a completely new libretto. Out popped a 1,622 smash. If all that one needed was a new script, well then, why not the same for Dick and Oscar's more modest darlings?

During the same year when *Crazy for You* took the town for a ride, the Rodgers and Hammerstein organization signed off on a proposal by British director Nicholas Hytner to remove years of alleged residual goo and cuteness from *Carousel* and to add a new opening scene at a sweatshop, all of which promised to reveal what was really a tougher-minded musical drama at heart. Many who saw the London production cheered the rediscovered "darker" realism. As originally written, the show opened onto residents of a Maine seaside town skittering around Billy Bigelow's carousel in carefree merriment. In grim contrast, the new Hytner version begins with a line of female workers at their looms, monotonously slaving away in a mill.

Typical of the good press it won was this from staff writer Mike Steele of the *Minneapolis–St. Paul Star-Tribune*: "For once you get a real sense of the people's emotional release and understand the intoxication of the merry-go-round."[9]

Hytner's *Carousel* was hailed by West End scribes, and hailed some more when it landed on Broadway. Everybody agreed how different and how much darker it looked. And the optimists at Happy Talk Central were proudly talking up a rediscovered classic that appealed to younger, more with-it crowds. Whether it in fact did appeal is debatable. It did not in San Francisco, where the national touring company played. On Broadway, however, Hytner's *Carousel* lasted for nearly a year at a respectable 377 performances.

Years later, those hard-as-nails Brits took a skeptical look at the team's groundbreaking hit *Oklahoma!* In it, Jud Fry, the lone farm hand who nearly goes crazy cooped up alone in his shack, supplies plenty of anchorage against the otherwise cheerfully amusing goings-on. Trevor Nunn, then with the National Theatre, made some minor script changes by moving several dialogue scenes and adding or cutting a few lines here and there. To his credit, Nunn assembled a stellar cast, with Hugh Jackman as Curly, and staged a work of penetrating authenticity true to the blazing original. Even then, when *Oklahoma!*, minus Jackman, got to New York after a wham London reception and run, some shrugged. Nunn's memorably rich staging outlasted *Carousel's* by a mere 41 shows. Neither picked up a penny in profits.

In a more important historical sense, both revivals accomplished what the impractical dreamers on the Avenue of the Americas may have to gratefully accept: warmly received subsidized runs that give serious musical theatre buffs the rare opportunity to study and enjoy the mastery of two giants in first-rate productions. Preserving rather than recycling the canon would surely be the more honorable course. Or would it?

Ted Chapin, in concert with Mary Rodgers, who herself is thought to wield the most authority of all the heirs, would move fearlessly ahead in their dubious quest to darken the image — as if somehow, someway, a musical by Dick and Oscar could be turned into a musical by ... well, how about by Kander and Ebb? As if somehow, more gritty embellishments could bring out some shadier Brechtian undertones. Were those two men really that sweet? Not so Mr. Rodgers in his personal life — a good place to start, so let them push that around a bit.

About life behind the scenes, Ms. Rodgers, seemingly eager to prove that her father was anything but a one-woman simpleton who turned out really cute ditties about birds learning to pray, began talking more openly to the press about his miserable moods away from the piano. In fact, about her entire family's dysfunctional imprisonment. She talked about being raised in a dreadfully unhappy household over which the brooding shadow of her composer father — happy only when he was writing songs—forever hung. She suffered his various phobias and neuroses, one being an evident aversion to her obesity, about which he made ugly jokes.[10]

On a PBS Television special honoring the one hundredth anniversary of the birth of their father, Mary and her sister Linda shared lots of unpretty stuff. Said Mary in a glib tell-all-mood bordering on a *Saturday Night Live* monologue, "I don't think anybody ever knew who he really was with the possible exception of one of the five psychiatrists he went to, and I'm sure they didn't know. He was just all locked up in there, grinding out gorgeous stuff ... a neurotic, a drunkard or both.... He was deeply neurotic, deeply, and very unhappy unless he was working."[11]

Ms. Rodgers had also spoken freely to Meryle Secrest, author of the 2001 Rodgers biography *Somewhere for Me.* In it, concerning the overweight issue, reported Secrest, "Mary did not think their father would have noticed at all if his wife had not been so 'busy' pointing it out." Rodgers told Secrest, "I think she shouldn't have had any children, and under a truth serum would have confessed she didn't want any."[12]

"It was a drug-infested family," disclosed Ms. Rodgers. Her father lived in a paranoid state of losing his power. "The very thought that someone might change a chord, let alone a phrase without his approval, would lead to an explosion of rage.... They [Dick and Oscar] irritated each other often enough. It was clear to everyone that Rodgers was the dominant partner in the relationship and expected everything to go through him first. He would get extremely upset if he was not the first to know."[13]

Not even Mary's handsome playboy son, Tony-award winning composer Adam Guettel, could escape the notoriety or the psychological wounds. Like his tell-all mother, Guettel shared with the press the tabloid details of a life of drugs, metrosex, and of his "death-defying addictions" sponsored by the lavish trusts left him by his grandfather, whose curse in a strange eerie way he seemed to have inherited. To Jesse Green, then at work on a gushing profile of him for *The New York Times*, Adam revealed, "I've lost a good 20% of my singing ability by frying my voice with alcohol and cigarettes and pot."

In calling Adam's famed grandfather "arguably the greatest American composer and arguably an alcoholic, a womanizer and an all-around tyrant," Green advanced a totally new theory about why it became so difficult for Rodgers to pin down his elusive first partner, Larry Hart, for songwriting sessions: "The wayward Hart did everything possible to get away from him when he couldn't face the music. Even Rodgers' piano seemed desperate to escape."[14]

Author Secrest zeroed in on the long-rumored Richard Rodgers sex scene, constructing tales of serial affairs on the tiniest of foundations. In the back of Ms. Secret's sexually straining tome, every index entry under "womanizing" leads only to fatuous innuendo and hearsay: how his hormones were cooled by Shirley Jones telling him how like her father he looked. How, with another actress, a warm friendship rather than anything else was formed. Or how he carried on somewhere in a back corner at Sardi's, where he was thought to have had a private room — though for whom and when, it is not made known. Secrest never appears to have corralled a single willing participant face to face to actually say the words "Yes, we had sex." "Okay, he seduced me." "Oh, I know all about that room over Sardi's!" What she has uncovered are possible actions bordering on what today might be called first-stage sexual harassment around a photocopy machine.

None of the crumbs of rumor Ms. Secrest amassed appeared to have satisfied the hunger of others to recast the musical theatre's most prolific composer as just another rascal. After all, if that's what he really was, there must be a lot more worldliness to his music — and maybe more sophistication to the shows he turned out with Oscar.

As for Mr. Hammerstein, neither can he escape the in-the-bedroom radar. Thanks to one Judy Critchen, we learn that the man who waxed lyrical about traditional love and marriage "had a secret long-term affair with a beautiful showgirl," and that Mr. Rodgers was very protective about it.[15]

No matter. Stuck with the life-affirming themes and the generally decent characters with which Richard and Oscar imbued their musicals, no matter how much "goo" or "treacle" can be directorially removed or concealed from any of them, we are still up against essentially romantic works from a bygone era.

The best of these works is bound to suffer the same stigma that was starting to dog *Flower Drum Song*: "Too quaint."

And that is history. And that is art. And that is a legacy both inspiring and problematic. And at his desk high above the Avenue of the Americas, Ted Chapin would have none of it. That was yesterday, and today was here — with new directors and new ideas and exciting new opportunities to rethink and restage the canon. And during a very candid interview one afternoon, Mr. Chapin was clearly embarrassed by the Chinatown show. He did not even bother to disguise his disdain. It was now 1996, and a revival of *The King and I*, starring Lou Diamond Phillips, had just come triumphally to town. High on the return of Dick and Oscar to a Broadway House, Chapin let on that a young "Asian" writer whose name he declined to disclose had approached him about "revising" *Flower Drum Song*. Chapin referred to the 1958 musical as "a naive, old fashioned, antifeminist story with a truly great score.... We're eager to see a new approach. It's one that really could stand changes— in fact, it needs changes."[16]

There next to Mr. Chapin sat Mary Rodgers, who might have wondered to herself how a show could be "anti-feminist" when it was written well before the "feminist" movement broke out publicly in slacks. She was ready, just the same, to display the same sort of progressive attitude towards modern-day directors wanting to rethink and even rewrite. "We don't want a long list of dead workhorses on our hands," she said.

It was not the first time that somebody had aired a desire to revamp the Mei Li saga. Back in 1985, a young filmmaker then on the rise, Wayne Wong, shared the notion in an interview with the *Seattle Times*, which reported that he "confessed a real love-hate relationship with *Flower Drum Song*, the ... borderline racist Rodgers and Hammerstein musical that hokes up San Francisco's Chinatown. Wang even wants to remake it."[17]

In 1996, R & H still had one more chance to take a look at the original work in a full-blown quasi civic light opera staging out on the West Coast. In San Mateo, south of San Francisco, the Peninsula Civic Light Opera would be doing it during their upcoming annual summer series. A conservative group with ample resources, PCLO producers were not prone to taking risks, yet they prided themselves on their tinkering before and during rehearsals with scripts, once talking up dozens of dialogue changes they were allowed to make to *Meet Me in St. Louis*— they came in with a second act that ran longer than the first.

Fearing that *Flower Drum Song's* controversial Bay Area history might cause some of their subscribers to nervously avoid it, PCLO officials went out of their way to meet with local Asian American groups and individuals in an effort to hear them out on the project. They took extra measures to demonstrate a sensitivity to the feelings of others. And from there, they took a fussy PC pen to the script, censoring words or phrases they thought might cause audience discomfort.

Actor Jared Lee, who took on the role of Wang Ta, observed a number of revisions made during rehearsals: "The main objective was to tell the story in the best possible way. Any changes to the script were done to accommodate that. Some of the original dialogue was replaced with dialogue similar to the movie version because it made more sense. It was a wise choice, in my opinion. Another obvious change was the deletion of the term 'oriental,' which was changed to either 'Asian' or 'Chinese.'"

The second act ballet was completely axed. About this, reflects Lee, "I don't think the artistic staff thought it was a necessary element in telling the story. I think the ideas that were supposed to come across in the ballet were incorporated when changes to the dialogue were being made."

They rounded up a largely Asian cast. They engaged competent directors. And they delivered a respectably mediocre production which bore, with little juice or jazz, the polite imprint of timidity and hesitation — when it might have jumped higher in spots, turned bawdier in others. On the plus side, the big dance numbers hit the mark often enough to keep the show energized and give it polish. To their credit, they managed to ring plenty of laughter out of "The Other Generation." And "Sunday" was surreally wonderful.

Not nearly as engaging was "I Enjoy Being a Girl," delivered with temporizing modesty. The book scenes, too, were directed in a stodgy, dutiful fashion, with too slavish a devotion to a sacred cow. Sparks rarely flew over the stage. Characters were not directed up and delineated out for amusing contrast. Worse still, by failing to incorporate the ballet, the producers deprived the production of the poignancy it can give to an otherwise carefree show.

Still, they filled the handsome stage sets with color, the efficiently sung numbers fairly sold themselves, and the audience greeted the final curtain with grateful applause.

"I thought the show went over especially well with our audiences," says Jared Lee. "As for the cast, I don't think I've ever worked with a happier group of people. The entire cast was very proud to be a part of the production. I think the traditions and strong sense of family that many of the actors brought with them made the experience all the more enjoyable. I think we all saw the cast as being one big happy family. To this day, we have FDS reunions."

That 1996 production in San Mateo, California, may well have been the last one of *Flower Drum Song* ever to be seen anywhere. The show received only one review, which to the big guns at Happy Talk may have felt like the kiss of death. Wrote Betsy Hunton in a discouraging 2½ star notice headlined "Tuneful but Dated" for the *San Mateo County Times*, "It has attracted attention from Ted Chapin, the president of the Rodgers and Hammerstein Organization in New York. Chapin, who planned to come to see the performance, says that his group is interested in a possible Broadway revival.... If somebody is investing megabucks in a Broadway revival, it needs to be sensational. Chapin ... and friends ought to hang onto their money."[18]

Actually, they moved their money into a far different direction. The most dramatic chapter in the history of New York revivals was about to unfold.

Enter the mysterious "Asian" writer.

12

Songs for Sale

"An extraordinary kind of snobbery now dictates the choice of musicals fit for stage revival," observed Sheridan Morley in the *Spectator*. "Briefly, anything by Sondheim is politically acceptable, as are early Rodgers and Hammerstein's, but only provided you pre-announce your intention to 'rediscover' them. *The King and I* is just about permissible still, but God help the manager who tries to revive *Flower Drum Song* (racially impure), or anything much by Jerry Herman or Julian Slade or Ivor Novello or even Noel Coward."[1]

And God help him who stays too true to the original text. The term "rediscover" increasingly signaled an intention to purge a libretto of older sensibilities. One of the longer-lasting revivals, *Annie Get Your Gun*, came back to town with a worked-over book by Peter Stone, eliminating perceived racial slurs against Native Americans. Two songs were thus cut, one of them, the melodically haunting "I'm an Indian Too," deemed an embarrassment by modern-day standards of ethnic etiquette.

When playwright David Henry Hwang knocked on the doors of the Rodgers and Hammerstein Organization in 1996, the year when Gene Kelly died, he had a more radical idea in mind: a complete rewrite of *Flower Drum Song*. And what he best offered R & H were the perfect credentials to do it. He was, after all, the country's—no, the world's—most famous Chinese American dramatist, having scored an early-career home run in 1988 with his *M. Butterfly*, said to have been written in only a few weeks. Based on a real-life incident of a diplomat falling in love with a Chinese male transvestite, the overnight success had put Hwang on the map at the age of 32. Within his own race, he was without competition of note.

When Hwang spoke to Mary Rodgers and Ted Chapin about his life-long love-hate affair with their moribund Oriental property (the movie version, that is) and of his desire to fix it, they sat fairly transfixed, all ears. They could see modern-day salvation for their neglected little musical. So could James Hammerstein, son of Oscar, who had directed various stock versions of the show during its infancy and who had always loved it. He had reportedly wanted to revise it himself.

In his youth, Los Angeles–born Hwang felt a rare social recognition from the movie despite misgivings with stock characters and synthetic motifs. "It loomed large in my life," he told Michael Phillips, drama critic for the *Los Angeles Times*. "As a boomer Asian-American, you didn't often see people that looked like you on TV. And the idea that the younger generation, at least, was portrayed as American was unusual. So growing up, the musical represented one of the few positive portrayals of people that looked like me."

However ... during Hwang's college days pursuing a bachelor of arts degree in English from Stanford University, he joined the growing ranks of his disillusioned compatriots who looked to the film as "something to be demonized." He started wondering why, in his own home, his family's heritage had been so "downplayed." His father, a native of Shanghai, was a hard-working banker. His mother, Dolores, was a pianist who had grown up in the Philippines. Hwang's maturing sense of ethnic pride was inflamed by the student protests of the era. "Here we were starting to claim our own voice as Chinese-Americans. And *Flower Drum Song* was a remnant of the way we were portrayed by white artists."[2]

The budding playwright in Hwang carried him, at the age of 23, clear to New York City, where his 1981 off–Broadway play, *Fresh Off the Boat*, won an Obie. Seven years later, *M. Butterfly* landed with a 777-performance boom at the Eugene O'Neill. It became the talk of the theatre world, and its author was the first (and still only) Asian American playwright to win a Tony. Hwang was thrust overnight to celebrity status. Two follow-up works from the same clever pen did not, however, bolster the young writer's reputation: the embarrassingly ill-conceived *Face Value*, a 1992 try for a New York return that could not get past a nasty critical lashing in Boston; and *Golden Child*, another Obie winner which failed to sustain crowds beyond a couple of months.

Did we have here a one-hit wonder? By 1996, when Hwang sat down with the folks at R & H Central to sell them on his youthful vision for a revamped *Flower Drum Song*, he tactfully linked his inspiration for the idea to his having seen earlier the same year the Broadway revival of *The King and I*. Curiously, from his statements made to the press, Hwang revealed scarce knowledge of Mr. Lee's novel, and he believed that Mr. Lee, like himself, had been born in Los Angeles.[3] (Lee was born in the Chinese province of Hunan.)

Rodgers and Chapin apparently were in the perfect mood to dream along. Basking in the glow of yet another likely *King and I* revival success, they could also wonder in frustration why none of the other shows by Dick and Oscar had ever done nearly so well on return visits to Times Square. Another empowering development that favored Hwang's overture was that, by 1996, Rodgers and Chapin now enjoyed elevated control over the musicals through the recent death of one of their most ardent protectors, Dorothy Rodgers, wife of Richard. Mrs. Rodgers was known to have resisted revisionist proposals such as the one now being advanced by Mr. Hwang, which was not completely without precedent. In fact, wholesale overhauls were a regular practice of some note in other quarters where older musicals from the 1920s and the 1930s, especially, more frequently underwent major face lifts en route to Revival Row.

"She was a formidable woman," said Mr. Chapin of the late Mrs. Rodgers. "She wanted to keep her husband's works from being forgotten, and wasn't eager to see changes made. Meetings with her and the Rodgers and Hammerstein folks were relatively rare."[4]

Would Dorothy Rodgers have turned Hwang away at the receptionist desk? Today, her daughter, Mary, is not so sure she would have. "My mother loved the successful Rodgers and Hammerstein shows, but always maintained an open mind to new interpretations. She was in on the early discussions of the Nick Hytner *Carousel*, and I'm only sorry she never got to see it."

Richard Rodgers' will, as explained by Chapin to *Los Angeles Times* writer Diane Haithman, dictated considerable wiggle room for such rethinking, in spirit encouraging his heirs to "do what they feel he would have agreed to."[5] Another section of the will, as quoted by author William Hyland, appears to stipulate a less flexible course, stating, "The artistic integrity and reputation of the musical compositions and lyrics written by me and the manner in which my works will be performed or otherwise presented after my death is of great importance to me."[6]

Just what Oscar Hammerstein's will allowed was not disclosed, although estate cooperation appears to have been granted by Hwang's having received amiable encouragement from James Hammerstein, with whom he was rumored to have already worked in casual association on an early treatment of a proposed rewrite. "No one wanted to revive the original, which I felt would probably come off as pleasant and amusing, but a bit of a museum piece, if done as originally written," contends Hwang. "My intention was to make a musical which was more emotionally moving in the tradition of the great R & H libretti."

Quite obviously, R & H did not need much persuading to support the total makeover of a work they held in low regard. Here potentially was another big event to drive their publicity machine. Another opportunity to keep Rodgers and Hammerstein in the news and maybe get their names onto another theatre marquee.

Hwang was given the firm's blessing to proceed. He returned, many moons later, with a first draft that did not please them at all. "It was completely unproducable," said Mr. Chapin, "because as good a playwright as David is, he didn't know how to structure a musical."[7] So, to learn the basics, Hwang was introduced by R & H to stage director Robert Longbottom, whose limited track record in New York houses had impressed some of the most important critics. In 1997, Longbottom had scored two modest take-notice achievements. The first was the offbeat new musical *Side Show*, which garnered a host of admiring notices. The second was the troubled musical *Scarlet Pimpernel*, which brought him in during a big shutdown for revamping. He revised and restaged it, and managed to turn a lot of the reviewers who had dissed it when it first arrived in town into reformed fans after it reopened. Longbottom also oversaw *Pimpernel's* national tour.

A Broadway veteran, Robert Longbottom had performed in numerous shows himself, most notably with an international touring company of *A Chorus Line*. He knew his way around Gotham. Commercially, he had made a certain splash directing live holiday productions at Radio City Musical Hall.

Speaking to the *Chicago Tribune*, Longbottom dismissed the original *Flower Drum Song* as hopelessly out of date: "It presented San Francisco's Chinatown as an early version of Disneyland. People would never buy it today."[8]

While Chapin and staff were critiquing Hwang's emerging vision of what the new non–Disneyland *Drum* might look like, news of a possible revival on Broadway was slowly trickling out through the media and setting the theatre world abuzz. The Chinese American community, as well, took hopeful note. In the fall of 1997 at the Davies Symphony Hall in San Francisco during the second annual Golden Ring Awards for Asian/Pacific artistic achievement, one of the honorees that year was author C.Y. Lee. Another three were alumni from different versions of *Flower Drum Song*: Pat Suzuki from the stage show and Nancy Kwan and James Shigeta from the film. At one point, described by *Asian-Week* as "perhaps the evening's most riveting moment," David Henry Hwang presented special Golden Ring awards to the three actors.

Following a film clip of the movie, Mr. Lee and the three other honorees walked out onto the stage to take a well-deserved bow. "The cheering Davies crowd immediately rose to their feet."

Mr. Lee then took the mike to announce that Mr. Hwang had rewritten his musical with the "blessings of Rodgers and Hammerstein."[9]

Disparate generations of Asian Americans bridged a huge cultural gap that strange preemptive night: one original cast member — the lady who had belted out "I Enjoy Being a Girl" and put the show on the map; two stars from the movie; the author whose novel had inspired it all; and a young playwright wishing to make their circle of creativity ethnically complete.

M. Butterfly's creator pitched his work in progress to whomever would hear him out. To Monica Eng, of the *Chicago Tribune*, he explained, "The basic idea is that I am taking all the songs ... and writing a completely new script for it. The reason I started to think this was interesting is because it is based on a novel by C.Y. Lee, and I think it is really a great novel and something that I believe has been neglected in Asian-American studies because of its connection with the musical."[10]

That curious assertion evidently resonated with Ms. Eng, who stridently remarked that the original show, developed by "two white men about Asian-Americans," with "song titles like 'I Enjoy Being a Girl' and 'Chop Suey,'" represented "a veritable politically incorrect mine field for a culturally sensitive writer."[11]

Hwang's second proposed rewrite met with approval at the R & H office. Readings ensued, the first in the spring of 1999 and the second in the fall. Around a table sat a group of actors, recruited for the project with no guarantees that any of them would go as far as the new show might. The read-throughs were done mainly for the benefit of Hwang and Longbottom, so they could hear the dialogue and get a sense of the libretto's development.

Central to Hwang's version was an aging male opera performer named Wang who persists in performing, six nights a week, in a run-down club in San Francisco's Chinatown, circa 1960, before a pitiful handful of patrons— the erroneous implication being that Chinese opera had died within the old pagoda-topped neighborhood. Wang's more progressively inclined son, Ta, was a low-key playboy who put up striptease and standard nightclub entertainers one night a week at the same venue. And, of course, Ta's idea of how to attract a crowd paid off.

The plot's early trajectory followed Wang converting to the modern way, by comical accident becoming a late-blooming jokester dispensing pop-schlock fare. This brought him to a semi-breakdown in the second act when he suffered an identity crisis and tried explaining it to his son.

Kim Varhola, one of the actors who took part in the first reading, observed early drafts of Hwang's script (which would be watered down), and was struck by its probing nature:

"It was very direct with its idea of race, and there were some very strong scenes that dealt with not being white — what it feels like to be different and to walk into a situation knowing that you look different and knowing people are looking at you because you're different."

Varhola valued a scene where Ta himself starts to question "the integrity of what they're doing," when he wants to leave the club and is challenged by his now-converted father: "You walk out that door and you become just another Chinaman." The scene led into Wang's sitting down before a mirror and chanting to himself while he applied makeup, in the tradition of Al Jolson going into blackface. The women who appeared in the scene, Varhola says, came across "as almost like a Greek chorus, behind him chanting the words with him."

Wang was basically saying to Ta, as Varhola explains, "Hey, this is what I have to do in order to be accepted in this country. I have to become a comic version of myself. I have to become a grotesque version of that, through the eyes of a white American vision.... We're turning into some kind of a strange oriental minstrel show."

Kim Varhola hailed from a new generation of highly trained Asian American actors, making the job of casting such a show a treat compared to what producers had endured forty years earlier, having to tear through dozens of local dance studios and dramatic societies, and having to walk the streets of Manhattan and talent-scout other cities in order to find a few viable candidates. All that Varhola knew about the new musical was her brief encounter with the film: "I rented the movie and fell asleep, it bored me so much."

Another actor at the table was Thomas Kouo. He watched as Hwang and Longbottom proceeded with the necessary process of revising and honing. For, as Kouo reminds us, "The arc of musical theatre is very specific." Kouo saw the work lose some of its biting reach. Originally, he said "it was a lot more controversial, very poignant. I think what he did was soften a lot of it. He left the messages in there, but he padded it enough so that people could go see this thing and have an enjoyable time and still get the message without having it beaten over their heads."

By then, the venture had hit a responsive chord in Gordon Davidson, who ran the Center Theatre Group in Los Angeles — itself the city of Hwang's birth and a town where a fair number of Asian Americans patronize theatre. Davidson's early participation had been solicited by Ted Chapin back in 1998, when he took in the New York readings and liked what he heard. He began to visualize the show trying out in one of his theaters on Grand Avenue.

Lucky breaks tend to converge in twos and threes. About six months

Looking on while Hwang, center, makes a point during a Los Angeles rehearsal are director-choreographer Robert Longbottom, left, and producer Gordon Davidson (Craig Schwartz/Mark Taper Forum).

after the second reading, a new Disney musical, *Aida*, opened on Broadway. Notwithstanding a scathing blast of critical dismay, the box office (no respecter of reviews) did not lack for thousands of Disney aficionados. Nothing was about to dissuade them. Their reliable allegiance combined with another shrewd marketing job on the public would turn a plodding third-rate tuner into a bona fide must-see Disney destination for out-of-towners, if not for the more discriminating locals. This was a very good omen for Hwang and his *Drum* dream.

For among a triumvirate of writers responsible for *Aida's* leaden book, there is the name David Henry Hwang. He had been brought in during out-of-town regional theatre break-in travails, to make things sound more authentically Asian and to help lend a little understanding to the interracial love story. Hwang helped them turn a cardboard story into a more — well, textured cardboard story.

Never mind that *Aida* would survive on Magic Kingdom showmanship, on outlandish costume design that folks left the theatre singing — all the way back to Peoria and to San Francisco — and on a few good Elton John and Tim Rice songs more than on anything else. Hwang was now a certified contributor to a soon-to-be certified hit. And what he likely gained in the adventure was a shrewd understanding of the saving graces of manipulative commercialism, an act of shameless salvation that stretches back to the days of celebrated Broadway director wunderkind George Abbott. Good pop songs. Sassy dancers. Cheap trendy jokes to make things sound hip. A cartoonish flair for resolving ridiculous plot contrivances. Fast-moving orchestrations. And all of it cleverly employed to disguise a threadbare libretto. Hwang cut his musical theatre teeth not so much on Rodgers and Hammerstein as down a Disney assembly line.

Not a month after *Aida* grabbed the boards, Gordon Davidson's Center Theatre Group out in Los Angeles made known its 2000-2001 season. On the bill was a May 13 to June 24 date for the "revised" *Flower Drum Song*, touted as the first stop on the road back to Broadway. It was to be co-produced by two east coasters, Benjamin Mordecai and Tony Petito, between whose prior respective offerings in Times Square playhouses the box office rarely tingled. Queried by *Los Angeles Times* theatre writer Don Shirley for specific examples of changes Hwang had made, Davidson answered, "The older generation of Chinese Americans in the script will be aficionados of Chinese Opera, instead of a contemporary nightclub."[12]

From the reading tables to a staged workshop at the Michael Bennett Studios they went, into the summer of 2000. Hwang continued laboring over revisions. Dancer Eric Chan, engaged for the workshop, was moved by the script's deeper relevance. "David's incredible writing. It was honest. It was real.... We didn't have to go, 'Oh, yes, sir!' 'Oh, no, sir!' 'Me no understand!' It was all of everybody's journey, of what America meant. Coming to America — Italian, Russian, Jewish. We all had a through-line of trying to fit in coming to America. And that, to me, was the most beautiful and amazing through-line that connected us all."

Benjamin Mordecai's support gave the project a semblance of east coast approval and money. Ironically, here entered a man from the academic sphere up at Yale — a sphere where theatre traditions and respected legacies such as those of Richard Rodgers and Oscar Hammerstein are usually honored and preserved. To the bizarre contrary, Mordecai was throwing his modest force behind the total elimination of a libretto for a hit Rodgers and Hammerstein musical from the so-called golden age of American musicals. Actually, Mr. Mordecai prided himself on playing both sides of the street, academic-regional theatre to commercial sector. At Yale, he taught theatre management. Down in Manhattan, he dabbled in the role of producer, having brought to town a number of plays, among them *King Hedley II*, Lanford Wilson's *Redwood Curtain* and Hwang's short-lived 1998 drama, *Golden Child*.

Mordecai favored the recent trend in producing affiliations between regional stages (for tryout purposes) and Broadway. "Before 1980," he told

Frank Rizzo of the *Hartford Courant,* "there were two very-well defined worlds.... But in truth, that was really from a money perspective. The writers, actors, directors, designers and audiences floated back and forth between the two worlds. The only thing that wasn't floating back and forth were the [financial] management [people]."[13]

A survey of Benjamin Mordecai's track record as lead producer of New York openings does not put him in a league with major impresarios— nowhere near. He appears to have had only one commercial hit, although his name is listed along with the usual cabal of allied producers on a number of critically endorsed plays which mostly had short-lived runs. Mordecai's most successful show as lead producer was August Wilson's *The Piano Lesson,* which turned a handsome profit off a nine-month run. Of the offerings his Yale Repertory Theatre was instrumental in first producing before their transfer to New York houses, another work by Wilson, *Fences,* enjoyed a 15-month stay on Broadway. Its lead producer was Carol Shorenstein.

Crossing the street once again, Mordecai planned to head up the production team for a projected run of *Flower Drum Song* that would follow the scheduled tryout in Los Angeles. He and his colleagues decided to conduct test marketing with a focus group of women in New Jersey. The gender preference, according to Gordon Davidson, was because "women are the primary buyers of theatre tickets."[14] Did the name of the show itself strike an urge to book seats in advance? None of the ladies who lunched in New Jersey that day could relate very well to the old title.

"It's really a new musical," remarked Mordecai to the *Los Angeles Times.* "And to reinforce that idea, we thought of a title change early on. I wanted to know what we might lose by changing the title and what might be gained."[15]

However, Hwang favored the title as was. As for all the Asian Americans out there harboring negative thoughts derived from the movie, Hwang clarified: "If you scratch the surface, you will find a number, like me, who secretly liked it."[16]

To Hwang they deferred. The title stayed put. "It has pedigree," said Davidson, "even if people aren't quite sure what it is."[17]

As a September 2000 workshop neared, the search for seasoned actors to deliver a one-two punch to jaded backers intensified. A call was put out for Jodi Long, who had appeared in the original version of the musical as a child when she joined her father in a touring two-city production. Long was also up at that time for the TV version of *South Pacific* to play Bloody Mary, and because she had already auditioned the year before for the same *Flower Drum Song* role (Madame Liang) and was turned down for being "too young," she thought they were out of their minds.

"They're never going to use me!" she told her agent. "They said I'm too young! I don't even want to go in."

This time they persisted. Long was urged to reconsider.

"Let me read the script," she said, relenting. During her first audition, which she had done dressed as herself, she had not seen the new script and assumed the part of Liang would be similar to one from the original. "I didn't know what Madame Liang had incarnated into and I wasn't going to play her like Hall."

Now, as she looked over the revised text, Long immediately saw how she could play the part. She grew excited.

"I know this woman.... She just seemed like all those women that I kind of grew up backstage with."

This time, Jodi Long went in costume — all of it her own design. "I kind of put up my hair like my mother did and put on big false eyelashes. I did a whole character thing for Madame Liang. And I went in and sang 'Grant Avenue.'"

It was a fait accompli. Long had created on her own the exact same character that audiences would eventually see her play. "That was all mine," she states. "I walked in as my idea of Madame Liang. And once they saw me next to Sandy, they were like, 'Oh, my God! Of course!' It was the sense that Linda Low is the younger version of Madame Liang."

Another echo from the original production (national tour) showed up at auditions in the form of Alvin Ing. Forty years after understudying for Wang Ta on the national tour, now he was cast to play Ta's uncle, Chin. And he was assigned to sing part of "You Are Beautiful" with Ta. One day after rehearsals, Ted Chapin told Ing he had a gift in the archives.

"I've got the perfect song for you!"

"Yeah?"

"Yes," said Chapin. "I'll let you know."

A little later, Ing was handed the sheet music for "My Best Love," the lyrically inconclusive ballad that had been dropped from the show's first out-of-town shakedown up in Boston.

Clearly, Mary Rodgers and Ted Chapin, never above meddling in things, were having their way here and there. "They were very much involved," recalls Ing, fondly describing Mary Rodgers as "a feisty lady — strong personality. Loved the show."

To Thomas Kouo, Mary Rodgers was "the royalty of musical theatre.... She's engaged from the very beginning. They have to have her blessing."

Gordon Davidson was there every day.

Ted Chapin was around a lot.

The two workshops drew full houses, purposely stocked with backers and more producer types taking a look-listen. The days of the single
force — of a David Merrick or a Cameron Mackintosh — live on only in history books. From all the comped-in attendees with billfolds and checkbooks at the ready, they failed to raise the money needed for a direct Los
Angeles-to-New-York transfer. However, they did get pledges for backing
from sources in Singapore, interested in the show eventually coming their
way, and this was sufficient to fund the Ahmanson Theatre premiere in
Los Angeles.

By now, defenders and critics of a rewrite were forming on the sidelines. To the media at large, the story had long legs because of the R & H
factor. To many students of the genre and to Rodgers and Hammerstein
diehards in particular, the undertaking bordered on heresy. Wrote a letter writer to the *San Francisco Chronicle*:

> That David Henry Hwang had the audacity to approach the Rodgers
> and Hammerstein estate and request permission to rewrite is over-
> shadowed only by the estate's puzzling willingness to do so.... It's a
> blatant attempt to go back in time and develop a new culture on con-
> cepts that didn't exist at the time the piece was created.... What's next?
> Shall we rewrite *Finian's Rainbow* since the racial issues it confronts no
> longer exists as they did in 1948 and the Irish jokes are not PC? Maybe
> we should integrate Catfish Row so that an equal number of whites,
> Asians and Latinos reside alongside Porgy and Bess.[18]

Probing the issue of revised revivals in a *Hartford Courant* article,
writer Frank Rizzo asked, "Has a major revision of a problematic musical
ever succeeded?" To which, in offering examples like *Golden Boy, Mack and
Mable, Merrily We Roll Along, Follies,* and *Dear World,* he answered, No.

As for *Flower Drum Song,* Rizzo placed it, too, in the "problematic"
class, terming its score "much admired," its script "well intentioned but
misguided ... dated and racially tricky."

"What is the net effect of all these revisions of shows that were far
from perfect when they were originally produced? If Broadway history is
a guide, their chances are slim at best."

Better to spend the time and the money on living writers with contemporary ideas, Rizzo urged. "I hope that Herman's *Miss Spectacular* finds
a home as well. And I think of the scores of theatre artists who are itch-
ing to create something brand new, to have their voices heard and their
shows seen. It makes one want to give these shows their first chance."[19]

Oddly, in a sense Hwang was swimming up the same stream with a
new work of his own, except that he had the songs of Dick and Oscar —
his passport to Broadway. Music theatre fans everywhere could, in the

affirmative, ponder the prospects for a better book more deeply rooted in C.Y. Lee's novel. Maybe this time, Helen Chao's suicide would make it to the stage. Maybe Mei Li would be accused of stealing a clock, and in the pathetic aftermath, the house servant who had staged the theft would suffer the whip-lashings of her deaf-and-dumb husband provoked to an angry sense of retribution. Maybe this time, Wang Ta's father, on the brink of losing his son, would take the son's advice and see a western doctor about having his terrible cough examined.

Maybe.

Hwang talked on and on about his new pet project, "almost a total rewrite," stressing a rare sense of theatre destiny: "It's the book Oscar Hammerstein would have written had he been Chinese American."[20] Elsewhere, he happily noted the wonderful advances Asians had made. Now *they* had the keys to the *Drum* car, and they could drive it however, wherever they wished.

On their own, the Singapore "investors" were having grave second thoughts. And they did not have much trouble acting on those thoughts and pulling out, for the money they had pledged had never been sent. This caused Mr. Mordecai, reportedly responsible for raising $2 million for the L.A. tryout, to bow out, too, throwing the enterprise into limbo. Rodgers and Hammerstein treated the setback as a momentary bump in the road. Chirped their public relations man, Bert Fink, "Nobody is backing off because of the materials. They're backing off because they couldn't get all the elements together in a timely fashion.... I would just say, 'one hundred million miracles are happening every day!'"[21]

To skeptical outsiders, the project looked doomed. Rumors circulated that the New York workshops had really not impressed many theatre insiders.

Out on the west coast, Gordon Davidson, struggling to rekindle his foundering career as a leading regional theatre figure, was by now a firm believer in Hwang's dream. In his mind, Davidson was cutting and crimping and compromising, thinking smaller. Dreaming like Mordecai and all the others of a way back to the greatest theatrical thrill of all. To that place where art and commerce gloriously converge. Where the taste of rave reviews is the sweetest of all aphrodisiacs....

Ah, yes, one can never have enough opening nights on Broadway.

13

Way Out of Town

Standing placidly aloof from the asphalt symphony of downtown Los Angeles is a small round-shaped building sporting a tan stucco facade, the Mark Taper Forum. It and two larger, more conventional theatres— the Ahmanson and the Dorothy Chandler Pavilion — share a plaza of spacious fountains and promenades called the Music Center, which together bring the performing arts into one leisurely location. Here on balmy evenings before taking in plays, concerts, ballets and opera, Angelinos can sit down at outdoor tables to dine and converse, their socializing pleasantly removed from the whizzing traffic on Grand Avenue, two flights below.

The Taper, a collegial space with an intimate thrust stage, is a friendly destination for new work seeking a test audience. Here was where David Henry Hwang's new *Flower Drum Song* would have its world premiere.

On a sunny August morning in 2001, across the street in a rehearsal annex, a gong rang out and producing director Gordon Davidson, who had run Center Theatre Group for over thirty-five seasons, welcomed a new cast to the first rehearsal of the new "Rodgers and Hammerstein" musical. Perhaps to prepare them for the grueling eight-week rehearsal period that lay ahead, the Taper chief stressed the value of trial and error: "We're as interested in the process as we are in the final result."[1]

Davidson's long, once-illustrious career as L.A.'s most prodigious theatre producer had been heading south for a number of thin seasons. Now he was once again dreaming, just as eager as the youngest performers in the company, reaching for that magical something new to send to New York — with his name on it — as he had done long ago. His Center Theatre Group had developed an impressive number of New York–acclaimed works (not all of them money makers), including *The Catsonville Nine* (1972); *The Shadow Box* (1977); and *Children of a Lesser God* (1980). Some of them

Davidson himself had directed. With musicals, he had fared far worse, having produced and sent east the first "Chicano" musical, *Zoot Suit*, which folded after a month.

In the 1990s, luck struck again; Gordon Davidson was instrumental in nurturing Tony Kushner's *Angels in America* on its fateful journey from San Francisco, where it received its first reading, all the way east to ultimate acclaim. In fact, the Taper Forum was the first to present both halves of Kushner's work. *Angels,* like the Taper-originated plays *The Kentucky Cycle* (1993) and *Shadow Box,* won a Pulitzer prize.

And still, Frank Rich, one-time drama critic for the *New York Times,* beating an old elitist drum, would write that "Los Angeles is no theatre town."[2] Rich likely knew his arrogance would go uncontested by Angelinos, who themselves suffer a strange interiority complex whenever glancing eastward. Even the late David Shaw, media columnist for the *Los Angeles Times,* often made it crystal clear that in his estimation *The New York Times* was the country's best newspaper.

Of course, people like Frank Rich conveniently overlook the realities not just of Davidson's once-prolific Center Theatre Group, but of other L.A.–based producers like the Los Angeles Civic Light Opera's late Edwin Lester (*Kismet, Peter Pan, The Song of Norway*) who sent money makers to New York houses. In its heyday, Davidson's organization was the central component of a thriving local L.A. theatre scene, mostly played out in a few hundred 99-seat houses, where a special arrangement with Actors Equity (since altered slightly) allowed its members to appear for free in limited runs at their discretion. Today, the same actors appear for little more than carfare. Some with day jobs in television and cinema enjoy working the boards and will willingly act for a bus coupon or two, which brings to mind similar sacrifices made off off Broadway in Mr. Rich's own bailiwick.

Now — into a new millennium — Mr. Davidson was vexed by a growing parade of negative notices from pointedly disillusioned critics and theatregoers desiring more than another salute to Stephen Sondheim or some self-wallowing monologue by a trendy local polemicist. The town had grown tired of Davidson's choices— either too obscure or too conventional. Along with original dramas that failed to fly, there were tepid revivals of old musicals and the national touring companies of confusingly ill-conceived new ones like Cameron Mackintosh's dull-as-a-sermon *Martin Guerre.* Through it all, subscription audiences guaranteed the nut and helped prolong the labored illusion of a prospering operation in touch with its patrons.

Transferring *Flower Drum Song* from the Ahmanson — too expensive — to the far less costly Mark Taper Forum, Davidson was able to sketch out a budget that made feasible the premiere. As he faced the freshly assembled cast that promising summer morning, he smiled upon a lovely coalition of experienced pan–Asian faces. Most came with credible professional resumes. Among the 23 members in the room, one was an international musical theatre star. Some were familiar to TV viewers. Some had played minor roles in movies. Many had toured with *Miss Saigon*; a few had opened with the show in New York. Some had worked in Disney musicals. One had appeared in *Rent*, another in the revival of *Annie Get Your Gun*. There were alumni from *The Lion King*, from *Sunset Boulevard* and from *The King and I*. A couple had never worked outside California.

Davidson had the luxury of precedent on his side — a score by two giants of musical theatre from a hit show. Even then, incredibly, he still worried that the brand new script by a *Chinese American* dramatist might antagonize somebody out there in his Asian American audience base. So, well before opening night, Mr. Davidson conducted a series of informal get-togethers with interested Asians to demonstrate his sensitivity to their feelings. At the same time, the gesture might rally more customers to the box office and to the subscriber lists. Produce and promote.

Had they not succeeded in eradicating all alleged racial slurs? Reported the *Los Angeles Times*, "The Taper approached community relations with unusual care, organizing at least one panel discussion with actors and community members to ensure anyone who might be offended would be on board in time for opening night.... While this crowd is solidly behind the new flowering of *Drum*, publicist Fritz Friedman acknowledged that concerns about Asian stereotypes were raised at an earlier panel discussion."[3]

While Davidson and colleagues worked the Asian-populated room to promise everyone present an ethnically enlightened new script, the show's author brushed elbows with a group of prospective movers and shakers who just might be persuaded to pull out their checkbooks and become investors. Hwang shared his own personal history leading up to the epochal moment. During college days, he said, "Asian Americans were just beginning to write about ourselves, and I think it was necessary for us to demonize the highly visible efforts of non–Asians to write about us."[4]

The cast consisted mostly of New York–based actors. Naturally, they were all hoping to land a big hit in Los Angeles and be offered repeat roles in a Broadway-bound production. With the right reviews and box office, maybe prospective backers with big bucks would finally come through.

Of locally based thespians, screen and TV personality Tzi Ma, cast to play Wang, was a close friend of Hwang's, the two having worked together on several projects. *Drum* would be their fifth. And for Ma, it would be his first major role in a musical. In quick fashion, he learned to sing and dance. "I've never seen anybody work so hard in my life," says cast member Ronald Banks.

Only a handful among the cast of 21 had participated in the first New York reading. One of them was Thomas Kouo, who had expectations of going with the show all the way to a New York opening, for Robert Longbottom had several times told him, "When you get to Broadway, you'll have been in every production."

Beyond Davidson's good wishes to all — beyond Longbottom's promises to select actors — a certain insecurity soon dogged nearly every phase of the project as, indeed, it does many shows in tryout. One of the recipients of this ambivalence was Jodi Long, who did the New York workshop and had, by that point, auditioned twice. Still not enough. In order to appear in L.A., she was made to audition a *third* time.

"I was so annoyed at the whole situation, because I felt I had done my job in the workshop."

To enhance her frustration, Long was about to board a plane for Scotland. In order to placate the "producers" (Davidson, she suspected), the actress would have to delay her trip. She was told they needed to see her read with a number of actors being considered for the role of Wang, against whom she would be playing.

"I was so pissed off, and I canceled my flight to Europe. They knew all of this. I was just so annoyed because it was like the last minute."

The audition was at the Carnegie Hall Rehearsal Studios. Long walked through a narrow hallway into a large rehearsal space that was painted bright yellow. "I looked up and said, '*Love* the *yellow!* Emperor's yellow. That's good luck!' just like Madame Liang would say, and they all cracked up. Then I said, 'Do you want me to sing 'Grant Avenue' *again?*'"

Nobody expected to see Long enter in the hair, makeup and costume of her character. They turned sheepishly apologetic. "Jodi, you are a goddess!" said Tara Rubin. "You raise the bar!"

"I knew that going in as Jodi Long was not going to get me the part. I had to go in as Madame Liang."

After auditioning but still without a definite offer, Long swept out onto the streets of the big city and bolted up 57th to indulge in a shopping spree at Bergdorf Goodman's. From there to the Zen Institute she went, for meditation. Emerging from the Zendo, she checked her cell phone. There were two urgent messages from Robert Longbottom to call. When she reached Longbottom, he said, "Jodi, I'm so sorry we had you come in again. What were we thinking? Of course, you have the part."

One who never faced a tryout panel was international star Lea Salonga, of *Miss Saigon* fame, on whose mere name the producers no doubt were banking to lure devoted fans. Longbottom approached Salonga personally, inviting her to lunch where he offered her the part of Mei Li, sans audition.

Salonga had been sent a script the year before, when she was tied up with *Saigon* in the Philippines. She found it quite amusing.

When the Taper rehearsals got underway, Hwang and Longbottom were still striving to find a grounded center for the piece. The focus had not yet been mastered: How deeply could they risk committing themselves to Wang's journey as Hwang had originally conceived it? How willing were they to follow his opera-to-nightclub turnabout and the mental breakdown it caused him?

The closer they got to opening night, the farther from the crisis they retreated. The gradual erosion of that dramatic premise was observed firsthand by, among others, Ronald Banks, who had joined the company just one day before rehearsals commenced. Banks had been offered the role of Chao, a character just written into the libretto, who works in a fortune cookie factory and harbors grave and bitter doubts about life in the United States. The part served to set up a minor second-act romantic triangle between Mei Li and Ta.

Enthralled with the chance to work on a show which could take him all the way to New York, a place he had never been, Banks gave up six contracts, including two opera engagements, in order to sign on. He was also auditioned to understudy two parts. One of them was Wang, and this gave Banks a rare glimpse into the character's rapidly diminishing trajectory.

The script Banks was handed to study and read was "darker and more tragic." He was immediately moved by the sad spectacle of Wang "turning his back on Chinese Opera which he had spent his entire life being devoted to" and having to grapple with his son's commercial pandering to American audiences. "And all of a sudden, to become Sammy Fong portraying all the worst versions of Asian stereotypes was more than even Wang could take."

Or, evidently, the show.

"In the scene I read, because of this sort of wrenching transition, Sammy Fong/Wang has a breakdown, à la *Follies*, and it comes when he's facing his son, Ta. It was a very dramatic scene."

That one audition read-through was the last time that Banks ever saw the scene; it did not make it into the Taper rehearsal script.

The director and writer were tossing and turning between a number of situations they had embedded into their "revisical"— the Mei Li romance with Ta; the father's comical journey from old-opera holdout to all-out American lounge buffoon; the feisty agent's pitch to go U.S.A. all the way and open Club Chop Suey; her romance with Wang; and Chao's late-arriving declaration of love to Mei Li, complete with pleading offer to accompany him on his return to China.

All the while Hwang was continually coming up with funnier lines, he thought, dashing them off on tiny slips of paper and handing them out to actors to memorize and implement.

"He's so quick to relook at things," said Longbottom. "Before we'd ever read through the first scene with the company, David had the pencil out, cutting. I've never seen anything like it. He's always a step ahead of me, asking questions, 'What do you think of this?' 'Could we do without it?'"[5]

Hwang was so open to tinkering with the dialogue that when Sandra Allen, in her own words "notorious for changing my lines," by accident did just that, she was sometimes encouraged not to worry about it. "He was so great in saying, 'That sounds great, too.'"

While Hwang fussed over the new jokes and Longbottom refined the dances, a fundamental reason for their ongoing vacillations became apparent to some, like Ronald Banks, who himself had the time to sit out in the seats and watch the endless tinkerings. Hwang could write all the lines of dialogue he wanted until kingdom come; he could not, however, alter a single line of the lyrics. "One of the reasons it got lighter," remembers Banks, "is because they could not really change the music that much."

At the rehearsal hall one day when Longbottom was staging "Don't Marry Me" between Jodi Long and Tzi Ma, with Hwang looking on, Banks observed the director struggling to set the number and conceding, "What we are faced with is that David's dialogue is often better than the song it leads up to."

Around and around this unsolvable paradox circled Hwang like a writer lost in a loop, pencil and pad in hand, flinging out new zingers to displace other new zingers flung out the day before, bouncing about the theatre, gazing at the action from different vantage points, wondering and creating and wondering — when to feel satisfied, when to feel a completeness of treatment.

He was coming up against a daunting challenge, likely unforeseen when he set out to save the show from itself: Striving to fit old-fashioned songs into a modern libretto, to somehow find a way for fresh dialogue and aging verse to join in narrative wedlock, Hwang would wrestle with disparate elements to make them work together and never, apparently, feel satisfied. How could he? Some of the juxtapositions were effective, even stunning. Others were awkwardly forced. A couple of songs were left behind: the comedy rant against those vulgar Americanized kids, "The Other Generation," and the soft-shoe charmer, "Sunday."

"The Next Time It Happens," an excellent old tune out of the failed *Pipe Dream*—became a new tune for Lea Salonga to sing. Sing it she did, never convinced that it belonged.[6]

Alvin Ing was handed the long-forgotten throwaway "My Best Love" to sing. It gave modest substance to his curiously fragmented role, which required only two brief appearances during the show.

"I Enjoy Being a Girl" was the production's closest thing to a known classic, and it went to Sandra Allen, cast to play the new version of night-club stripper Linda Low. The multifaceted Allen, who had done stunt work in films, suffered no identify crisis over the number, into which she threw herself body and soul. "I love singing the song because I'm really girly. I love being girly, and I have no problem with it and I don't have a problem with you knowing that I'm being girly, because at the same time, I'm some-body who has different sides to my personality.... But for Linda, that is all who she is and that's fine for her."

What about those who call the song sexist and outdated?

"Everyone is entitled to their opinion. I think that there are women who are fine with being feminine and fine with believing in maybe an older view of ideals, and in an old school kind of way, and that's who they are, and that's okay."

Lea Salonga was encouraged not to copy vocal performances off either the original cast or movie albums of the show, but to make them her own.[7]

Let some of it be hers? She would have to, for a few of the songs were practically stood on their heads. They had to be in order to fit the radically reconfigured landscape of the play. Salonga's "A Hundred Million Mira-cles," which opened the show, had matured from a soft, sentimental ditty to a defiant pro–Western anthem set against a backdrop of Chinese Com-munist repression. No way could Salonga have sung it the way Umeki did even if she wanted to.

The fairly close-knit cast, sharing a dream of Asian affirmation in a work written by one of their very own, felt part of the process. During informal discussions, some of them expressed how it felt to be Asian Amer-ican on American soil, while Hwang listened with compassion, all too eager to invest every line of his script with a pro–Asian authenticity. A few others grew tired of all the soul-searching time-outs—"What does *this* mean to the Asian American experience?" "What does *that* mean?" And Ronald Banks observed some testy "talk backs" between certain members of the cast and director.[8]

Robert Longbottom's demanding stage pictures and overall direction casused acute cast dissension during the Los Angeles rehearsals (Craig Schwartz/Mark Taper Forum).

Aside from Longbottom's token deference to such ethnic ramblings, he was a different theatre animal at heart, a throwback to the old-style Broadway taskmaster not above berating the dancing feet. Certainly, his coddling of the leads did not extend to the ensembles, with whom his communications grew tense and ugly. Admired by some of the dancers, among them Eric Chan, for his painterly choreography, Longbottom was decidedly less respected for his abrasive outbursts.

Those "visually stunning pictures," as Thomas Kouo described them, came at a steep emotional price to the women in the ensemble.

"He was not the same person that I worked with in New York," says Kouo, noting how Longbottom's personality had changed from warm and supportive back east to caustic and tyranical out west.

"The relationship between him and the cast definitely suffered."

How ironic that, for all the company's agonizing over how to come off looking as politically correct as possible, the man who was directing them was about as far from PC as a director could be. Those who were shielded from Longbottom's darker side hold a more benign view of such behavior, which, it can be readily argued, is deeply entrenched in showbiz tradition. "Bobby is very old school," as Jodi Long puts it, likening him to a ballet teacher telling a student how bad she is in order to shame her into practicing harder. "In any kind of rehearsal creative process, there is always going to be conflict. For me, it comes with the business."

Behind closed doors, the director, whose "old school" ways in the worlds of Ronald Banks "seemed especially to rub some of the female dancers the wrong way," began to badger and bawl them out, never quite happy with some of them. During one very confrontational meeting over the matter, which had reached a boiling point, the criticisms turned so brutal that the women insisted on calling for a rep from Equity to be present to witness the reprimands. The request was unprecedented, and the women were berated for complaining.

One dancer, distraught, stood up and repeated the demand: "You can't do this without the Equity rep!"

Growled one of Longbottom's production assistants, shaking his finger at her, "This is not a democracy! You are not allowed. You do whatever Bobby says you do. You sit down and shut up!"

He repeated his warning a second time.

Secretly tape-recorded by one of the dancers, the confrontation was reported to Equity to no avail.

As recounted by Blythe Matsui, "Equity just slapped him on the hand, from what I understand."

Matsui watched the director turn "into a certain kind of person where you forget about human decency…. Your main goal is to get your picture, get with your vision. It had to be there, that whole type of obsession."

As recounted by Matsui and confirmed directly or implicitly by others interviewed on the subject, Longbottom's tirades brought several women to tears. And he never apologized.

Tzi Ma was appalled by the situation, particularly by the way the women were callously pushed around "like little objects." It pained him to see how some of the cast members, both men and women, were being treated, and he urged them to stand up for themselves. "It was a nightmare."

Ma himself, with a lot more clout as one of the leads, refused to be ridiculed or humiliated, and on a few occasions his discontent with Longbottom's limited approach to interpreting Hwang's script—"a Chinese/ Chinese American story" as Ma proudly viewed it—escalated from tactful suggestions to confrontation. During a dress rehearsal, Ma became so incensed over Longbottom's insistence that he wear a "ching-chong" hat over his pompadour that he walked off. Intervention from Davidson brought Ma back.

New to musical theatre, Ma was amazed at the extent of Longbottom's power. He had never seen anything like this. He was also amazed at how little direction this director actually gave. Most of the choreography, as Ma observed things, was staged and set by Longbottom's two assistants. And most of the scenes between Ma and Jodi Long were self-directed by the two actors. Moreover, the original blockings suited a proscenium stage presentation rather than the Taper's thrust. This never made sense to Ma, who in vain urged Longbottom to make better use of the thrust. When Gordon Davidson watched a run-through of the first act, he prevailed on Longbottom to do just that, and much of the show was reblocked.

The accumulation of Ma's heated disputes and confrontations with Longbottom seems to have landed him outside the director's favor, even though, during the opening night party, Longbottom told Ma, "You're gonna be great on Broadway!" He would hear that same victory promise over and over again. "As a matter of fact," recalls Ma, "this was expressed by all the powers that be, Gordon, Ben, David, Bobby, that I was going to B'way from one time or another during our successful run at the Taper."

Those big guns and a few of the more privileged actors never witnessed the director's tirades. "He definitely tiptoed around Lea and the writer," says Matsui. "Whenever the production staff was in the room, he would treat us to the T, very very sweetly. But when they left the room, of course, all hell broke loose. We had a lot of incidents that they were very difficult to get through."

Nothing like an incident, though, about to occur thousands of miles across the country — an incident that would make all their Taper troubles seem like minor plot turns in a harmless little song and dance show. Less than three weeks into rehearsals came the morning of September 11, 2001.

14

The L.A. Embrace

Some first heard about it on their radios, waking up to the unbelievable and rushing to their television sets to watch it occur before their eyes. Others received frantic calls from friends: "Turn your TV on! Go look!" And within a few nation-shattering minutes, they would all share one horrific nightmare as they watched the two tallest buildings in New York City leak smoke and flames and then collapse into mountains of twisted steel and glass, trapping and killing thousands of people beneath their devastating remains. The Twin Towers of the World Trade Center, their structural integrity breached beyond salvation, had minutes earlier been flown into by a couple of hijacked jetliners piloted by terrorists.

This was not an Orson Welles *War of the Worlds* radio show from the 1930s. Not a Hollywood disaster flick or a sick video game. Not a shameless MTV aberration. No, this was the worst foreign attack ever to befall the United States—caught by the cameras of live television coverage and witnessed by millions of shocked Americans.

As it happened, rehearsals had not been scheduled as usual at the Mark Taper Forum that tragic Tuesday morning; instead, that week the cast had come in on Monday and was not due back for two days. When they reconvened on Wednesday morning, an emotional paralysis gripped the company. "We sat around and talked and cried and consoled each other," recounts Ronald Banks. "There was lots of sorrow, anguish and anger, and the cast members from New York were especially upset because at this point they had no word from friends and family."

A panicking girlfriend of Lea Salonga's had called her from New York, about to board an airliner and dreadfully resolved: "I've accepted death," she said.[1]

They shared their feelings about waking up to the horror. Ronald

Banks told his fellow actors, "I turned on the TV and watched the towers come down as it happened." The others repeated the same tale, each in their own words, each seeking a personal catharsis. "Later that day," continued Banks, "I tried to give blood at the Red Cross, but they were swamped."

Eric Chan remembers a deafening silence after the opening number: "You could hear a pin drop, because everyone was going through the same thing ... we had this kind of spirit, and our country was going through hell."

It was too much for the company to continue that day. Around noon, Robert Longbottom sent them all home.

The next week, they paused during a rehearsal to conduct a company memorial for the lost. They prayed. They sang. They lit candles. Like every other American, they felt as if their world would never be the same again.

There are those who believe that the show proceeded determinedly up an even more comedic road after September 11, owing to the mood of the country and to a feeling among the creative staff that audiences would now much prefer levity over drama.

Previews were scheduled to begin in three weeks. Five days after 9/11, the first major news story about the historic "revival" in the making — "Let the Debate Begin"— appeared in the *Los Angeles Times*. The L.A. hype machine had swung into full, irreversible action. Gordon Davidson, in generous cooperation with hometown journalists, began talking up the next Taper offering. There were tickets to sell, previews to pitch, an opening night to ballyhoo. In the *Times* story, written by drama critic Michael Phillips, one could read that "America's premiere Asian American dramatist is redefining himself as Mr. Musical." As Phillips saw things, "It's a case of a major Chinese-American writer taking a familiar title away from the white devils of Broadway."

All participating writers and interviewees seemed happily amenable to the idea of revamping the 1958 script. Phillips quoted actor Tzi Ma, "no fan" of the R & H version, now quite high on the treatment that his longtime friend and theatre associate David Henry Hwang had wrought. "I thought, wow, this is not the original *Flower Drum Song*. Not everybody's going to like it, but that may be because people will recognize something of themselves in it."

Hwang told Phillips, "I actually assumed we'd be getting more flak about this new version, but people seem to accept the idea in fairly measured fashion. I think people are able to have some perspective on it — accept it as an artifice of its time, appreciate what was useful and important about it."[2]

Over at the Taper press mill, they had designed and were sending out beautiful yellow and red fliers, headlined "Enchanting, Melodic, Passionate.... Combining the splendor of Chinese opera with the pulsing rhythm of American life, one of Rodgers and Hammerstein's most captivating treasures is made enchantingly new again."

The flier pitched the story as follows: "Mei Li, a young refugee from Communist China, arrives in San Francisco's bustling Chinatown in search of a better life. She steps on shore and is immersed in everything American, including an immigrant's delicate balancing act between tradition and the natural desire to assimilate. She finds herself falling magically in love."

Program magazine stories all skirted any controversy inherent in the project. Former *Los Angeles Times* drama critic Sylvie Drake surveyed the Rodgers and Hammerstein legacy in adoring prose, talking up their biggest hits. *Drum*, of course, was not among the favored; Drake relegated it to the new role of a "re-imagined" musical.[3]

In another Taper program article, "Vision and Revision," Christopher Breyer erroneously stated, in blatant contradiction to all historical accounts, that Oscar Hammerstein had "labored mightily to fix the troubled production when it floundered out of town." Fact had no place in these puff pieces. Unquestioningly, Breyer quoted Hwang mischaracterizing the 1958 opening night reviews as "mixed." And he passed along the self-serving remarks which Hwang and his colleagues had been dispensing to the press, one being the aura of assumed collaboration with the ghosts of giants past: From David Chase, the show's musical director, came the bizarre assertion that one could feel "like Rodgers and Hammerstein wrote this show today with David and Bobby and myself."

Two other *L.A. Times* staffers who helped spin the advance were theatre author Barbara Isenberg, looking back in a Taper program story on Gordon Davidson's thirty-five seasons at the helm of the organization, in which *Drum* was mentioned without note; and Diane Haithman, in a *Times* piece which appeared on the day of the show's opening, interviewing C.Y. Lee, Hwang and a few of the cast members.[4] Alvin Ing spoke about getting aced out in his youth time and again by blond, blue-eyed actors who were cast to play Asian characters in *The King and I*.

Jose Llana, like most of his acting peers too young to have seen the original stage version of *Drum*, did what unfortunately too many people do when they believe they understand the show simply because they have seen the misleadingly inferior movie. Comparing his encounters with the film to Hwang's script, Llana talked up the latter as being "much, much better than the original one. That was somewhat saccharine and innocuous."

And novelist Lee, ready to flack, spoke of having granted writer Hwang complete autonomy, and quipped, "I might as well keep quiet and let him surprise me!"

Mr. Lee would find plenty to be surprised by when the show opened that night.

On a dark minimalist set composed of simple Chinese motifs sufficient to stir the imagination, there hung a large banner of Mao Tse-tung in the background. A circle of slave laborers toiling under the thumb of their oppressors sang "A Hundred Million Miracles," not with the innocent hope as it was originally conceived, but with defiance. Powerful, stridently anti–Communist, the number called to mind the song "Red and Black" from *Les Misérables*. And it charged the first moments with a riveting sense of direction pointing to a minefield of probing drama. Mei Li's dissident father grabbed hold of the Mao banner and ripped it down. Quicky he was apprehended by guards, subdued and hauled off to be murdered for treason. Rarely do musicals open in such a compelling manner.

"A Hundred Million Miracles" as rewritten by the pen of David Henry Hwang. That's a banner of Mao Tse-tung in Tiananmen Square (Craig Schwartz/Mark Taper Forum).

Take-charge star Jodi Long, center, playing showbiz agent Madam Liang, infused the revival with comedic gusto (Craig Schwartz/Mark Taper Forum).

Rarely, too, would a musical's initial imagery so mislead. What began with a roar deflated all too quickly into a minor hoot as Mei Li, no longer the submissive country lass of the original work but a strong-willed woman ready to make a mark in the land of freedom and opportunity, journeys to the States. Arriving in Chinatown, she is charmed into penniless show-biz work (although the sort of work is not specified) by a fractious old opera singer and his playboy son, themselves in a family feud over how to make real money entertaining American audiences in their rundown Chinatown venue. Old world yin and yang versus Great American Songbook & striptease.

Mei Li's first number, "I Am Going to Like It Here," foreshadows script contrivances ahead. The lyric's sweet allusion to all the people seeming "so sincere" strikes an oddly irrelevant chord against the boisterous and bawdy manner in which Mei Li had just been befriended by the people about whom she was now singing.

Leading the musical parade are the shimmering new orchestrations supplied by Don Sebesky, enriching the Richard Rodgers melodies with fresh luster. Among the elevated treasures is "You Are Beautiful." Indeed, as each old-new song is delivered, it offers the pleasure of rediscovery.

Sandy Allen's unapologetically brash rendition of "I Enjoy Being a Girl" is a warmup for Jodi Long's "Grant Avenue," delivered with the zip and boom of a take-charge star. Here I am. You're gonna watch me! Long plays the aggressive nightclub agent Madame Liang, pitching to Wang the idea of turning his moribund old opera barn into a trendy night spot. The moment she rips into "Grant Avenue" is the moment the show takes off.

Any misgivings about the script are rendered fairly mute by Ms. Long's presence. Her blood seems theatrically infused from Channing to Tomlin … to Long. She steals the show the old fashioned way, and she does it partly — as she will later explain, looking back at magical connections — by allowing her childhood idols into her singing soul: "I invented it from all the people that I grew up with — my parents' generation, and that I saw backstage at Forbidden City. And a little Pat Suzuki — oh, yes, I always felt Pat Suzuki was up on that stage with me because I saw her do 'Girl' and 'Grant Avenue' for so many times when I was a kid."

In Long, a star. In Salonga, the power and lure of celebrity. And in Tzi Ma, a late-blooming theatre buffoon who holds his own. And therein lay an asset in threes and another problem for logic-centered students of the modern school: What exactly to make of these characters, who appear happily stranded inside a busy contrivance without clear narrative aim? If we think too hard, the fun may shine false. What, for instance, to make of Wang's improbable conversion from old-opera troubadour into brash Yankee funny face? Let go of it for the moment, and let the party have its way. The three reigning personalities — Salonga, Long and Ma — divert our minds, tickle our hearts. Together, they serve up a dandy little tour de delight.

Except that author Hwang wishes to be a part of it, too. He contributes now and then, sketching out soul-searching monologues wherein the principals pause at tidy intervals poignantly scored, to share deeper fears and wishes, all of them moody and pensive and fleetingly beyond the show's structural timidity. They are supposed to be caught up in what it means to be Chinese in America, needing to honor homeland customs, dreading a cultural sell out to the West. Yes. Yes. Yes.

The songs are another source of fail-safe enjoyment — thank you, Dick and Oscar. "Fan Tan Fannie," a risque fashion show bordering on bare flesh; "Chop Suey" (horribly truncated, presumably to avoid calling too much attention to itself; after all, wasn't this one of the despised elements Hwang had intended to excise?); Alvin Ing's wistfully vague "My Best Love," stopping the action too warmly. Lea Salonga has two more big numbers — her first act closer, "The Next Time It Happens," the great, long-forgotten import from the failed *Pipe Dream*, which she revives marvelously; and "Love Look Away," one of the evening's sublime pleasures.

"Don't Marry Me," reassigned to Madame Liang and Wang, arguing over a late-developing romance, is only okay.

If a musical's book is to mean something, its characters have to mean what they are about, and these characters are mostly about alluding to serious issues between all the stock showbiz turns. Really, they are not so much characters as vaudeville monologuists for the author. Concepts or plot? Hwang's unconvincing, sometimes plodding patchwork gives lip service to the Mei Li–Ta romance. And in that romance, actor Jose Llana, his fine baritone voice superior to his perfunctory acting skills, comes across as too glibly tentative for the more anchored Salonga. Their story never advances beyond a dutiful outline, as if the author is bound by contract to do something with the two romantic leads from the original show.

Still, most troubling is the Disneyesque character transformation of Wang. Had Hwang retained his earlier drafts depicting Wang's growing doubts and soul-searching breakdown before Ta, perhaps he would have

In a tricky character transformation, Tzi Ma, in the role of Wang, shucks aside Chinese opera to try his hand at night club schtick in "Gliding Through My Memories" (Craig Schwartz/Mark Taper Forum).

given us reason to feel more empathy. Here, there is too little to root for. In fact, Tzi Ma out-Sammy Fongs Sammy Fong. And the script shreds off from there into George Abbott confetti.

Altogether, the show moves glowingly along in a bright, engaging manner, full of breezy jokes and sassy dames in amusing gear, elevated now and then through some thoughtful asides. Too, it was much easier to be bowled over by all of this in the cozy Taper setting, where the intimate relationship of audience to players is closer to a small-town community theatre experience.

In Los Angeles, the musical worked wonderfully well on opening night and on almost every night that followed. Insecure, "not a theatre town" Angelinos were in no mood, apparently, to question a show that hoped to be a New York hit. Neither were the critics. Insecurity — of which there is plenty in Lotus Land for all of its entertainment-world dominance — does not breed the sort of independence of thought that will often set a panel of New York theatre judges pointedly at odds with each other.

So the L.A. critics stood and high-fived this one. Switching roles from feature writer to reviewer, the *Los Angeles Times*' Michael Phillips called Hwang's show "wholly revised and gleefully self-aware ... a few tons shy of a mega-musical — no fake helicopters here, no power ballads saccharine enough to stop Communism dead in its tracks— it's a raffishly entertaining response to the 1958 original."[5]

Other notices were in collegial lockstep, heralding a big local hit. "Wildly entertaining," said *Entertainment Weekly.*[6] "Marvelously effective," reported the *Daily News.*[7] "A bold theatrical operation, an artistic success," heralded *Variety's* local guy.[8] The *Hollywood Reporter* called it "while not perfect, an exhilarating accomplishment."[9] *Backstage West* found it "the most exhilarating musical show we've seen all year."[10] And the ordinarily left-wing, we-hate-mainstream-musicals *L.A. Weekly* joined the dragon parade, declaring, "It contains a hundred million miracles ... frequently mesmerizes and deserves a complimentary pass into the annals of American musical theatre history ... a fascinating tug and pull, not just between East and West, between tradition and assimilation, as in R & H, but between the agony of immigrants to America and the American musical comedy machine that inflates them into stereotypes. The machine wins."[11]

Thomas Kouo: "I think opening night represented for us in the cast, and I speak for myself, a lot of grief. We were a very close cast, because we had gone through a lot together. We were all aware of the fact that perhaps no one will ever know what we went through together in that cast to get to that point.... I think that's something that made the L.A. production special."

Eric Chan feels that the intimacy at the Taper had a lot to do with the favorable reception. "Very difficult to be dishonest when you're sitting about twelve inches from an audience member."

On opening night, out in the audience sat some of the alumni from the 1958 production. Their reactions formed a split verdict.

Patrick Adiarte: "I loved it. In ways it was better than the original. Happily surprised at how different it was and how good it was."

David Lober: "Brilliant concept ... it had serious second act problems.... Got bogged down in polemics somehow along the way, and didn't move, and didn't have a real ending."

Chao-Li Chi did not attend the L.A. opening on purpose. He was appalled by his understanding of what Hwang had done to the script. "Unfortunately, this is where I'm intolerant." Chi views Hwang as being "rabid anti–Communist," and what, asks he, "has *Flower Drum Song* to do with refugees from Communist persecution? That I cannot swallow, and so I didn't want to go, because I had nothing good to say about it."

Based on what he had heard, Chi also objected to one of the show's central themes: "The idea is that they are from Chinese opera, which I know something about. But Chinese opera is revived by the present government, and it's flourishing."

In Hwang's radical departure from the original 1958 musical and the novel upon which it was based, Chinese dissidents resisting Communist oppression were portrayed in the opening scene (Craig Schwartz/Mark Taper Forum).

Any bad reviews? Only one lone scribe, Edmund Newton, a couple of weeks later writing in *New Times Los Angeles*, dared to question hometown euphoria: "A vaguely dispiriting affair that saps Rodgers and Hammerstein's frothy formulaic concoction of a lot of its fun."[12] Other disparaging remarks came mainly from newspaper letter writers, who continued tossing scorn at the Tinseltown parade. A few days before the show had opened, in response to one of the *Times*' feature stories touting the production, a letters-to-the-editor contributor wrote, "Being Jewish, I admit that certain aspects of *Fiddler on the Roof* cause me to wince as well; however, this does not invalidate the story's breathtaking authenticity when it was written by Sholem Aleichem a century ago ... and to sanction the sort of wholesale evisceration that Hwang has visited upon poor *Flower Drum Song* is to erase entire pages of human history and render pointless the whole concept of musical revivals."[13]

After the show opened, another disgruntled *Times* letter writer called it "an absolute disaster," complaining: "All the charm, warmth, humor and fantasy of the original are lost on his new libretto.... In his great arrogance, he thought he could improve the show by making it modern with no reference for the original novel by C.Y. Lee.... The fact that the original shows a 1950s America that the Asian-American community was just as vital a part of society as any other is completely lost on him in his desire to make it PC."[14]

Nevertheless, Gordon Davidson's Taper hat trick was greeted by one sellout after another. "Only one or two nights of the entire run, we didn't get a standing ovation," says Ronald Banks. So popular was this *Drum*, originally slated to close December 2, that it would become the first-ever show at the Taper to be extended. This necessitated bumping the next-scheduled show into another theatre. Full houses and standing ovations continued apace.

Blythe Matsui felt that the closeness of the actors communicated well to audiences. She loved the "backstage antics of the cast members and the camaraderie of the girls. In that dressing room, I felt like those girls were my sisters. So valuable to me, because in *Miss Saigon* I never felt that.... When we were up there on stage, we were up there as a team, and that is so valuable when you're expressing it to someone else, expressing it to an audience. They feel that family; that's a big part of what I want out of my career — that feeling that we understand each other, we know where each other fits."

It all came to an L.A. end on January 13 — sweet for some, sour for others. Not all the performers, not anywhere near all, were offered the chance to move east with the show. Ronald Banks was one of the eliminated. His role was being rewritten for a younger man, to build up the relationship between Mei Li and Chao and create more triangular tension between them and Ta. "I was really honored to be a part of that production," says Banks. "A lot of really great people. It moved my career to another level, even if I didn't get to Broadway."

Incredibly, Tzi Ma was left behind, too. Despite his great reviews. Despite all the promises from the powers that be. Jodi Long feels that the decision may have been motivated by the prickly exchanges during rehearsals between Ma and Longbottom. "It was unfortunate, it was upsetting to me — for not only did we have a chemistry that worked for the show, we had also known each other and David for years." The three shared a rare history going back to their early New York days when both Long and Ma played concurrently in two Hwang plays at the Pacific Theatre, *Dance and the Railroad* and *Family Devotions*.

Hwang evidently did not make much of a case for his friend, even though, according to him, contractually he had the power to hold out for

One of the many left behind in Los Angeles: screen and television personality Tzi Ma (Craig Schwartz/Mark Taper Forum).

anybody in the cast going all the way. "It's not unusual for cast members to be replaced between regional and Broadway productions, painful and difficult as those choices are. And, yes, I have casting approval, and so take responsibility for all decisions made."

He may have actually deferred to Mary Rodgers, who had all along envisioned another actor for the role of Wang.

"I have long been a fan of Randal Duk Kim," she said. "He was the most remarkable Kralahome in the 1996 revival of *The King and I* that I have ever seen — and he was happy to join the cast in New York."

One actor who had every right to feel betrayed — that is, if a director's word in a theatre is supposed to count for something — is Thomas Kouo. He had been assured by Longbottom on several occasions that he would be going all the way with the show back to New York. It did not happen.

"I was surprised with a few people that they decided to leave behind, myself being one. I'm not quite sure why he decided to leave me behind.... I hope that people don't forget where it came from.... Every single person that came through gave a special piece.... It's unfortunate that a lot of these people were not recognized from the work they put in, what they endured to get it there."

"I do believe those who spoke their mind did not get included in the Broadway cast," states Blythe Matsui.

Most of the ensemble waited in vain for good-news phone calls from their agents. Charlene Carabeo, Michael Dow, Thomas Kouo, Keri Lee, Blythe Matsui, Jennifer Paz, Robert Pendilla, Chloe Stewart, Christine Yasunaga — they were all left behind. Four of seven men in the chorus and only *two* of eight women — Susan Ancheta and Kim Varhola — were retained. Half of the entire Los Angeles cast would not be going forward with the show they had helped turn into a promising hit.

Recounts Matsui: "Other cast members started to call me. 'I got let go, what did you get?' Weird, I pretty much got the last call that I wasn't going to be going to New York. Terrible. Of course, I was definitely hoping that would become a reality also. I didn't expect it, but in a way I did."

More important to Matsui, she came out of the ordeal with her integrity intact. She had spoken up against a director's hostile ways, determined to maintain her own ethics and peace of mind rather than pander in silence just to land a shot on Broadway.

"It comes to a point where you want to be healthy," she explains. "You don't want to just swallow it. It scars you. I know certain Fosse dancers who are scarred permanently. They're terrible people because they don't know how to be healthy, to stand up for yourself, to say this is not right, this is human decency.... Most of all, I've learned that I want to be healthy. Business doesn't matter that much to torment myself. What matters is that you were in there giving your heart."

Why *were* so many let go? When queried about this, in reply Mary Rodgers addressed only the Tzi Ma issue in her deference to Kim, concluding evasively, "The rest of the principals remained the same."

Some of the rejected became so distraught, they rode around on trains the whole day fighting to escape their failed Broadway dreams. Trains not to Christopher Street or Lincoln Center, to Midtown or Times Square. Trains just to Wilshire and Western, to Vermont and Melrose or Hollywood and Vine....

Have a nice day.

15

Back to Broadway

New York is a place that can instill fear and dread and a glaring loss of perspective into otherwise confident egotists. Indeed, not a few creative giants nearing Broadway opening nights have been known to rewrite their brightest ideas into theatrical mush. There's something about a town whose mood is hard to read because new shows are routinely fizzling — and clicking — for no logical reasons.

Something about maybe how people in collaboration agree to collaborate down the final stretch through a minefield of precarious audience reactions and the marathon script conferences that can ensue during final previews. When all is tried and discarded and tried a different way, nobody knows exactly what makes a "hit." Only the box office knows, and it is not speaking.

No wonder Richard Rodgers once quipped that he wouldn't open even a can of sardines in Manhattan. That was on a day when new shows first tried out up in Boston or New Haven. Now, most new musicals go through "development" from workshops to regional theatre productions before final script tinkerings during "previews" in the Broadway houses in which they will open.

And here, at last, in the fall of 2002 were Messrs. Hwang and Longbottom, who by all accounts dug each other's company. They were not a little apprehensive with their Grant Avenue ticket as they faced their Boston in New York. For, judging by the way they carried on, they — or those who caused them to carry on that way — were anything but confident. Was their great west coast success really as good as those have-a-nice-day L.A. writers had said it was? "It's really not *that* good, guys," one can hear a thousand self-appointed theatre mavens telling them. "Here is what you still need to do." And so on. Perhaps the new producer, Benjamin Mordecai, was already injecting his own suggestions as producers are known to do. Heck, maybe Mary Rodgers and Ted Chapin, in whose backyard Hwang and colleagues were now working, were passing along "notes."

True, they were in a bigger house, not quite twice the seating capacity of the Taper Forum. They were in a bigger theatre town, *the* town. And they were starting over again by all reports, quivering at the knees 24/7, facing a much larger stage, wondering professionally how best to fill it with their little Taper trick. All of which had done zilch to calm Hwang's chronic penchant for daily revisions. In fact, from inside accounts, Hwang never called a halt to his incessant tinkerings. Well, the absence of a clear narrative focus can cause a librettist to endlessly rewrite in the elusive search for a center that was never staked out in the first place. And defining such a center takes a degree of gumption and real risk; it is much easier to hedge one's bets and load the singing basket with a little of this and a smudge of that. And at that, Hwang possessed a certain facilitating talent, placing him somewhere between poet and pitchman.

Hwang's initial focus on Wang's anxiety-ridden journey from opera holdout to cheesy nightclub takeout had been slowly watered down to the point of near-inconsequence.

"While I thought the idea of Wang's breakdown remained valid from the point of view of his character," explains Hwang, "it threw off the dramatic balance in Act II.... We didn't have enough songs to support two big book scenes, both the Linda-Ta breakup and the Wang breakdown, so in the end, one had to go." That dramatic journey, says Hwang, "was sadly sacrificed."

Lea Salonga remembers an unsettling feeling shared by many that they had not reached the artistic finish line when they all met up at the Virginia to begin pre-previews rehearsals. She notes how things were constantly evolving, clear up to opening night. How, in particular, certain story lines were still not registering well.[1]

One of them was the sketchy-as-a-rumor romantic triangle involving herself (playing Mei Li), Ta and Chao, the fortune cookie maker. Salonga was high on a younger actor being brought in to play Chao, for this gave Mei Li a more visibly dramatic choice between Ta and another man vying for her affections. Nonetheless, Chao's late-breaking declaration of love still did not become a triangular threat until well into the last act.

"Because the Chao character was basically played as a joke in L.A." points out Hwang, "Mei-Li's decision to stay in America was much less difficult and therefore less meaningful. I definitely stand by all the script changes that were made between L.A. and N.Y."

On a more daunting level, however, Hwang remained constrained by lyrics he could not change, and beyond or because of this he seems to have sacrificed his bite in a schism of structural styles. His adaptation strove to be both a standard book musical (in its laying out of the Mei Li-Ta romance) and, at the same time, a modern concept show (in its deference at intervals to personal soliloquies). Although the latter asides lent a serious air, they also made the book scenes between Ta and Mei Li feel more artificial, and they failed to generate real audience empathy for a particular plot.

Cast and crew had to be wondering as opening night approached if the critical scrutiny they were about to face would overlook such flaws. Surprisingly, one of their first critics, one whom they could not ignore, was novelist C.Y. Lee himself. On the eve of the New York premiere, when Lee and Hwang sat down with USA Today's Elsa Gardner for tea and conversation in a midtown café, Lee told her how "shocked" he was, when he first saw the show in L.A., by Hwang's opening scene depicting the ripping down of the Mao Tse-tung banner. Lee felt offended, he said, not just by the imagery but by the insult to the famed Communist leader.

"Mao did a lot of damage to China," said the 84-year-old author, "but people still worship him because he helped make China a very powerful country."[2]

To Gardner, Hwang revealed that on the road to the Big Apple he had revised "about a fifth" of the script, still a work in progress. The changes included the deletion of the banner defamation. In its place, the prisoners now all carried copies of Mao's little red book. This placated the offended Mr. Lee, whose pointed remarks to a reporter — for him, a rare excursion into public candor — confirmed the apolitical nature both of the novelist and of his 1958 novel. Said Lee, "Everyone in China hates that book because everyone suffered from the cultural revolution."

Emboldened, Mr. Lee took surprising belated aim at the original Flower Drum Song, about which, all these years later, he now harbored grave second thoughts: "The version that Rodgers and Hammerstein and Fields did was a lot of fun," he noted, "but my original idea was to show both the cultural conflict and the closeness of the Chinese family. That's easier to do in a book than on the stage, but David managed to simplify it. He added feeling, so that you really see the relationships and the love between these characters."

Alvin Ing, the actor who had played the banner-defacing dissident, now played the only character who dared toss his little red book to the ground in scorn, resulting in his being dragged off to be murdered. Ing was left a little baffled by the revised scene, wondering how the musical would go over in China if it were presented there anytime soon. "Ten years ago, I could have been shot for that!"

Hwang's literary kowtow to Mr. Lee was not the only concession he would make. Behind-the-scenes forces pressing him and Longbottom to change things only grew more insistent and widespread as they came closer to the opening night showdown. They labored to give more flesh and bones to the rather limp Mei Li–Ta story by adding dialogue and by reinstating a song not used in Los Angeles from the original, "Sunday."

Jodi Long felt that the song's insertion between "Grant Avenue" and "Fan Tan Fannie" retarded the momentum of the first act, "which had been like gangbusters in L.A. That was R & H. They really wanted 'Sunday' in because, I guess, that was Richard Rodgers' favorite song. And so David and Bobby said, 'This is the only way it's going to fit in here.'"

At one point during the L.A. run, Long and Ma pitched the idea of *their* doing the number. "We were all talking about it. How do we get 'Sunday' in the show? Well, maybe we could do a little medley with 'Don't marry me.'"

Lea Salonga, in amused recollection, admits to not having been too impressed with the staging of song, which showcased Llana while leaving Mei Li semi-stranded on the sidelines as a virtual prop.

And they ditched one of Salonga's biggest numbers, "The Next Time It Happens," that marvelous refrain from *Pipe Dream* which has a way of invading numerous rethought R & H offerings (*State Fair*, for one). Vibrantly melodic and freshly modern-sounding still, it was arguably in sync with Hwang's modernized take. Salonga, though, was not surprised by the loss, now matter how thrillingly it landed on the ears of musical theatre fans. She agreed with the creative staff that it did not feel compatible with the rest of the score.[3]

Also falling victim to the scissors were all the dance routines that had been performed back in Los Angeles by the actor Tzi Ma. Ma's New York replacement, Randal Duk Kim, was not a dancer, and so out went Wang's footwork.

The cast worked feverishly into and through three weeks of promising previews to master mountains of script alterations and tons of new dance steps. Sandra Allen recalls a round-the-clock barrage: "I was being thrown dialogue, pages of it, up until opening night, and I believe my last changes were made press night, which is the night before opening. I had new lines even then. So I feel I had one of the hardest jobs. I had to keep up with the dance changes, dealing with my singing, dealing with my dialogue changes and all the scene work."

Why so much, so fast, so late? "The show was way too long," answers

Allen. "They clipped some stuff.... I can remember big chunks of chore-ography being taken out in New York and then added and then reposi-tioned that I can't believe I ever got through it. At times I thought my brain was going to explode from the sheer fact that we had a show that night and were rearranging everything. I was just hoping that I would be in the right spot and that I wouldn't get smacked in the head with a foot or something."

Oh, the theatre. Lerner and Loewe had once waged rewrite war there while wrestling with *Camelot*, into and far beyond opening night. Now Longbottom and Hwang were there, faced with having to refit their show from a thrust stage layout to a conventional proscenium. Not an easy task, especially for a director noted for superfluous perfectionism and clever-ness. This unwieldy penchant of Longbottom's had already shown its face in at least one of his previous stagings, *The Scarlet Pimpernel*. In that musi-cal's overwrought second act, the director overplayed his hand, embellish-ing a delightfully fey first-half romp until it became a campy caricature of itself.

Longbottom was also known for favoring androgyny. In *Flower Drum Song*, he alluded to it through the character of gay costume designer, Har-vard, a narrative interpolation of Hwang's which added yet one more ill-fitting layer to the cake. The show is supposedly set in the year 1960, making the inclusion of this character relevant neither to Mr. Lee's conservative novel nor to life in Chinatown during the period it covers.

Overall the changes appear only to have exaggerated a disjointed structure crying out for unity. Measure by measure, Hwang was embel-lishing his patchwork.

On the dramatic front, Jodi Long has a different take on Hwang's tin-kering with the character of Chao. She believes that, while making him "more of a threat to Ta," they also made him more angry because of his inability to fit in. "In a sincere effort to deepen the drama of the piece, they sacrificed what I thought was the sweet innocence of the version we did at the Taper."

The departure of Tzi Ma was another question mark in Long's mind. "In his heart, Tzi, I felt, was much more the character. Tzi was born in Hong Kong. He is steeped in Peking opera tradition. A serious actor, he can also be a hambone, which is important for the character of Sammy Fong."

On the production level, Eric Chan grew nervous over the ramping up of everything: "Bigger. Bigger. Bigger. Bigger. Louder. Louder. Bigger. More! More! More! It was Broadway."

Chan sensed that "too many cooks" had their hands in the stew, and that the musical was losing some of its lustier, easygoing charm. What troubled him the most was a feeling that Robert Longbottom was himself losing control to all the cooks—namely, to Rodgers and Chapin and Mordecai, as well as to a conglomerate of investors, each elevated to the modern-day status of "co-producer" ad nauseam.

Recalls Chan, "I met a lot of people during the opening party who would say, 'Oh, I'm one of the backers of the show!' 'Ooops, oh, nice to meet you!' I met people backstage who were giving tours—'Oh, I'm one of the backers!' 'Oh?'"

Quite a new experience for Eric Chan, since he had worked for Cameron Mackintosh, himself a rarity among contemporary producers who rarely shared power with others.

Chan noticed changes that he felt were not made by Longbottom. He asked the director's assistant, "What's going on?"

The answer: "Well, Bobby has no say in this."

Jodi Long has speculated that Longbottom was possibly reined in because of his abrasive behavior toward the female dancers during the L.A. rehearsals.

"There were so many things that were wonderful about this production," stresses Chan, "but then all of a sudden you would have these things that were against it."

The cast was kept in a state of creative panic during previews, when they were often playing to sold-out houses and drawing standing ovations as a rule.

Kim Varhola remembers it feeling obvious to everyone that the Los Angeles reception was about to repeat itself. "We got spoiled. We thought we had a hit, because during previews, I couldn't get tickets for my family.... We were just going to take off. The audience reaction during previews was amazing. They loved the show. They laughed and they were totally enthralled by the show."

They averaged about 86 percent capacity those three break-in weeks, which would have kept the weekend seats filled. As opening night neared, news and website reporters came out to interview key figures with the company and interested Asian scholars and authors at large. The theatre community took Hwang on his word and pondered the long-term ramifications of this revolutionary new *Flower Drum Song*—indeed, the most radical rewrite in Broadway revival history.

Most everyone welcomed a reformed musical free of insulting stereotypes. Gen Woo, speaking for the Organization of Chinese Americans to staff writer Cheryl Lu-lien of the *Baltimore Sun*, talked about the original show: "I was embarrassed particularly by the character [Mei Li], who was

fresh off the boat. She was such a demure, non-aggressive character it per-
petrated a stereotype of Asian females not having strength. It didn't give
me a sense of pride seeing her."[4]

In the same story, Linda Low was termed another unacceptable character, having been discredited by critics in general (none named in particular) as "the embodiment of another type of Asian woman — the wily,
highly sexualized Suzie Wong-type."

Argued Josephine Lee, associate professor at the University of Min-
nesota and author of *Performing Asian American: Race and Ethnicity on
the Contemporary Stage*, "Asian America women are seen as hyper-
feminized, very dependent, purely sexual beings without a life aside from
her sexuality."

Ted Chapin, who participated in the *Baltimore Sun* interview, was
obviously eager to (kind of) agree. He talked about the original R & H
show as containing characters "constructed in a perfunctory way ... 'I am
father; I believe in tradition;' 'I am the son, I want to marry the hot girl.'"

About the oft-maligned song "Chop Suey," Hwang shared a complex
rationale he had worked out for keeping it, guilt-free, in the show. "It's
somewhat problematical in 2002 to have a bunch of Asians on stage singing
about chop suey. It's like having a bunch of African Americans on stage
singing about watermelon." In order to make the number fit, Hwang
named the night spot "Club Chop Suey." Rationalized he, "It dovetails
rather nicely with the historical reality that there was a series of Cotton
Club–like nightclubs that featured all–Asian revues in the '40s and '50s
called the 'Chop Suey Circuit.'" And with that handy precedent, Hwang
now could see the song being used without causing one more anti–*Drum*
thesis to be written by another insulted Asian grad student.

Four days to go before the critical countdown, and the mighty *New
York Times* gave Hwang a chance to describe the show's genesis in his own
words. Hwang repeated most everything he had heretofore told everybody
else who would listen, this in a front page Sunday Arts and Leisure splash,
headlined "A New Musical By Rodgers and Hwang."

"Among a spate of race-based issues," he wrote, "... I find that much
of my work has involved a search for authenticity.... How do we regard
the jokes about laundries and restaurants and Confucius that were characteristic of the period? ... I have become less interested in seeking some
holy grail of authenticity and more convinced of the need to create characters who burst from the page to stage with the richness, complexity and
contradictions of real people.

"At its core, a stereotype is bad writing: a one- or two-dimensional cutout
devoid of humanity, and therefore prone to demonization. Whether your char-

acters are cooks, laundrymen, computer scientists or gangsters, if they are well written, they will exude humanity, which is ultimately the most effective weapon against stereotypes, and the most visceral measure of authenticity."[5]

There to judge for themselves how "authentic" Hwang's latest work might be, on opening night, October 17, 2002, were Pat Suzuki, Arabella Hong, Baayork Lee, and others from the old show's alumni. There, too, were the dozens of upbeat, well-wishing friends and relatives of the company, R & H fanatics, theatre followers and wide-eyed tourists. Inescapably there, too, were the critics from the current-day press, who collectively did not find much authenticity in the new show. Altogether, their reactions comprised a checklist of complaints that could fill an entire chapter in a book titled *How Not to Write a Musical.*

"The modest production superimposes a paint-by-the-numbers showbiz quality on the clash-of-cultures generational story," wrote Linda Winer in *Newsday.* "... We feel knocked around by the flip-flopping styles, which begin with a generic, knee-jerk cartoon scene of Communist Chinese oppression before getting comfortable with fabulous club numbers that slyly mock stereotypes and enjoy them.... Most disturbing is a first-act change in Wang's character, from bitter proud traditionalist to vaudeville hotshot, that should have audiences suing for emotional whiplash."[6]

From the similarly unimpressed *New York Daily News*, Howard Kissel called the show "an entertaining, albeit vulgar revival, which reinforces one's sense that nowadays Broadway can do showbiz themes smashingly. Less glitzy areas elude it."[7]

Clive Barnes, sitting — or slouching — in for the *New York Post*, found the new version ("humdrum") to be no more memorable than the old one. He was, however High on Sandra Allen, noting, "She also gets to sing the great little number, 'I Enjoy Being a Girl.' Girl? Is that politically correct? Oh well."[8]

Variety's Charles Isherwood took Hwang's contrivance apart, offense by offense. "A compendium of cardboard characters and corny jokes ... structural ingenuity can't make up for the bland characterization and an endless barrage of wise cracks that belie Hwang's stated desire to bring more depth and emotional integrity to the musical."

Puzzled by the insertion of the "flaming queer costumier Harvard," Isherwood considered it another glaring affront to the writer's touted campaign to rid the script of stock cartoons.

The salvaged work of Dick and Oscar, in Isherwood's view, gave the show its only valid pulse. "It's only when they're [Salonga or Llana] performing these still-vital sounding songs that either of the characters exhibits fresh theatrical life."[9]

The new Linda Low: Sandra Allen, a one-time stunt actress, also enjoyed being a girl (Craig Schwartz).

Michael Kuchwara's Associated Press review summed up the evening as less than engaging. "Tastefully pleasant ... and curiously sedate.... It's now an Asian *Rags* by way of *Fiddler on the Roof*.... Hwang has tossed out the original story by Hammerstein and Fields and replaced it with a new tale that manages to weigh down the evening with even more plot and some unconvincing funny business.... These showy, razzmatazz numbers seem anemic.... Then there's Allen Liu as Linda Low's gay confidante, Harvard. Talk about stereotypes. If you are going to perpetuate one at least give him better jokes."[10]

The one notice everyone, of course, awaited for by sacred tradition was the verdict from the *New York Times*. It was issued by Ben Brantley, not a happy theatregoer that night. To begin with, Lea Salonga, in Mr. Brantley's eyes, had turned meek little Mei Li into a feminist-approved character, "her speech, as crisp and confident as a television anchorwoman's." Complained Brantley, "Striking tai chi poses in a Mao suit for her opening number, she might be auditioning for a new, improved Charlie's Angeles team."

As for other characters and situations, Mr. Brantley enumerated a number of convoluted liberties taken: "'I Am Going to Like It Here,' a valentine to American culture, is now a bleak reprise for a group of oppressed workers in a fortune-cookie factory.... The production numbers seem stranded between sardonic kitsch and sincere showmanship.... Listening to the lines, you remember that Mr. Hwang also contributed to the puerile humor of Disney's *Aida*."[11]

Lea Salonga remembers waiting anxiously to see what the *New York Times* would have to say. And once Brantley's blast landed on the deflated company like a nuclear missile, she wondered apprehensively if they could survive it.[12]

On the upside, the company did garner, soon after, a couple of major media endorsements, one from *USA Today* ("rapturous!")[13]; the other from *Time* magazine, whose Richard Zoglin took issue with all the nasty notices, accusing the dart throwers who produced them of being "suddenly quite protective of a musical play they never much liked in the first place."

In Zoglin's eyes, the musical had been "rescued from the dustbin of theatre history and made relevant again without getting weighed down by PC. This new Broadway revival is a work of bravery and intelligence, and real faith in the possibilities of theatre."[14]

Yet Zoglin's rave was not without serious and telling qualms which only, to the careful reader, reinforced the formidable doubts of the naysayers. And another affirmatively mixed notice, from John Heilpern in the weekly *New York Observer*, lauded Hwang's deft prose while belittling the dated songs that came with it, effectively addressing a problem that Longbottom had acknowledged as far back as the L.A. rehearsals. "The one thing he can't do is rewrite the sacred and sometimes hokey score to his own profounder purposes," wrote Heilpern. Nonetheless, the director and writer, thought he, worked "brilliantly around the score to create a new Broadway show of high and low seriousness, which was Rodgers and Hammerstein's intention in the first place." As for the "cliched" character of Harvard, "which Broadway show resists camp nowadays?" asked the defending critic.[15]

Outside the mainstream press, within the Asian American community there were marked differences of opinion. Carl Wong, analyzing for the online magazine *Film Score*, found "many pleasures to be had," but on balance concurred with the not-impressed, offering his own savvy observations: "The revival ... is a nice try, but ultimately, I think it works about as well as the original book would have. Hwang, the talented but didactic playwright of *M. Butterfly*, is too heavy-handed to take on what is essentially a romantic comedy.... Trying to use the songs from *Flower Drum Song* and turn it into *Carousel* is a Sisyphean task at best.... By the end of the musical, the characters may look fondly on the theatre's operatic past, but it's too little too late ... never light on its feet.... Without the pretensions and the baggage of the actual stage show, the music really does hold up well."[16]

John Kuo Wei Techen, founding director of Asian Pacific American Studies at New York University, accused all Hwang's critics of being "clueless" in an essay published by the online Maynard Institute. Argued Techen, if the original musical was "kitsch, then Hwang's version camps it up by playfully reconstructing the story line and making the whole story over the top."

He called the critics "querulous," believing that they should have been asking the question — was Hwang's show "successful as camp? The audience I witnessed definitely suspended their disbelief and had fun."[17]

Baayork Lee, from the original cast, spotted the difficulty inherent in wedding a modern treatment to the older score. "Those songs are written in a lighter vein. David's writing is darker, so it's hard to make all of that come together."

Pat Suzuki, who ended up seeing the show "inadvertently" seven times with that many Japanese fund-raising groups, loved it. "It was a hoot," she declares. And Arabella Hong, a three-time attendee, found the updated story to be "very effective," the production numbers "imaginative," but the singing, overall, "better in the original." She does feel that the critics "tore it apart unnecessarily and said things they really needn't say."

Why were the all-important first-night notices so utterly downbeat compared to the Los Angeles writeups? In the face of chilly reviews, conspiracy theories help at least to salve wounds. One reason for the jilting reception could be the so-called New York–L.A. rivalry, said to turn the critics in each town against work emanating from the other. Of course, this does not account for certain shows that do well with critics in both cities, and some do.

"I think they were gunning for it," surmises Patrick Adiarte. "I really thought it would do well."

Perhaps all the pre-publicity generated by Hwang himself had something to do with it, suggests Adiarte.

Might it have been Hwang's comparing himself to Hammerstein?

"You're talking about somebody who taught Stephen Sondheim how to write. Give me a break."

The quirks of the individual stringers were also advanced as a reason. Pat Suzuki feels that some critics secretly envy "golden boy" David Henry Hwang's success and refuse to give him a fair shake. One cast member suggested that a certain critic for one of the major newspapers is known to harbor a personal dislike for Robert Longbottom. And, as an equal opportunity snubber, Clive Barnes has long been observed to selectively nap when he should be consciously critiquing. In fact, if Barnes did doze off at the *Flower Drum Song* kickoff, he might have been dreaming of the original, for in a waking state he wrote, "What the passing of a half century of musical theatre has taught us is that even minor Rodgers and Hammerstein is pretty darn good."[18]

Or maybe all the last-minute changes were the real culprit. Drama critic Michael Phillips, who had reviewed the show in Los Angeles for the *Los Angeles Times* and was now writing for the *Chicago Tribune*, filed a follow-up report full of nit-picking comparisons. The dismayed Phillips reported a "pushiness" about the production which he felt "diminished its effect. Now, with a few extra million and an overriding impulse to impress, director/choreographer Robert Longbottom's staging has become larger and more opulent, with lots more pan–Asian cheesecake in the nightclub numbers, more but not better material for the creaky gay swisher character, and longer, gabbier book scenes 'amplifying' the love story between Mei Li and Ta ... the pacing is off; lines that were made for simply tossing off, and quickly, now go drip ... drip ... drip. I would suggest coffee. Speed counts for a lot with musical comedy."[19]

Eric Chan, of another mind, compares L.A. to N.Y.: "Having a romantic dinner in a very small quaint French restaurant is very different from having a romantic dinner at Balthazar."

For a few promising weeks, the latter looked to be the entree of choice for New York audiences. Looked to. During the first month, some nights the house climbed to nearly 100 percent capacity. Maybe they could prove those critics wrong and be another *Cats* or *Mama Mia* ... or, going back in time to another commercially quirky era, *Hellzapoppin. Time* magazine–blessed? *New York Times*–doomed? "After the reviews came out," remembers Kim Varhola, "our attendance level went down. But more importantly, the response level went down. I can't tell you why; maybe these people read the reviews and because the critics didn't like the show, they're not supposed to like it either."

The lush early turnouts did not last long. Into the second month, overall attendance dropped sharply — into the mid–70 percent range.

Through December they danced and sang, hoping for an award or two at the next Tonys not too far around the corner. That could reboot public interest and bring back the full houses and standing ovations. Just give the fickle public a Tony-mandated reason to believe in the show. In the meantime, the cast gave it all they had, having been assured by the producers that plans were under way to stay on the boards through at least the following summer, at which time a national touring company would be formed for dates in the States and in Asian countries.

Then came an especially dark, cold winter of little sympathy, casting long, lingering shadows over David Henry Hwang's now beleaguered *Flower Drum Song.*

16

Lost on a Bigger Midway

Lead producer Benjamin Mordecai took the show into New York with momentum on his side: a flush $4 million advance, much of it generated by block discount sales to group fund-raising parties; the imagery of a record-breaking L.A. run; and those magical three words, "Rodgers and Hammerstein." The right word-of-mouth combined with respectable reviews might duplicate the California turnouts.

Two weeks before the Virginia Theatre opening, the *Wall Street Journal* reported on the chancy prospects for box-office gold. Here, the show was venturing away from a season-subscription market into the trickier wilds of Times Square, where shows must motivate substantial ticket window trade. Ronald Lee, who managed block sales, told the *Journal* they were "selling like hot cakes for groups and theatre parties."[1]

Further noted was the "surprise" over the unusually high percentage of ticket orders coming in from "the Asian-American community that once eschewed the show"— the unfounded claim itself something of a surprise given the show's strong reception, as late as nine years previous, at Oakland's Woodminster Summer Musicals, where Asians made up 25 percent of the audience.

Curiously, the *Journal* accepted without question the argument that offensive stereotypes had previously hurt the show. The *Journal* projected that Hwang's corrected version, eliminating such insults as women being called "local egg rolls," might attract a larger percentage of Asian Americans than the mere 3.5 percent who usually purchased theatre tickets. "Backers are betting that a massive make over ... can change the public perception of it, as well as bring in a new crowd."

Mordecai had committed "about 10 percent" of his $1.5 million marketing budget to Asian neighborhoods around town. Already his staff had rounded up more than a dozen groups to host fund raisers tied into performances of the show — another boon to box office ledgers. And Hwang's new script generated plenty of free publicity, spurring comparisons with its predecessor. Commented Fay Matsui, executive director of the Museum of Chinese in America, the original *Flower Drum Song* "was very stereotyped high pidgin. It became embarrassing." She herself pushed a block sale of tickets, all of which were snatched up "almost immediately."

The groundwork had been laid for strong potential support from New York's Asian districts. Still, the producers would need every shred of patronage they could extract from the musical's natural audience base. This latest R & H revival would be going up against at least *seventeen* musicals already on the boards— many of them long-run, market-shrewd survivors that still dominated ticket windows and scalper boards. And eight more tuners, new or revived, were slated to open by year's end. "There are so many musicals in the market place," remarked Broadway press agent John Barlow, "that the consumer needs a compelling reason to go. That means rave reviews, a star and awards."[2]

At the outset, Mordecai's property had a couple of rave notices to hype. It certainly had a bona fide star in the person of Lea Salonga. Awards? If any were to be, that would have to wait for the next Tonys, for which nominations would not be announced until nearly seven months after the show opened.

Though the reviews were on balance problematical, still there was enough praise scattered throughout the better ones to provide eye-catching quotes for ads, fliers and posters. The publicity department skillfully pulled out enough positive words and phrases to lend the sure *image* of a hit — even if knowing theatregoers were aware that a grumbling majority of the show's critics were the heavy hitters— Brantley of the *New York Times*; Barnes of the *Post;* Kissel at *Woman's Wear; Variety* and *The Associated Press.*

Adroitly, Mordecai's PR flacks salvaged lines even from two downbeat reviews, lifting from each words which, when rearranged out of context, lent the impression of a widely acclaimed work. "Baby, Look at You Now!" shouted the *New York Times* excerpt. "This thoroughly revised *Flower Drum Song* is as transformed as Eliza Doolittle in Pygmalion."[3] Quite a feat to make that sound like a positive assessment, considering that *Times* readers checking out Brantley's capsule review of the show in the Sunday theatre listing would read about a "thoroughly revised revival" that seems "to have given up all evidence of a personality to call its own."[4]

Howard Kissel's dismissal —"a spicier but ultimately coarser treatment"— was brazenly contorted into a list of attributes by the Mordecai spin-

Jose Llana and Lea Salonga (Craig Schwartz/Mark Taper Forum).

masters: "A spicy entertaining *Flower Drum Song*! Lea Salonga is lovely and winsome, and the handsome Jose Llana sings beautifully. Jodi Long is wickedly hilarious ... Sandra Allen is dynamic singing "Girl" with true pizzaz. And Don Sebesky's orchestrations capture the great score sharply and wittily."[5]

The show's biggest boosters—*USA Today* and *Time* magazine — provided nearly camera-ready copy for the ad boards. Even then, some questionable tinkering with Richard Zoglin's *Time* notice distorted the use of the word "amazed" (from the sentence "We should be amazed that this song is back in tune") into the headline-grabbing "AMAZING!" on fliers and posters. From there, Mordecai's flacks followed their unethical inclinations to the max, touting "The Rodgers and Hammerstein Classic!" — itself another flagrant misrepresentation, for the original libretto was nowhere to be found at the Virginia.

From lesser sources came additional much-needed kudos. For instance, Jeff Lyons, of WNBC-TV, thumb-upped "an evening of enchantment ... works wonderfully. Filled with engaging characters, it's daring, vibrant and charming."[6]

The review "quotes" on *Flower Drum Songs's* official internet website would easily capture the interest of out-of-town theatregoers planning a weekend of New York shows. The logo itself—photo images of Salonga and Llana facing each other timidly like a couple of adolescents too shy to take their first kiss—was hardly the stuff to stir the modern-day customer. After all, weren't we supposed to have left the soft, sentimental fifties behind? The innocuous sweetness of it all called to mind a long-gone era of stout-hearted straitlaced romance. Evidently, nobody on Mr. Mordecai's staff paused to notice that mainstream American sensibilities no longer favored such tender rituals.

Here, in fact, was problem #1: *Flower Drum Song* was entering a market long removed from pre-feminist boy-girl niceties.

The reviews might be mulled over and debated for years to come. When a show draws marked criticism from the most respected sources, their words can cast shadows over its entire history, just as Kenneth Tynan's classic insult ("the world of woozy song") did over the original. Just as Brooks Atkinson's faintly repeated one-word qualifier—"pleasant"—would be quoted ad nauseam by *Drum* haters who had never seen the original but were hounded and haunted by its shoddy incarnation on celluloid.

Among the first-night appraisers dissenting to Hwang's treatment, no single reviewer's comments jump out. Yet all together, they allude to a random sampler straining to look modern while riddled by its own flimsy stereotypes and weighted down by the uneasy interface of old songs and new ideas. To be fair, many musicals have survived worse reviews to prove their worst critics wrong—well, at least as box-office prognosticators. According to the adjudication of the New York League of Theatre Producers on its website, the reviews for the hit show *Aida* came in at an average of 2.4 (5 being the highest possible mark); *Flower Drum Song* registered a 2.5.[7]

Audiences, of course, often ignore negative notices and turn ill-reviewed shows into hits through word of mouth. Andrew Lloyd Webber, who has reason to be thankful for this phenomenon, is notorious for having driven certain scribes into fits of sarcasm over his musicals, which managed, despite vicious criticism, to shatter Broadway records. Webber's *Cats* was the longest of them all. His *Phantom of the Opera*, which opened on 1988, is still on the boards.

If producer Mordecai worked the reviews to his advantage, what he did not do nearly so capably, according to everyone in the cast who granted interviews for this book, was to ballyhoo his property. Jodi Long questioned Mr. Mordecai's brand of promotion. "From the poster to the marquee," says she, "I thought they did a terrible job marketing the show for

Broadway." Remembering that pink-colored logo, Long laments the lack of timely pizzaz. "If they had marketed it in a way that was hip —*hip*, instead of looking like the Asian *Titanic*. It was terribly saccharine. It was so frustrating and sad because I think we all felt we had a good show. It just wasn't being promoted in a way that was going to really bring the people in."

Problem #2: The producers, entering a Big Apple market, were observed by the cast to be operating on a rummage sale budget. "We were told they went into the New York production lacking a million dollars," says Alvin Ing, who believed the missing money might have been earmarked for promotion. What struck Ing and his cohorts was the depressing lack of ads for the show. No television commercials and no posters on the sides of busses, recalls Ing with painful regret, feeling they were "definitely under-promoted."

Kim Varhola shares a similar frustration: "Why, when I go to Grand Central and there are fliers for all the shows, are there no fliers for *Flower Drum Song*? And why, on opening night, are there no noteworthy celebrities who have turned up to see our show?

"They told us there was no money."

Nonetheless Varhola, describing herself as "the third dancer from the left," asked Ben Mordecai face to face: What are you doing about marketing?

"He in turn told me that he was very satisfied with the way they were marketing the show. And that kind of ended."

Varhola could never understand pitching the show so heavily to local Chinese Americans: "Is this a viable market for our show? Yes, but I would suspect that they aren't our primary target audience.... We were not talking about the demographic of people who are going to shell out a hundred dollars to see a Broadway show."

Jodi Long shared a bright promotional idea with Hwang and Longbottom: When it was time for her to take a vacation, why not have the musical's *original* 1958 star stand in for her?

"Get Pat Suzuki!" she suggested. "She knows the song [Grant Avenue], she's seen the show many times. All she has to do is what I do. She can do it."

To Long's dismay, the idea was met with indifference.

"Come on, guys," she argued, "you'll get people coming to see the show!"

Cast members who had played the L.A. date were somewhat spoiled by the sellout crowds at the smaller Taper. The downward spiral in patronage, shortly into the show's run, was a morale-busting affair, and it only increased their discontent with the anemic promotion. "Nothing" is a word spoken over and over in a kind of slow orchestrated lament by dancer Eric Chan. He describes the many places where he looked for evidence of his show, and how he started to wonder if they were trying to hide it under a lotus leaf.

"There were so many things that were wonderful about this production," he stresses, "but you would have things that were against it."

Such as?

"I could never understand why I would never see any promotion of our show on Broadway. I was spoiled being brought up basically with Mackintosh, who is a genius at the machine of promotion. Here we are without anything. I'm going, "Well, what's happened?'"

He pauses ...

"Advertising? I'm talking nothing. We had a little thing on Times Square amongst the other millions of things.... Might as well have someone passing out leaflets on the corner."

Baayork Lee, from the original cast, saw the production and thought it had a fighting chance to succeed. Comparing it to the better promoted *Aida* with its "terrible reviews," she believes that *Flower Drum Song* deserved the better fate. "They fulfilled all of the needs of why people go to see shows; if David Merrick was the producer and Disney was behind it, this show would be running."

Most of all, Lee welcomed the opportunity the show afforded a number of talented Asians to practice their craft. "There are no shows that are taking the leap onto Broadway with Asians. We were so happy to have something, and that was the same thing in 1958.... We're working. Once every fifty years comes a show."

Certain shows, no matter their respective assets or lack thereof, may be easier to market than others. Eric Chan references the ageless disparity between commerce and culture: "You can have crap on a stick, but have the greatest promotion and you will sell out." One need only substitute personally despised titles for "crap" to readily agree with Chan's view.

He continues: "And you would have the most wonderful thing, without it, we had nothing."

Nothing.

There was a lot, unfortunately, that David Henry Hwang's new musical did not have. In fact, the show's principal liability may have been Hwang's inability to deliver a focused work of force, the sort of force that can sweep an audience into the realm of *character driven* verisimilitude. This liability, in turn, dogged whatever efforts the marketing staff made to define their product to the public. What may have hurt the new *Flower*

Drum Song the most was simply too weak an identity. What *was* the show? Was it a romance, complicated by the issue of how to assimilate into the American fabric? A vaudeville hoot about an aging opera singer's sudden conversion to nightclub clown? The saga of Chinese refugees questioning western values? A clever potpourri, concept-musical style, giving a stage full of Asian actors the rare chance to express themselves in a variety of emotions through soliloquy and satire?

Beware of musicals that are difficult to summarize in a few words. *Drum's* "theme" would be discussed in many nebulous terms. Actor Jose Llana talked up the script's "darker issues" when interviewed by Bud Wilkinson on his radio program *Broadway's Biggest Hits*.

"Those issues being *what*?" asked Wilkinson.

To which Llana evasively replied, "What it means to raise your children in an American society while appreciating the foreign culture that they came from."[8]

And therein, somewhere somehow someway, lay the "darker issues."

What exactly *is* Hwang's central point? Several critics noted the throwing of too many plot shreds at the audience. Worst of all, the least sustain-

Between Mei Li and Ta, played by Lea Salonga and Jose Llana, the drum became a politicized symbol of ethnic pride (Craig Schwartz/Mark Taper Forum).

ing shred received, ironically, the most stage time — the harmless little intended old-fashioned romance between the two would-be lovers. This meandering tale is too simple-minded to compete with the other issues and the bawdier characters that swirl around it. Indeed, Hwang's allegiance to the paper-thin Ta and Mei Li story seems to have trumped his better narrative instincts. Tzi Ma recalls, to his regret, how the easygoing Hwang time and time again has given into directors and producers pushing for changes upon changes. "David's first draft is always his best draft."

Jodi Long saw a distressing number of back-and-forth script and production alterations during the New York previews. She saw what she has seen too many times before, when sometimes "people start to worry about what's going to make a hit. It compromises the original creative impulse, and I think that in wanting to create something that is going to be a hit, they sometimes throw the baby out with the bath water. I missed the simplicity from L.A. When we got to N.Y., we were grappling with the bigger-more-better version."

Long cites as one example the restaging of Linda Low's number "I Enjoy Being a Girl" from a standard self-strip in L.A., with six other showgirls doing likewise, to an interaction in N.Y. with shirtless men assisting in the wardrobe removal. "I mean, what is sexy about a strip tease? The tease! Will she or won't she? Burlesque taught us that! When someone takes off your clothes, it's a whole other ball game.

"Maybe there was pressure from the producers, I don't know. But I wish the show had stuck to some of its original artistic impulses, which might have been less slick but were pure."

What could they go for, really? This was not a new musical, not with its dated songs; not a true revival, either, not with a totally new book. What it was, was an exuberantly reconstructed collage of too many disparate parts to take an audience on a satisfying ride to anywhere. And it had to compete with a pretty tough breed of newer, far less sentimental fare: the bombastic over-the-top *The Producers* fueled by the chemistry of two strong central characters; *Mama Mia*, a pop-driven story with a clearly defined premise (so well conveyed in the opening minutes as to be a textbook example of Oscar Hammerstein's mantra about establishing your theme within the first five minutes and sticking to it); the gritty, inventive *Urinetown*, turning the old Kurt Weill–Bertold Brecht up-with-the-oppressed-class light opera onto its head; and the cartoonish rock and roll romp *Hairspray*, which shamelessly indulges in camp to achieve a kind of oddball unity. Some shows make it big by going all the way.

Also vying for the consumer's dollar were the senior champions like *Phantom* and *Les Misérables*, must-sees still for visitors making their first trip to Manhattan. Add to that a host of revivals to choose from: *42d Street; Cabaret; Chicago; Oklahoma!; Into the Woods.* And don't overlook three Disney workhorses, not to be out-promoted by anyone. How many musicals can the average visitor take in during a single stay?

Most of the shows then on Broadway fairly dwarfed the less-hip ways of Hwang's "revisical." The real revivals, edgier or not, offered the patron a genuine look at yesteryear's gems, which *Drum* could not do. The new tuners on the block promised scores of recent vintage, which *Drum* could not promise. Indeed, on that tough thoroughfare where Benjamin Mordecai and producing colleagues played out their fate, their competition stared them in the face every night from another playhouse directly across the street, where endless lines besieged the ticket windows.

With a laugh of regret, Eric Chan recalls the production of *Hairspray*, whose blazing success was like a thorn in their side. "It didn't help having something like that. We thought *Hairspray* would win Best Musical; *Flower Drum Song* Best Revival. We thought we were going to make 52nd Street "the destination for great theatre" and then.... Our timing sucked. Everything was totally against us. The rough winter. The war. The economy. The recession. Oh, my goodness, I thought we had the sweetest story to be told."

Audience reception turned noticeably mute after the reviews hit the streets. Before opening night, a theatre is a different world—full of promise and hope when a brand new show on its stage, still technically a work in progress, can engender sympathetic crowd reactions and the best wishes of supportive friends and kin. And during previews, *Drum* had two things going for it: its rosy run back in L.A. and all of the Asians who had come out to take a look and cheer it on. The preview crowds loved what they saw and heard. Many no doubt dreamed that they were witnessing history in the making.

The pre-opening euphoria melted slowly away after the critical notices melted in. So, too, did the support of the Asian-American community to whom Mordecai had sold thousands of tickets early in the engagement. Inescapable is the conclusion that this show did not generate compelling word-of-mouth. By late December, attendance sank to a dismally unacceptable 55 percent. Rarely thereafter did it rise much higher. Compared to other musicals around town, almost week after week *Flower Drum Song* played to the smallest houses. It was not cutting it at the Virginia. Insiders wondered how long Mr. Mordecai, co-producer Michael Jenkins, *et al.* would be able to keep their costly experiment in operation.

A *Wall Street Journal* theatre survey of audience satisfaction at musicals, conducted near the end of *Drum's* run, asked how many audience members would recommend current shows to their friends. With 77 percent, *Drum* tied with *Urinetown* for the second to last place on the list, just above *Moving Out*.[9]

The crowds from Chinatown never materialized in force. New Yorkers routinely shunned the show. "Those people are hard-core theatregoers," remarks Sandra Allen. "Whereas in L.A., theatregoers are a little more laid back."

Allen sensed that many New Yorkers, whom she assumed had seen the original production, viewed the remake with skepticism. They turned "cautious," she says, recalling an air of apprehension out in the audience some nights.

Alvin Ing saw the old east-coast/west-coast rivalry at work again. He saw it in some negative notices, wondering why they, too, had to dredge up Kenneth Tynan's old "world of woozy song" crack. "Very unfair … what does that have to do with *our* show?"

Mediocre-to-awful business never helps the morale of a company; nor do the impressions taken away by paying customers who will share memories of empty seats. With too much competition on Broadway, *Flower Drum Song* did not apparently have what it takes—not as produced on limited funds—to go the distance.

Lea Salonga looks back ruefully. She remembers that a manager once told her that when people really want to see something, all they have to do is whisper their approval to others and crowds will quickly materialize. She concludes that perhaps the show just wasn't strong or unique enough to compete with all the other entertainments on the horizon.[10]

Pundits guessed that Mordecai and company should have left town by early January rather than stick around in desperation, hoping to reverse the downward spiral in business. "Swing by *Flower Drum Song* on a Wednesday night," quipped Michael Riedel in the *New York Post* in late January, "and I guarantee you'll be able to snag the entire orchestra. Last week's gross: $296,000 (how much longer can they go?)"[11]

A couple of weeks earlier, Riedel had reported that there was "more intrigue" surrounding the show's fate "than you're likely to find in a back alley of Shanghai. Last week, Rodgers and Hammerstein's rice-queen musical appeared to be headed out the door of the Virginia, a victim of Broadway's annual box office chill. The owner of the Virginia—Jujamcyn Theatres—told the producers … that the writing was on the great wall, and they should go out with dignity rather than bleed slowly to death."[12]

The bum houses triggered the threat of an eviction notice from the landlords, who could, per a below-box-office stop clause in the contract, legally usher an underpatronized tenant out the back door.

Even so, Riedel understood Mordecai's hesitancy to close based on tra-ditional business patterns. If the show could survive the winter months, salvation might return in the spring when tourists once again flocked to Times Square. Conceivably, it might then last out the entire year.

Hard to imagine that happening, however, in view of Mr. Mordecai's out-for-Krispy-Kremes marketing staff, whose mind-boggling ineptitude reached new lows on Presidents' Day. Mondays are usually dark, but sev-eral shows—including *Mama Mia, Phantom, Chicago,* and *Rent*—kept their doors open for the holiday trade. *Flower Drum Song* followed suit— but for some reason, while the other shows listed their added performances in the *New York Times* theatre section ads, *Drum* did not. According to Alvin Ing, there were around 175 people in the matinee audience. "Isn't that the stupidest thing you ever heard?"

Jodi Long had noticed the lack of a mention in the ad in Friday's paper. She assumed the error would be corrected, but there was nothing in Sat-urday's edition. Nor in Sunday's—when the show also placed a small dis-play ad which pitched student-rush discount tickets but, strangely, did not push the next day's added shows.

"The worst marketing job I'd ever seen," she declares. "This is the thing that made me nuts."

On Monday morning, during a blizzard that dumped three feet of snow onto the streets, Long got a call from the stage manager informing her the show would be going on that afternoon.

"To whom?" she asked.

"Oh, we're sold out!"

"Sold out?"

She was told that snow would not discourage New Yorkers. It did not discourage 175 of them from attending that afternoon.

She asked the stage manager why there had been no ads in the papers. "What are you talking about?" he replied.

"I don't think anybody knows that we have two shows today."

"We're sold out! We're sold out!"

Following the pitifully attended "sold out" matinee, Long went to the box office, inquiring about the night's haul.

"Are we sold out tonight?" she asked.

They looked at her querulously. "Jodi, we do not know what the pro-ducers are doing, because there's no ad. No, we're not sold out. We've maybe sold about 500 tickets."

Some of the other musicals in operation that Presidents' Day did sell out.

Backstage, Long vented her frustrations with the stage hands, who, because it was a holiday, were being paid double time. "It was unbelievable. Clearly, nobody was minding the store."

They kept the unminded store open for a another few weeks. Finally, the word was posted: The show would be shutting down on March 16. And it would lose all of the more than $7 million invested in it.

News of the imminent closing came as a "big shock" to the company, as recounted by Alvin Ing, for they had been told the production would continue on until at least the Tony Awards, when a Tony or two might reverse the lagging turnouts. Two weeks before the last performance, Mary Rodgers followed through with a cast party at her house that had already been planned. "She was charming and full of life," remembers Ing. David Chase sat down at the piano to play, and everybody sang along.

Spinning away in a prolonged state of denial, David Henry Hwang would continue serving as his own best press agent, claiming, despite hard evidence to the contrary, that in every city the show played on a short national tour after it left New York there were only positive notices. And not just positive, but "even more positive than they had been in L.A."

"New York," says Hwang, "remains a strange and disappointing anomaly — the only city where our production was not met with praise." He feels that the critics "seemed to perceive the new book as an exercise in political correctness, and therefore felt compelled to defend the original." He cites the absence of critical support from *The New York Times* as the likeliest cause for his doomed date at the Virginia. His *M. Butterfly*, which similarly "divided the critics," still excelled, he states, the difference being that "the *New York Times* supported *Butterfly*, but didn't like FDS."

Had the original Rodgers and Hammerstein musical been revived, Hwang is also certain that the same dreary reception would have befallen it. "I promise you ... they would've condemned that one just as fiercely!

"I'm not the person who started the 'revisical' craze," Hwang asserts, pointing to precedent in the 1974 revival of *Candide* at the Broadway Theatre. Nor is he the first to have been accused by the critics of "a P.C. exercise," recalling a similar reaction to the rewritten *Annie Get Your Gun*. History, Hwang believes, "will validate the opinions of those critics who did like the new book."

Looking back, too, with passion and pride, Eric Chan loved every minute of it. "I think the most genius thing was to have an all Asian cast come together to tell the story, and to hell with the rest. I thought we had a gorgeous thing. End of story."

17

Hwang Versus Hammerstein

Came the Tony Awards telecast in May 2003, and nothing. *Flower Drum Song*, no longer in operation, was left in the dirt. Rendered less viable commercially. Three of its contributors were snubbed when Tonys they might have won — Hwang for best "new" book, Gregg Barnes for costumes; Robert Longbottom for choreography — were handed to others: to *Hairspray*'s Mark O'Donnell and Thomas Meehan for book, Ivey Long for costumes; and Twyla Tharp, of *Moving Out*, for choreography.

Nothing for *Drum*, a rarity in musicals which that season technically could have been nominated for both best musical *revival* and best book for a *new* musical! The bizarre inconsistency reflected the no-man's-land nature of David Henry Hwang's inscrutable experiment; it also demonstrated once again the lunacy of Tony committee decision-making — this was the same body which had made it possible in recent years for a director of a *ballet* to win best director for a *musical*, the same body under whose aegis a work of dance, *Contact*, was nominated for best musical.

Where exactly did *Flower Drum Song* fit in? If it had been actually nominated that year in the best musical revival category, the show would have competed against *Gypsy*, *La Bohème* (a restaged, "reimagined" opera), *Man of La Mancha*, and *Nine*. The award went, surprisingly, not to the ground-breaking *Gypsy* (which Bernadette Peters evidently failed to persuasively revive), but to the mediocre *Nine*, fronted with masculine charisma by Spanish heartthrob Antonio Banderas, after whose early departure the show folded fast.

Flower Drum Song was out-nominated by new shows born of younger, more contemporary sensibilities, including *A Year with Frog and Toad* and *Hairspray*, and by legitimate, non-deconstructed revivals, against which its reformed personality may have struck traditionalist-minded Tony voting members as illegitimate. Not a single Tony — a long-lasting blow to Hwang's great adventure in historical revisionism.

Then came another major setback rendering the work even less commercially promising: the domino collapse of a planned national and international tour. West coast appearances had been penciled in at Gordon Davidson's Ahmanson Theatre (ironically, the venue in which the musical was to have originally premiered) and at the 2,994-seat Orange County Performing Arts Center, both of which operations drew from a large Asian population. From there, the company would head up the coast to play a "Best of Broadway" date at the Orpheum Theatre in San Francisco, as part of an eight-city national itinerary.

First to bail, about a month after the Tony Awards, was Orange County. Reports of a SARS epidemic throughout Asia caused the cancellation of engagements slated for Singapore, Hong Kong and China. As covered locally, the pullout of the foreign dates "rendered the entire tour economically impractical."[1] So everything fell down more or less at once. Into the Orange County theatre went, instead, a touring production of *Chicago.* The Ahmanson considered for a time mounting its own production of *Flower Drum Song,* but let that one go, too.

Up in San Francisco, a Japanese-American group tried in vain to salvage the Orpheum date. The Shorenstein-Nederlander management were said to want an "enormous amount of money," as recalled by Alvin Ing. And the capital wasn't raised. Reported the *San Francisco Chronicle,* SARS may have killed the Asian dates, "but money was the problem on this side of the Pacific. There wasn't enough interest in the show."[2] Other musicals, in fact, were drawing far more attention from the locals. *Urinetown* would extend its September run by 16 more shows at the America Conservatory–operated Geary Theatre, where the new musical would set a single-ticket sales record for ACT. And *Chicago,* the champion of all Broadway revivals, added performances before even opening at the Golden Gate.

Meanwhile, back on the *Flower Drum Song* front, one of its New York co-producers, Michael Jenkins, who manages the Dallas Summer Musicals, had been flying all over the country, feverishly scrambling to salvage what he could of the doomed national tour. Jenkins apparently remained in denial longer than any of his producing colleagues. He was still recovering from his very first taste of impressarioship on Broadway — a heady experience that can blind otherwise rational souls. Actually, Jenkins had raised about a third of the $8 million it took to book the Virginia Theatre and schedule the opening. According to the *Dallas Morning News,* the show had been "born with the financial and moral support of Mr. Jenkins and his Dallas Summer Musicals." Indeed, Mordecai had told the *News*, "Michael's dedication and his role as a producer of the show in New York have been what kept this together."[3]

Keeping it together, Jenkins was struggling to save face and a season of his own, for he had committed the show to his venues at the Dallas fairgrounds and Theatre Under the Stars in Houston. He managed to cobble together an alliance with two other regional producers like himself in Seattle and Sacramento for a scaled-down version of the show, and across the four dates the touring company would generate a politely mixed set of reviews ranging from delighted to dismissive. In Houston, for instance, Lee Williams of the *Houston Press* called it "a sweet production that never catches fire like it should," referencing "a mishmash of tales that never get a chance to gather the singular energy this show needs."[4]

Now, Jose Llana, the only lead from the New York cast who stayed on, was given "star" billing, though his name in the handbill appeared in type size no larger than all the other names. Alvin Ing and Allen Liu, two minor players from the New York company, also went out with the truncated tour. Jenkins engaged Longbottom's assistant, Tom Kosis, to direct and choreograph, and they overhauled the Mei Li role, resurrecting the spirit of Miyoshi Umeki in the form of Yuka Takara.

Laid bare in Sacramento at the California Musical Theatre, the show was now two steps removed from its warmly embraced Los Angeles premier. Two *big* steps removed. All of the high-voltage talent with the original cast was long gone. Without them, the production resembled a somewhat threadbare, hand-me-down musical. On the larger stage, the mix of ingredients from audience-pandering jokes to serious monologues was more glaring and harder to take. Ready to entertain, nonetheless, it was. The welcome spectacle of a proficient, talented pan–Asian cast was something of a modern-day novelty, especially for semi-hinterland crowds, and in startling contrast to other show biz quarters where young Asian-American wannabe troubadours still fight a hellishly futile battle for respect. As late as the year 2004, a group of Asian Americans in the San Francisco Bay Area, never having seen their own likenesses on *American Idol*, organized their own local version of the television program.[5]

A Chinese culture that discourages musical aspirations outside the concert hall evidently still persists. Ole Kittleson believes it does. *American Idol* judges agree by default. And a counter-productive circle of defeat is kept alive by the indifferent theatrical producers who give scarce attention to Asian performers, thus reinforcing the performers' negative attitude and leaving them with little incentive to pursue creative arts. As Baayork Lee describes it, too many potentially talented Asians end up with not enough hope to continue. Too many ask, "What are we studying for when there are no jobs?"

Asian Americans are still ranked high as martial arts experts and "submissive computer geeks." To this illicit fold add the name of 21-year-old William Hung, by day an engineering major at U.C. Berkeley, on the off-hours a career off-key singer who had his infamous moment being tossed off one of the early rounds of *Idol*. Undiminished in ego, the spurned Hung turned his bum date with *Idol* into a landslide marketing victory, turning himself into an overnight amateur hack star specializing in groan.

Not the sort of role model, sadly, in which a more talented young Asian American can take much pride or hope — unless the art of being amusingly the worst is to become the next new rage in America. (It is tempting to consider what a shockingly good boon to the box office Hung might be were he to be cast in a future revival of the original *Drum* as nightclub comic Frankie Wing, who sings the purposely amateurish "Gliding Through My Memories.")

There on the Sacramento stage — where, minus such an arguably apt cameo, our Mr. Hung would likely be caned off — thoroughly professional Asian actors do their level best to deliver clever lines from Hwang's musical hybrid. There, without Jodi Long and her like to bowl us over, we sit with more time on our hands to scrutinize an earnestly contrived libretto unable to resist burlesque — just in case everything else falters or fails. We watch actors as mouthpieces indulging a writer's overactive mind. We greet the return of Miyoshi Umeki's spirit in the form of Takara and suspect a telling insecurity on the road producer's part to bring back a better show. We are left with yawning time on our hands to nurse a distant desire for the simpler, unified beauty of the work of Mr. Fields and Mr. Hammerstein. And to consider that maybe *this* is gravitas enough.

There on the Sacramento stage, "Don't Marry Me" never sounded less amusing; "I Enjoy Being a Girl," never more lifeless. And the gratuitously interpolated "My Best Love" felt very — well, gratuitous. And what on earth is Harvard, the gay costumier determined by show's end to go home and come out to his straitlaced parents, doing in a musical set in the year 1960? And why is the resolve of Ta and Mei Li to turn their backs on the nightclub scene and hang out on Union Square Street corners singing authentic Chinese music not dramatized? How long, we are left to wonder, will the newlyweds last living off in-their-hat donations before returning to the great American songbook on a pagoda-land stage where fortune cookies are dispensed?

One lone voice in Sacramento, that of fortune cookie worker Chao (played by Bobby Pestka), cuts through all the varied shenanigans and concept-musical asides with deeply felt emotions. And he gives the show one achingly affecting voice. For a moment, writer Hwang has succeeded in bringing us face to face with an *authentic* character; and therein lies a hint of what his *Drum* should and could have been if only he had followed this one simple tale — or, indeed, *any* simple tale — all the way, allowing it

Against his contemporary inclinations, Hwang brought the curtain down an a happily-ever-after marriage (Craig Schwartz/Mark Taper Forum).

to dictate the final frame. Mei Li's exit with Chao back to China would have left Ta to ponder a real loss, and the audience to savor a bittersweet ending.

At the end of a couple of hours, the Sacramento audience gives the cast a few rousing calls for encores. No doubt, some could claim this version of the musical to be as respectably passable as critics of the original version claimed it to have been.

Comparisons are inevitable and will be made forevermore. History never completely goes away. Hwang's champions are unlikely to fade away, either, in rhetorical defeat. Dick and Oscar and Joe mined C.Y. Lee's novel for the generational conflict and for the three women who substantiated Ta's honorable quest for love. These themes, like it or not, still resonate today. The attitudes inherent in "I Enjoy Being a Girl" still resonate today — so much so that forty-five years after Pat Suzuki introduced the song, ladies of means who wish to accent their feminine anatomy resort to perilous foot surgery for "beauty's sake," as reported by Gardner Harris in the *New York Times*. "With vanity always in fashion and shoes reaching ionic cultural status, women are having parts of their toes lopped off to fit into the latest Manolo Blahniks or Jimmy Choos."[6]

Mail order brides? The market has never shut down. Today, "the industry markets stereotypes on both sides," according to coverage of the issue in the Associated Press. "They market to the women the image of wealthy American men and a better life. They market to the American men the image of docile women they can control."[7]

In his exploration of race in Broadway musicals, Kamal Al-Solaylee, writing in the *Globe and Mail*, found much to admire in Rodgers and Hammerstein. "The restraint with which *Aida* confronts issues like slavery or racism is a radical departure from the world of Richard Rodgers and Oscar Hammerstein, where issues are confronted head-on. While musicals like *South Pacific, The King And I*, or *Flower Drum Song*, suggest to our more sensitive ears stereotypical treatments of Asian and Asian-Americans, they were inseparable from their creator's progressive, liberationist views. Hammerstein in particular was a crusader for racial justice, a life-long commitment that's overshadowed by his reputation as lyricist of *Show Boat*."[8]

What might the great late theatre thinker and critic Walter Kerr have said about the David Henry Hwang operation? He had been a fancier of *Flower Drum Song's* understated, easygoing charm, and he was not one to suffer such subversive overhauls. When confronted with a return to Broadway of *Irene* and *Good News*, two reworked old treasures bearing additional songs from other shows and other trunks Kerr complained, "It immediately destroys the property, and the pleasures of the play at hand. We are not seeing *Irene* or *Good News* anymore. We're having a random and ultimately indigestible smorgasbord crammed down our throats. We're also being deprived of likely future revivals of the shows from which well-known goodies have been filched: who'll want to do them now that their tombs have been riffled?"[9]

Said Richard Rodgers: "When we can possibly get them performed the way they were written, we do so because we've found from experience, some of it painful, that the best way to project these things and get a response from a live audience is to do them the way they were done originally, after we got finished correcting them ourselves."[10]

Does the musical theatre community itself not bear a moral duty to honor and preserve its landmark achievements? To preserve the legacies of its most accomplished contributors down through time? If, indeed, Dick and Oscar are famously celebrated for having mastered the integration of book, music, and lyrics into the *musical play*, does the forcing of an entire set of songs into a drastically reconfigured libretto not undermine that legacy?

Answered Mary Rodgers, "The original seemed appropriate for its time and the revised version appropriate for its time."

Outside of the few newspaper letter writers heretofore quoted, only a few souls in positions of influence within the musical theatre community have taken more than a few moments or words to question or defend the long-term ramifications of subverting original work to serve modern-day agendas. Author Ken Mandelbaum expressed a preference for the earlier show. "One misses the rowdy gaudy fun of an original that — if now unproducable on Broadway — managed to raise similar issues in a far more entrancing fashion."[11]

For cabaret singer Michael Feinstein, the thought of going to see the new *Drum* was distressing enough. "I have very mixed feelings about rewriting the book of a classic Broadway musical because I have rarely had the experience of enjoying the revised versions. Unfortunately, I did not see the revival of *Flower Drum Song* because I had trepidation about going and ultimately waited too late and missed it."

Says Feinstein, "Shows like *My One and Only* and *Crazy for You* that morph from 'classic' shows like *Funny Face* and *Girl Crazy* are not created for people like me who like to experience the musicals elements in a more authentic way ... personally I'd rather see no revival of a given show rather than see one that is monkeyed with. I'm happier listening to the recording."

Author Ethan Mordden: "Apparently *Flower Drum Song* is half classic and half statistic, a much-loved show that most people don't ken. Obviously, casting a revival would be even harder than casting the original was, what with Actors' Equity and B.D. Wong examining birth certificates to ensure Ethnic Correctness, as in the case of *Miss Saigon*."[12]

Although Ivy Tam did not see the Hwang version, she heard discouraging things about it from friends who did. Tam resents in theory what happened, for she saw and loved the R & H version when it toured San Francisco in 1960; she still enthuses over its humor as if just returning from the theatre. Tam believes strongly in the acceptance of truth as portrayed in works of art, whether politically correct or not. Speaking about what Hammerstein and Fields wrote, she acknowledges how racially embarrassing it may strike some people as being. More important to her, however, is that it was true to life.

Ms. Tam wishes that Mr. Hwang would have started from scratch to create something totally his own, for she sees little value in trying to force a new story onto an old one.[13]

Had Hwang's adventure enjoyed solid New York success, it probably would have emboldened the R & H recycling bent. It would likely have given them additional leverage to push for a similar revamping of their other properties, like *South Pacific*, that are deemed long shots for Broadway revival. One of the many proposed new librettos for Rodgers and Hart's *Pal Joey*, to which Ted Chapin intriguingly alludes (the R & H Library controls the rights), might have been given the green light for development. Possibly Gordon Davidson would have reentered the picture, with a Michael Jenkins not far behind.

Chapin told Misha Berson of *Theatre* just as the new *Drum* was about to open at the Virginia, "Every musical produced by the giants of Broadway's golden era of musicals has been examined with the possibility of finding some new life in it. That will always be done, I think."[14] After the show closed, a less assured Chapin told *Variety's* Charles Isherwood, referring in general to Dick and Oscar's achievements, "They're staples, the reference points, and as with other great works of theatre literature, you check in with them periodically."[15]

On his own, Isherwood raised the specter of box office obsolescence. The same season, in a celebration of the one-hundred year anniversary of Richard Rodgers' birth, two of his other shows, *Oklahoma!* and *The Boys From Syracuse*, did not do well, either. "The question arises: Is this trio of flop revivals merely bad luck…. Or is it possibly that the sunny sounds of Richard Rodgers' music are fatally out of step with our wary media age?"

Maybe not — if ramped up almost beyond recognition and recast in the MTV universe. Several months later in London, a funky hip-hop version of *Syracuse* titled *Da Boyz* featured its tunes reinterpreted for younger crowds, who were observed to be liking it. Exuded R & H's Bert Fink, "We like to remind ourselves that the original was founded by two risk takers, and their families and heirs want that to continue."[16]

The implications of such fatuous spin are troubling, if not downright macabre. Again, does the Rodgers and Hammerstein office not bear a responsibility to preserve rather than dismantle the canon? With respect to what they did to *Flower Drum Song*, call it a self-serving act of artistic sabotage. Call it a sincere effort to bring a moribund near-forgotten work back to life — a worthy venture to give Asian actors, singers and dancers the unfortunately rare chance to perform in a Broadway revival. Call it whatever you wish. Arguably, the strange saga of the Hwang "revisical" comprises one of the saddest and most troublesome chapters in American musical theatre history.

At the center of audacity is this: If Rodgers, Hammerstein and Fields were guilty of slighting C.Y. Lee's novel in their comedic-romantic adaptation, Hwang's sin was the total betrayal of Mr. Lee's work. And everyone in places of power who assisted in its undertaking must share the responsibility with Hwang for the controversially bleak outcome and, worse yet, for its potential to further damage the R & H legacy.

Hwang squandered a golden opportunity to truly delve into Mr. Lee's novel and deliver the libretto Oscar Hammerstein, Asian or not, might have wrought in earlier years when he and Richard were in their creative prime. What seems so puzzling is why Hwang did not just write his own new musical by engaging — as a writer of his standing in the theatre should have no trouble doing — living, breathing songwriters to share in his vision. After all, he had no discernible interest in serving Mr. Lee's themes, plots or characters; he had, in fact, admitted to having not read the book before he thought up the project.

Equally puzzling was the reluctance of Mr. Lee himself to stand in the way of this wholesale deconstruction, to challenge or resist Mr. Hwang when he came calling. And, so, the playwright in high favor, smashing fortune cookies right and left, proceeded to bury the work of other men in order to lay claim to their valuable songs — his ticket back to Broadway.

Let it be argued that revivals which strive to restore once-cherished musicals to former glory belong in the hands not of opportunistic writers but of *directors*. It is, after all, the director's job to invest old scripts with new energy and force, to find fresh insights in long-neglected corners, new shadings between oft-spoken lines. To rechart a musical's journey with fresh vision — that's the real and honorable challenge facing every new generation of directors and actors, stage designers, choreographers, orchestrators and technicians. And, yes, *producers*. They are the only ones who can give an old show a new pulse. How many revivals are figured to have risen or collapsed owing to a particular *production* or to a certain *star*?

British wunderkind Trevor Nunn brought *Oklahoma!* back to life on the West End in a way that surprised and gripped audiences with a realism they hadn't before seen. Nunn was not interested in rewriting the show. He was interested in bringing to life a compelling story that had always been there — the tale in which the character of Jud Fry played, in Oscar Hammerstein's words, "the bass fiddle." Nunn's *Oklahoma!* was a full-bodied triumph, even if it lost something en route to New York. Gushed a grateful Mary Rodgers, "I've never seen a performance like Hugh's. I've never felt so moved. You tend to think of it as just being a cheerful little show, a little pure thing. It's actually very deep and very troubled in places and glorious in others. Trevor just found amazing things in it."[17]

Nunn, who directs straight plays as well as tuners and who declined an invitation to add his voice to others quoted in these pages, told the *Los Angeles Times*, "Our habit of mind is completely the same when it comes to American musicals. We say, 'How can we inquire into this masterpiece to discover fresh resonances?'"[18]

Much the same was stipulated by another Brit stager, Sam Mendes, who declared a fidelity up-front to the existing text and to structure, and an aversion to "rejiggering" works such as *Gypsy* and *Guys and Dolls*.[19]

Will the opinions of Nunn and Mendes prevail? Or will the future bring yet more improbable "revisicals"? Are we to end up having to settle more and more for the wonderful songs sans the dialogue and characters with which they came calling in the first instance?

Maybe the so-called golden age will turn out to have been not so golden after all, as new shows get written and the younger fans who embrace them create their own lists of favorites ... as the world itself in and around Broadway moves on. As it must. Maybe just the songs will increasingly show up in "rethought" shows, in effect, for sale to the favored few like David Henry Hwang with new librettos in need of ready-made scores. A new *South Pacific*? Don't count it out.

"That's a great show," protests Arabella Hong. "*Leave it alone*. Go write something else of your own. Let's preserve the classics. Rodgers and Hammerstein will always be the classics of musical theatre. They are the pillars of musical theatre."

Oscar Hammerstein: "Musical plays are not books written by an author with songs later inserted by a composer and lyric writer. The musician is just as much an author as the librettist. He expresses the story in his medium just as the librettist expresses the story in his. They weld their two crafts and two kinds of talent into a single expression. This is the great secret of the well-integrated musical play."[20]

Now there are two *Flower Drum Songs*. And both, according to Mary Rodgers, can be licensed and performed.

Who can predict what will happen? Broadway is forever open to what may come. Pat Suzuki's fondest memory of her days with *Flower Drum Song* were the "mechanisms around it" ... drops falling and rising, stage hands in the shadows ... the orchestra blaring below, "twenty-two guys underneath your feet!"—cast and crew working as one to create wonderful illusions. "You look backstage, and it's just a bunch of dead pieces of wood, or like a can of paint, or lights that, unless they're turned on, don't do anything. Those are the things, the makers of magic, that you remember most of all. They were the most mystical things."

...Like a light from the past waiting mystically to be turned back on. Who knows? In time, maybe a Trevor Nunn will search the original 1958 text of the Mei Li–Wang Ta story and be moved, by unexpected "fresh resonances," to find the right actors and the right beat to bring it back to life in an all-new production. Maybe they will have themselves a giddy romp going for the comedy without fear of a student protest. Maybe the songs will once again enliven the story for which they were created. And, in a sense, the old flats and drops will once again come alive....

And maybe then, with a little luck on Broadway, audiences will discover, too, a certain special magic seen and felt by those who were there opening night many seasons ago—when a delightfully different new musical breezed gently, exotically, across the boards with a smiling Asian face.

Notes

Abbreviations for frequently cited sources:

FDS   C. Y. Lee, *The Flower Drum Song*
LAT   *Los Angeles Times*
NYT   *New York Times*
SFC   *San Francisco Chronicle*
SFE   *San Francisco Examiner*
SFM   Meryle Secrest, *Somewhere for Me*
RHF   Stanley Green, *Rodgers and Hammerstein Fact Book*

Unless otherwise noted, all quotes are from author interviews and correspondence, conducted during 2003–2004, with the following:

Patrick Adiarte
Sandra Allen
Ronald Banks
Eric Chan
Chao-Li Chi
Dean Crocker
Arthur Dong
Michael Feinstein
Scott Henderson
Arabella Hong
David Henry Hwang
Alvin Ing
Ole Kittleson
Thomas Kouo
Baayork Lee
Jared Lee
David Lober
Jodi Long
Wonci Lui
Tzi Ma
Blythe Matsui
Mary Rodgers
Harriet Schlader
Lea Salonga
Pat Suzuki
Ivy Tam
Jeannette Thomas
Kim Varhola

(For the record, included among those who did not respond to interview requests is C. Y. Lee, Robert Longbottom, Gordon Davidson, Benjamin Mordecai and Michael Jenkins.)

(Interviewees who declined to be quoted directly are paraphrased and endnoted.)

Chapter 1

1. SFM, p. 331.
2. "General Foods Presents Rodgers and Hammerstein" television program, 1953.
3. RHF.
4. *Ibid.*
5. Video copy of *Ed Sullivan Show*, 1955, author's collection.
6. *American Decades*, p. 24.
7. (And succeeding quotes.) Jon Whitcomb, "Mr. Words & Mr. Music," *Cosmopolitan*, August, 1958.
8. (And succeeding quotes.) Cleveland Amory, "The Nicest Guys in Show Business," *Holiday*, February 1959.
9. "Playing the Race Card," *The Globe and Mail*, May 6, 2003.
10. SFM, p. 335.
11. SFM, p. 334.
12. RHF (And succeeding *Cinderella* reviews.)

13. Rodgers, *Musical Stages*, p. 294.

14. SFM, p. 337.

15. Associated Press story by Michael Kuchwara, *Charleston Gazette*, October 20, 2002.

16. SFC, October 9, 1957.

Chapter 2

1. "Fortunate Son," SFC, September 18, 2002.

2. FDS, p. 3.

3. *Ibid.*, p. 6.

4. Bill Moyers, *Gold Mountain Dreams*, PBS documentary, 2003.

5. (And following quote.) *Unbound Voices*, p. 300.

6. FDS, p. 76.

7. Bill Moyers, *Gold Mountain Dreams*.

8. Quoted in exhibit display at the Chinese Historical Society of America Museum in San Francisco.

9. Nee, *Longtime Californ,'* p. 83.

10. (And succeeding Forbidden City coverage.) *Forbidden City, USA*, Video, Deep Focus Productions, 1989.

11. Author interview with Jodi Long. Long recalls that C. Y. Lee told her he could not afford to patronize the club and never did. Mr. Lee did not respond to three written requests for interviews for this book.

12. "C.Y. Lee: Chinatown Journalist," interview with Lia Chang, Maynard Institute website, *www.maynardije.org*

13. *Ibid.*

14. "Fortunate Son," SFC, September 18, 2002.

15. *Associated Press*, October 20, 2002.

16. FDS, p. 59.

17. *Ibid.*, p. 29.

18. *Ibid.*, p. 5.

19. *Ibid.*, p. 39.

20. *Ibid.*, p. 129.

21. *Ibid.*, p. 144.

22. SFC, September 18, 2002.

23. (And all succeeding review excerpts.) *Book Review Digest 1957.*

Chapter 3

1. FDS, p. 82.

2. *Ibid.*, p. 65.

3. *Ibid.*, p. 117.

4. *Ibid.*, p. 90.

5. *Ibid.*, p. 233.

6. *Ibid.*, p. 238.

7. *Ibid.*, p. 239.

8. *Ibid.*, p. 239.

9. *Ibid.*, p. 243.

10. *Ibid.*, p. 244.

11. "They're Back—Rodgers and Hammerstein," *Newsweek*, December 1, 1958.

12. Author interview with Arthur Dong.

13. Cleveland Amory, *Holiday*, February 1959.

14. "They're Back," *Newsweek*, December 1, 1958.

Chapter 4

1. "R. & H. Brand on a Musical," NYT, November 23, 1958.

2. *Time*, December 22, 1958. The succeeding biographical information about Miyoshi Umeki and Pat Suzuki prior to their work in *Flower Drum Song* was gleaned from this source.

3. Author interview with Pat Suzuki.

4. SFM, p. 341

5. These incidents at Forbidden City recalled in author interview with Ivy Tam.

6. *Time*, December 22, 1958.

7. *Ibid.*

8. SFM, p. 341.

9. *Time*, December 22, 1958

10. Beck, *The Richard Rodgers Reader.*

11. "Old Friends in New Jobs," *Dance* magazine, December, 1958.

Chapter 5

1. *Gene Kelly: Anatomy of a Dancer*, PBS documentary, 2004.

2. Yudkoff, *Gene Kelly, p. 239.*

3. LAT, April 11, 2004.

4. *Gene Kelly: Anatomy of a Dancer.*

5. SFM, p. 340.

6. Citron, *The Wordsmiths*, p 295.

7. Hirschhorn, *Gene Kelly*, p. 223.

8. NYT, November 23, 1958.

9. *Ibid.*

10. Author interview with Arabella Hong.

11. Fordin, *Getting to Know Him* , p. 341.

12. SFM, p. 341.

13. *Ibid*, p. 341.

14. *Ibid.*, p. 343.

15. Fordin, *Getting to Know Him*, p. 342.
16. NYT, November 23, 1958.
17. *Ibid.*
18. *Ibid.*
19. *Newsweek*, December 1, 1958.

Chapter 6

1. *Variety*, October 29, 1958.
2. *Boston Herald*, October 29, 1958.
3. *Boston Globe*, October 28, 1958.
4. NYT, November 23, 1958.
5. *USA Today*, October 16, 2002.
6. *Newsweek*, December 1, 1958.
7. NYT, November 23, 1958.
8. Citron, *The Wordsmiths*, p. 297.
9. *Ibid.*, p. 297.
10. Fordin, *Getting to Know Him*, p. 338.
11. The intermission feedback incident was recalled in author interview with Arabella Hong.
12. Rodgers, *Musical Stages*, p. 295.
13. *Newsweek*, December 1, 1958.
14. Mordden, *Rodgers and Hammerstein*, p. 196. Of two other accounts: C.Y. Lee remembered Hammerstein writing the new lyric overnight, Rodgers composing it in the ladies room at the Shubert in 30 minutes (*Associated Press*, 10/20/02). *Newsweek's* account (12/1/58), reporting that it took Hammerstein four days and Rodgers six hours, appears the most plausible, given their well-known work habits.
15. Frederick Nolan, *The Sound of Their Music*, p. 205.
16. Yudkoff, *Gene Kelly*, p. 239.
17. *Newsweek*, December 1, 1958. Although cast members and theatre historians downplay Gene Kelly's actual participation as director, Richard Rodgers, in his autobiography, *Musical Stages* (hardly a trustworthy source given the composer's penchant for publicly upbeat statements contrary to his private utterances), writes, "We were confident he [Kelly] could do a beautiful job. He did" (p. 295). Rodgers told author Clive Hirschhorn (*Gene Kelly*, p. 224) that the show "required the surefire touch of an experienced professional to spark it all off, and in Gene Kelly we got a man who was not only experienced and professional to the very marrow of his bones, but hard-working and inspired. Without him, who knows how it all would have turned out."

Chapter 7

These biographical sketches of the seven first-night critics were based on material about them supplied by Steven Suskin in his book *Opening Nights on Broadway*.
1. Suskin, *Opening Nights on Broadway*, p. 358.
2. RHF.
3. *Ibid.*
4. *Ibid.*
5. Suskin, *Opening Night on Broadway*, p. 428.
6. RHF.
7. *Ibid.*
8. Hammerstein and Fields, *Flower Drum Song*, p. 9.
9. *New York Theatre Reviews* — all of the seven first-night notices are excerpted from this source.
10. RHF.
11. *The New Yorker*, December 13, 1958.
12. *The Reporter*, January 8, 1959.
13. *Variety*, December 3, 1958.
14. Hammerstein and Fields, *Flower Drum Song* — dust jacket copy.
15. *The Christian Science Monitor*, December 6, 1958.
16. "Mark of the Masters," *Life*, December 22, 1958.
17. Suskin, *Opening Nights on Broadway*, p. 570.

Chapter 8

1. LAT, June 6, 1960.
2. *Los Angeles Examiner*, June 6, 1960.
3. *San Francisco News-Call Bulletin*, August 2, 1960.
4. *Ibid.*
5. SFE, August 2, 1960.
6. *Oakland Tribune*, August 2, 1960.
7. SFC, August 3, 1960.
8. *Variety*, June 7, 1961.
9. "Drum Song Role: Orientals Are As You Find Them," *Variety*, June 28, 1961.

Chapter 9

1. Forbidden City activity recalled in author interview with Ivy Tam.
2. RHF
3. *Ibid.*

4. Lee, *Orientals: Asian Americans in Popular Culture*, p. 175.
5. Hammerstein, Oscar, and Joseph Fields, *Flower Drum Song*, p. 36.
6. Lee, *Orientals*, p. 174.
7. *Ibid.*, p. 173.
8. FDS, p. 180.
9. Lee, *Orientals*, p. 179.
10. Joanna Lee, from her presentation to the National Asian American Telecommunications Association in San Francisco, December 13, 2002, as viewed on www.naatanet.org.

Chapter 10

1. Author interview with Scott Henderson, September 9, 2003.
2. *San Diego Union*, September 1, 1961.
3. *Ibid.*, from undated photocopy of news article, circa September 15, 1961.
4. *San Diego Evening Tribune*, July 15, 1966.
5. *St. Louis Post Dispatch*, August 22, 1961.
6. *Ibid.*, August 10, 1965.
7. SFC, February 7, 1963.
8. *San Francisco News Call-Bulletin*, February 7, 1963.
9. SFE, February 7, 1963.
10. *Ibid.*, February 6, 1963.
11. SFE, September 17, 1964.
12. SFC, September 16, 1964.
13. Victor G. and Brett de Bary Nee, *Longtime Californ,'* p. xiii.
14. LAT, June 22, 2003.
15. "The Play's the Thing," Dwight Chapin's column, SFE, April 6, 1983.
16. Press release from KolmanRaush Associates, San Francisco, undated [1983].
17. *Asian Week*, April 7, 1983.
18. SFE, April 6, 1983.
19. *Asian Week*, April 7, 1983.
20. *Ibid.*, March 31, 1983.
21. *Ibid.*
22. FDS, p. 35.
23. *East/West*, March 23, 1983.
24. *Philippine News*, April 6–12, 1983.
25. *Asian Week*, March 31, 1983.
26. *Ibid.*, April 7, 1983.
27. As reported in Dwight Chapin's column, SFE, April 6, 1983.
28. *Asian Week*, April 7, 1983.
29. *Ibid.*, March 31, 1983.
30. SFE, April 8, 1983.
31. SFC, April 9, 1983.
32. *The Peninsula Times*, April 8, 1983.
33. *Asian Week*, April 14, 1983.
34. *Oakland Tribune*, April 11, 1983.

Chapter 11

1. *San Diego Evening Tribune*, August 21, 1981.
2. *San Diego Union*, August 21, 1981.
3. E-mail to author from Jeanette Thomas, dated December 18, 2003.
4. RHF — all review excerpts from this source.
5. Suskin, *Opening Nights on Broadway*, p. 506.
6. SFM, P. 340.
7. *Minneapolis–St. Paul Star-Tribune*, November 10, 1996.
8. North, *A Chronicle of American Musical Theatre*.
9. *Minneapolis-St. Paul Star-Tribune*, November 10, 1996.
10. SFM, p. 176.
11. PBS Masters series celebrating the 100th anniversary of Richard Rodgers' birth.
12. SFM, p. 298.
13. *Ibid.*, p. 307.
14. "A Complicated Gift," *New York Times Magazine*, July 6, 2003.
15. SFM, p. 268.
16. *Minneapolis–St. Paul Star-Tribune*, November 10, 1996.
17. *Seattle Times*, October 6, 1985.
18. *San Mateo Times*, July 28, 1996.

Chapter 12

1. "Mimicker, Mime and Magic," *The Spectator*, October 10, 1998.
2. LAT, September 16, 2001.
3. *Chicago Tribune*, November 15, 1998. Elysa Gardner in *USA Today* (10/16/02) wrote that Hwang had not read Lee's novel "before conceiving the project."
4. *Minneapolis–St. Paul Star-Tribune*, November 10, 1996.
5. "A Different Drummer," LAT, October 14, 2001.
6. Hyland, *Richard Rodgers*, p. 320.
7. *Theatre*, February 2002 issue, viewed on-line.

8. *Chicago Tribune*, August 22, 2000.
9. *Asian Week*, October 22, 1997.
10. *Chicago Tribune*, November 15, 1998.
11. *Ibid.*
12. LAT, April 14, 2000.
13. "Fences Are Falling Between Nonprofit, Broadway Theatres," *Hartford Courant*, September 24, 2000.
14. LAT, October 14, 2002.
15. *Newsday*, November 2, 2000.
16. *Ibid.*
17. LAT, October 14, 2001.
18. Letter from Tom Rizzo printed in the SFC, August 21, 2001.
19. "Trouble with Troubled Musicals: Revisions Seldom Work," *Hartford Courant*, November 19, 2000
20. LAT, October 14, 2001.
21. *Newsday*, December 21, 2000.

Chapter 13

1. LAT, October 14, 2001
2. Rich, *Hot Seat*, p. 30.
3. LAT, October 14, 2001.
4. *Ibid.*
5. LAT, September 16, 2001.
6. Author interview with Lea Salonga.
7. *Ibid.*
8. Incident recalled in author interview with Ronald Banks

Chapter 14

1. Author interview with Lea Salonga.
2. LAT, September 16, 2001.
3. *Performing Arts Magazine*, October 2001, p. 12.
4. LAT, October 14, 2001.
5. LAT, October 15, 2001.
6. *Happy Talk* (*www.rnh.com*) Vol. 9, no. 2.
7. *Los Angeles Daily News*, October 16, 2001.
8. *Variety*, October 15, 2001.
9. *Hollywood Reporter*, October 15, 2001.
10. *Happy Talk*, Vol. 9, no. 2.
11. *L.A. Weekly*, October 17, 2001.
12. *New Times Los Angeles*, November 1, 2001.
13. Steve Kluger, letter to the editor of the LAT, September 23, 2001.

14. Jason Kim Roberts, letter to the editor of the LAT, October 27, 2001.

Chapter 15

1. Author interview with Lea Salonga.
2. *USA Today*, October 16, 2002.
3. Author interview with Lea Salonga.
4. *The Baltimore Sun*, October 20, 2002 (and succeeding quotes to next notation).
5. "A New Musical by Rodgers and Hwang," NYT, October 13, 2002.
6. Reprinted in LAT, October 18, 2002.
7. "*Flower Drum Song*— The Reviews Are In," *Asian Week*, December 13–19, 2002.
8. *Ibid.*
9. *Variety*, October 15, 2002.
10. Associated Press, October 17, 2002.
11. NYT, October 18, 2002.
12. Author interview with Lea Salonga.
13. *USA Today* (excerpts at *www.broadway.com*), October 18, 2002.
14. *Time*, October 28, 2002.
15. *New York Observer*, October 28, 2002.
16. www.filmscoremonthly.com, November 2002.
17. "FDS: Chinatown, C.Y. Lee & D.H. Hwang." www.maynardije.org/news/features/021122/_flower/essay/flower_p3/
18. *Asian Week*, December 12–13, 2002.
19. *Chicago Tribune*, December 8, 2002.

Chapter 16

1. (And succeeding quotes.) "Hollywood Journal," *Wall Street Journal*, October 4, 2002.
2. *Ibid.*
3. Flower Drum Song website (since removed).
4. NYT, February 16, 2003.
5. Flower Drum Song website.
6. *Ibid.*
7. www.ibdb.com (League of American Theatres and Producers, Inc.)
8. *Broadway's Biggest Hits* radio broadcast on KNBR, San Francisco, March 16, 2003.
9. *Wall Street Journal*, Zagat Theatre Survey, March 14, 2003.
10. Author interview with Lea Salonga.
11. *New York Post*, January 29, 2003.
12. *Ibid.*, January 15, 2003.

Chapter 17

1. *Orange County Register*, June 29, 2003.
2. SFC, July 16, 2003.
3. *Dallas Morning News*, August 31, 2003.
4. *Houston Press*, January 29, 2004.
5. "Asian Voices Find a Stage," *San Jose Mercury News*, December 22, 2003.
6. Quoted in the *San Jose Mercury News*, December 7, 2003.
7. LAT, July 6, 2003.
8. *The Globe and Mail*, May 6, 2003.
9. NYT, January 4, 1976.
10. From Tony Thomas interview with Richard Rodgers, broadcast in Canada by the CBC, February, 1960 — available on F/CD 8108: Facet.

11. As quoted in *Broadway.Com*, October 18, 2002.
12. Mordden, *Rodgers and Hammerstein*, p.199.
13. Author interview with Ivy Tam.
14. *Theatre*, February 2002 issue, viewed online.
15. *Variety*, March 3–9, 2003.
16. SFC, May 30, 2003.
17. PBS pledge break during broadcast of the new movie version of the Trevor Nunn–directed *Oklahoma*, KCSM-TV, November 29, 2003.
18. LAT, March 17, 2002.
19. "West of West End, LAT, May 11, 2003.
20. *Holiday* magazine, February 1959.

Selected Bibliography

American Decades 1950–1959 Detroit: Gale Research, 1994.

Beck, Geoffrey, editor. *The Richard Rodgers Reader.* New York: Oxford University Press, 2000.

Book Review Digest 1957 New York: H.W. Wilson.

Bordman, Gerald. *American Musical Theatre.* New York: Oxford University Press, 1978.

Citron, Stephen. *The Wordsmiths: Oscar Hammerstein II and Alan Jay Lerner.* New York: Oxford University Press, 1995.

Fordin, Hugh. *Getting to Know Him: A Biography of Oscar Hammerstein.* New York: Random House, 1977.

Ganzl, Kurt. *The Musical: A Concise History.* Boston: Northeaster University Press, 1997.

Green, Stanley. *Broadway Musicals: Show by Show.*4th ed. Milwaukee: Hal Leonard, 1994.

_____, editor. *Rodgers and Hammerstein Fact Book: A Record of Their Works Together and with Other Collaborators.* New York: Drama Book Specialists, 1980.

Hammerstein, Oscar, and Joseph Fields. *Flower Drum Song: A Musical Play* New York: Farrar, Straus & Cudahy, 1959.

Hirschhorn, Clive. *Gene Kelly: A Biography.* New York: St. Martin's Press, 1985.

_____. *The Hollywood Musical* New York: Crown, 1981.

Hyland, William G. *Richard Rodgers.* New Haven: Yale University Press, 1998.

Kao, George. *Cathay by the Bay: San Francisco Chinatown in 1950.* Hong Kong: The Chinese University Press, 1988.

Lee, C.Y. *The Flower Drum Song.* New York: Farrar Straus & Giroux, 1957.

Lee, Robert G. *Orientals: Asian Americans in Popular Culture.* Philadelphia: Temple University Press, 1999.

Lim, Genny, editor. *The Chinese American Experience: Papers from the Second National Conference on Chinese American Studies.* San Francisco: San Francisco Chinese Historical Society of America, 1984.

Mordden, Ethan. *Rodgers and Hammerstein.* New York: Harry Abrams, Inc., 1992.

Nee, Victor G., and Nee, Brett de Barry. *Longtime Californ': A Documentary Story of an American Chinatown, 2nd* Boston: Houghton Mifflin, 1974.

New York Theatre Critics' Reviews. Vol. 19. New York: Critics Theatre Reviews, 1958.

Nolan, Frederick. *The Sound of Their Music.* New York: Walker & Co., 1978.

Norton, Richard D. *A Chronicle of American Musical Theatre*. New York: Oxford University Press, 2002.

Rich, Frank. *Hot Seat: Theatre Criticism from the* New York Times, *1980–1993*. New York: Random House, 1998.

Rodgers, Richard. *Musical Stages: An Autobiography*. New York: Random House, 1975.

Secrest, Meryle. *Somewhere for Me: A Biography of Richard Rodgers*. New York: Alfred A. Knopf, 2001.

Smith, Cecil, and Glenn Litton. *Musical Comedy in America*. New York: Theatre Arts, 1981.

Suskin, Steven. *Opening Night on Broadway*. New York: Schirmer, 1997.

Swain, Joseph P. *The Broadway Musical: A Critical and Musical Survey*. New York: Oxford University Press, 1990.

Tung, William. *The Chinese in America*. New York: Oceana, 1974.

Yudkoff, Alvin. *Gene Kelly*. New York: Back Stage, 2001.

Yung, Judy. *Unbound Voices: A Documented History of Chinese Women in San Francisco*. Berkeley: University of California Press, 1999.

Useful Internet Sources

www.asianweek.com

www.broadway'sbiggesthits.com — CD reviews, show reviews and information.

www.chsa.org — Chinese Historical Society of America.

www.ibdb.com — a comprehensive resource of historical information on shows and personnel, easy to search.

www.rnh.com — Everything you could ever want to know about the world of Rodgers and Hammerstein.

www.theatremania.com — Lively information in feature-coverage format and reviews about New York theatre.

Index